Unlocking the Secrets of Prompt Engineering

Master the art of creative language generation to accelerate your journey from novice to pro

Gilbert Mizrahi

BIRMINGHAM—MUMBAI

Unlocking the Secrets of Prompt Engineering

Group Product Manager: Niranjan Naikwadi

Publishing Product Manager: Nitin Nainani

Book Project Manager: Aishwarya Mohan

Senior Content Development Editor: Debolina Acharyya

Technical Editor: Reenish Kulshrestha

Copy Editor: Safis Editing

Proofreader: Safis Editing

Indexer: Manju Arasan

Production Designer: Jyoti Kadam

DevRel Marketing Coordinators: Vinishka Kalra

First published: January 2024

Production reference: 1111223

Published by Packt Publishing Ltd.

Grosvenor House

11 St Paul's Square

Birmingham

B3 1RB, UK

ISBN 978-1-83508-383-3

www.packtpub.com

To my incredible wife, Maria Olga – you are my rock and my best friend. Thank you for always believing in me. To my son, Daniel, and daughter, Andrea – you both make me strive to be a better person every day. Your unwavering belief in me gave wings to this dream. This book is for you.

– Gilbert Mizrahi

Foreword

In the dynamic and fast-evolving landscape of AI (artificial intelligence), Gilbert Mizrahi's latest book on the new discipline of Prompt Engineering stands as a beacon of practical knowledge and insight. As Founder and CEO of Aptima, Inc., I have known the author for more than 20 years since we were colleagues in the Company, inventing novel ways to engineer productive collaborations between humans and machines. It is my distinct honor and privilege to introduce this comprehensive and pioneering work.

Gilbert has always been at the forefront of innovation and technology since his days at Stanford, and this book is a testament to his deep understanding and insightful approach to large language models (LLMs) and generative AI. This work is not just a technical guide; it is a journey through the complex world of prompt engineering, underscored by a commitment to sound practices and a deep understanding of the transformative power of AI.

The book begins with a solid foundation in the basics of LLMs and moves through the intricacies of prompt engineering with the precision and clarity rarely found in the computer science and engineering field. His emphasis on ethics throughout the book is particularly commendable, ensuring that as we advance technologically, we do so with a conscientious mindset. As we experience throughout the book, prompt engineering is akin to crafting a meticulous recipe, where each ingredient – or, in this case, each element of the prompt – must be carefully honed to guide LLMs towards desired outcomes.

As we delve into the subsequent chapters of this incredible journey, the book masterfully decomposes and then synthesizes the core concepts. It also highlights innovative applications of prompt engineering across various industries. We are given a vivid glimpse into the future where prompt engineering could revolutionize fields like healthcare, offering compelling applications in clinical decision support, patient education, and drug discovery.

Gilbert's foresight in anticipating future trends and breakthroughs in LLMs underscores the need for collaboration and continual learning in this field. His exploration of the diverse applications of LLMs illustrates their potential to fundamentally transform nearly every industry and domain. The book not only serves as a technical guide but also as a behavioral compass in the digital age, emphasizing the need for wisdom, care, and transparency as these capabilities advance.

In conclusion, Gilbert Mizrahi's book is an indispensable resource for both newcomers and seasoned professionals in AI. It is a guide to understanding and mastering the art and science of prompt engineering to establish a fruitful dialog between the human user and the artificial intelligence, and a reminder of the collaborative effort required to harness its full potential responsibly. This book is a beacon for those navigating the evolving landscape of AI, reflecting a profound understanding of the technological, ethical, and practical aspects of LLMs.

I recommend this book to all who seek to explore the extraordinary possibilities of AI and prompt engineering. It is with great pride that I introduce this significant contribution to the field of AI, celebrating the achievements of a long-time colleague and friend.

Daniel Serfaty

Founder and CEO

Aptima, Inc.

Contributors

About the author

Gilbert Mizrahi is a product strategist, educator, and seasoned entrepreneur with a proven track record across a variety of industries. He brings a wealth of knowledge and experience in interactive data visualization, product strategy innovation, generative AI, and **Software as a Service (SaaS)**. As a co-founder of Twnel, Gilbert steers product R&D, leveraging his expertise in artificial intelligence to craft cutting-edge solutions that enhance communication and productivity for businesses. His passion for data science and product growth is mirrored in his ventures.

He holds a master's degree in operations research from Stanford University and a bachelor's degree in industrial engineering. Gilbert's extensive background includes serving as a mentor at MassChallenge and Newchip Accelerator, business strategy and product development consultant at Looi Consulting, and holding senior research and technology positions at Aptima Inc.

Gilbert's forward-thinking approach, entrepreneurial spirit, and dedication to fostering innovation make him a vanguard in the application of generative AI and strategy in product development.

About the reviewers

Daniel Mizrahi, a software engineer at Google, specializes in automating third-party service deployments to Google Cloud. Over the past two years, he has focused on creating systems that not only enhance operational efficiency but also pave the way for more advanced cloud-based applications. His experience has given him a profound understanding of the nuances of modern cloud-based systems.

Before his current role at Google, Daniel was on the Amazon Prime Video team, working specifically on a portal for content providers. This experience honed his skills in creating user-focused software solutions and deepened his appreciation of the intricate relationship between software engineering and digital content distribution.

Daniel holds a master's degree in computer science from the University of Southern California with a focus on machine learning and artificial intelligence. Daniel's academic background forms the bedrock of his technical expertise.

Divit Gupta, a seasoned IT professional with 20 years of industry expertise, excels in driving strategic architecture initiatives and providing leadership in multi-pillar sales cycles. With a global impact, he spearheads technical partnerships, defines team vision, and champions new strategic endeavors.

As the host of popular podcasts such as Tech Talk with Divit, Live Labs with Divit, and Cloud Bites with Divit, he showcases Oracle's technological initiatives and leadership. In 2022–23, he served as Oracle TV's correspondent for Cloud World. His passion for knowledge sharing extends to international conference talks, technical blogs, and multiple books on emerging technologies.

A recognized expert, Divit presented on Oracle Database technology at Oracle CloudWorld FY 2023. Holding over 40 certifications from Microsoft, Oracle, AWS, and Databricks, he remains at the forefront of technology.

David Santiago Castillo, with an extensive tenure of over a decade at Twnel, is a seasoned software developer who has played a pivotal role in the evolution of the company's communication platform. Twnel, initially founded as a messaging platform, has since transformed into a cutting-edge solution that automates business processes through conversational user interfaces. In the rapidly evolving landscape of AI and natural language processing, David has been at the forefront of harnessing the power of large language models to enhance and expand Twnel's automation capabilities.

Table of Contents

Part 2: Basic Prompt Engineering Techniques

3

Creating and Promoting a Podcast Using ChatGPT and Other Practical Examples   73

4

LLMs for Creative Writing   99

5

Unlocking Insights from Unstructured Text – AI Techniques for Text Analysis   115

Part 3: Advanced Use Cases for Different Industries

6

Applications of LLMs in Education and Law   139

Part 4: Ethics, Limitations, and Future Developments

10

11

Preface

The advent of **large language models (LLMs)**, such as GPT-4, Bard, and Claude, represents a seismic shift in **artificial intelligence (AI)** capabilities. Fueled by vast datasets and compute power, these models can generate astonishingly human-like text and engage in complex dialogue. However, their potential is only fully realized through the art of prompt engineering – the process of carefully crafting the prompts that activate the models. Prompts encode instructions, context, examples, and guardrails to channel the models' capabilities for specific tasks. Mastering prompt engineering unlocks the immense power of LLMs for a myriad of applications, from content creation to data analysis and beyond.

This book serves as a practical guide to prompt engineering across different domains. Through concrete examples and real-world case studies, readers will learn effective techniques for decomposing problems into discrete prompts, providing relevant background knowledge, iteratively refining prompts, and shaping model outputs. The journey equips readers with strategies to tap into the versatility of LLMs with properly engineered prompts. By following the techniques in this book, anyone can harness the problem-solving skills of AI systems such as GPT-4 and Claude to build solutions that create real value.

Who this book is for

Unlocking the Secrets of Prompt Engineering is written for anyone who wants to become an expert at crafting prompts for AI systems such as ChatGPT. Whether you're a total beginner or have some experience in prompt engineering, this book will help you master the art and science of creating effective prompts. I've designed it for a broad audience, including students, researchers, entrepreneurs, marketers, customer service agents, and other professionals who want to utilize the power of prompts to get the most out of AI. My goal is to provide actionable strategies and techniques you can apply right away to improve your prompting skills. By the end of the book, you'll know how to structure prompts that clearly communicate your intent, include the right amount of context and examples, and elicit the desired response from an AI system. The practical knowledge in this book will make you a prompt engineering pro!

What this book covers

Chapter 1, Understanding Prompting and Prompt Techniques

This introductory chapter provides a comprehensive overview of LLM prompts and the foundations of prompt engineering. It explores the components of prompts, different prompting techniques, LLM parameters, and a systematic framework for experimentation to craft effective prompts. The chapter also discusses challenges such as verbosity and inconsistency that need to be addressed. By equipping you with core knowledge about prompt engineering and how to guide LLM behavior, this chapter lays the groundwork for harnessing the power of AI for diverse applications in the following chapters.

Chapter 2, Craft Compelling Content Faster with AI Assistance

This chapter explores leveraging AI tools such as ChatGPT to generate, outline, and draft initial versions of content including social media posts, sales copy, video scripts, and articles. It covers providing context and examples to guide the AI, personalizing messaging, customizing the tone and voice, and refining the raw AI output. While AI shows promise to enhance human creativity and productivity in content creation through these techniques, human oversight remains critical. The key lessons focus on thoughtfully combining AI assistance with human creativity and intent to develop engaging and high-quality content.

Chapter 3, Creating and Promoting a Podcast Using ChatGPT and Other Practical Examples

This chapter provides practical examples of leveraging AI tools, for example, ChatGPT, for tasks such as crafting an engaging podcast and job interview questions. It explores prompts and techniques to identify podcast topics, potential guests, and promotional content. For job interviews, it covers how both interviewers and candidates can use AI to strategize relevant questions and thoughtful answers. The key lessons focus on using AI to accelerate preparation, idea generation, and content creation for podcasts and interviews while enhancing human creativity.

Chapter 4, LLMs for Creative Writing

This chapter explores how writers can leverage AI tools such as ChatGPT to enhance different aspects of the creative writing process. It provides examples of crafting prompts to generate ideas, characters, and plots for fiction as well as techniques for writing original poetry. The key lessons focus on using AI to spark imagination while retaining authorial vision and voice. With the right balance of human creativity and AI assistance, these models can accelerate idea generation, improve drafts through editing, and open new creative frontiers.

Chapter 5, Unlocking Insights from Unstructured Text - AI Techniques for Text Analysis

This chapter explores key applications of AI techniques such as sentiment analysis, data classification, data cleaning, and pattern matching to extract insights from unstructured text. It provides examples of using these techniques to perform tasks such as gauging emotion in content, categorizing data, resolving inconsistencies, and extracting structured information. The key lessons focus on leveraging

AI to automate the analysis of qualitative data, saving time and effort while improving accuracy. With the right techniques, AI enables anyone to unlock value from the proliferation of unstructured text data.

Chapter 6, Applications of LLMs in Education and Law

This chapter demonstrates applications of AI systems such as ChatGPT in education and legal domains. It provides examples of using these tools to generate personalized course materials, practice questions, and rubrics tailored to learning objectives. For legal professionals, the chapter explores leveraging LLMs for research, drafting documents, intellectual property management, training law students, and other emerging use cases. However, human validation of AI responses remains critical. When thoughtfully implemented, tools such as ChatGPT show immense potential to assist professionals in education, law, and other fields by automating repetitive tasks and enhancing productivity.

Chapter 7, The Rise of AI Pair Programmers - Teaming Up with Intelligent Assistants for Better Code

LLMs such as GPT-4 are transforming coding by generating functional code blocks, explaining code, debugging, optimizing performance, and translating between programming languages. This chapter provides case studies demonstrating the use of AI to rapidly develop website code and Chrome extensions, allowing developers to focus on design rather than rote coding tasks. AI coding assistants such as GitHub Copilot leverage GPT-3 and GPT-4 to provide autonomous code generation tailored to developers' needs. While AI can accelerate development, human oversight is still needed to review and refine the generated code before deployment. AI is unlikely to wholly replace developers soon, but it can augment human creativity and problem-solving abilities in coding. The future will involve fluent human-AI collaboration, with coders and assistants working together symbiotically.

Chapter 8, Conversational AI – Crafting Intelligent Chatbot LLMs

Chatbots powered by LLMs such as GPT-3/4 and Claude are transforming conversational AI and enabling more natural, human-like digital experiences. As demonstrated through the detailed examples in this chapter, these powerful generative models allow bots to truly understand natural language, hold free-flowing conversations with users, and complete sophisticated workflows from commerce transactions to personalized assessments.

The key to unlocking their capabilities is thoughtful prompt engineering. Developers can inject critical context, domain knowledge, business logic, data sources, and more into the prompts to shape the bot's behavior. While interacting in the playground provides a glimpse of the potential, custom solutions built on LLM APIs open up many more possibilities.

Chapter 9, Building Smarter Systems – Advanced LLM Integrations

This chapter explored various techniques for integrating LLMs into practical workflows to unlock new possibilities. Easy-to-use templates such as SheetSmart simplify setting up formulas in spreadsheets to prompt LLMs such as GPT-3.5 in bulk. More powerful automation platforms such as Zapier and Make enable connecting web applications into pipelines with LLM APIs. This allows automating processes such as generating competitive intelligence briefings by ingesting data sources into an LLM.

For full customization, developer tools such as LangChain, Flowise, and Langflow provide frameworks for building sophisticated LLM applications involving reasoning, conversation, and contextual recommendations. The walk-throughs in this chapter demonstrate sample integrations for extracting insights from customer data to enrich CRM systems and conversing with PDF documents using LLMs.

Chapter 10, Generative AI – Emerging Issues at the Intersection of Ethics and Innovation

Generative AI introduces profound challenges around trust, accountability, bias risks, economic impacts ranging from productivity gains to job displacement, massive computational needs threatening sustainability, subtle societal risks, and philosophical questions around machine creativity. Solutions require collaboration on ethics by design, algorithmic assessments, thoughtful regulations, inclusive governance, and upholding human rights. The choices made today on AI ethics and governance will have profound implications. With humanism guiding development, these technologies can be steered toward uplifting and enriching society.

Chapter 11, Conclusion

Prompt engineering represents a breakthrough in guiding generative AI systems such as LLMs to automate tasks and enhance human capabilities across industries. Meticulously refining prompts based on outputs is key to steering these models, much like adjusting ingredients when cooking. For now, human expertise remains essential to oversee AI's nascent abilities. Looking ahead, techniques such as conditional and causality prompting could enable more reliable, personalized applications. Healthcare and other fields, such as engineering and finance, exhibit immense potential for prompt engineering to assist professionals. However, we must acknowledge the current limitations and implement thoughtful governance to manage risks responsibly. Platforms integrating models with services and tools customizing outputs by training on unique data will expand the possibilities further. While focused on text generation, prompt engineering will grow even more versatile as multimodal LLMs advance.

Overall, this book provides an introductory survey of techniques to ignite exciting possibilities for transforming nearly every facet of life and work through thoughtful prompt engineering.

To get the most out of this book

To get the most out of this book on prompt engineering, you need access to OpenAI's ChatGPT, Anthropic's Claude 2, and Google's Bard. We start from fundamentals, so no deep technical expertise is required. You should be keen to engage creatively and iteratively in crafting effective language model prompts. An inquiring mindset will be rewarded as prompt engineering develops skills in articulating tasks and unlocking capabilities. Our goal is to set you on a self-directed journey.

We primarily focus on crafting prompts for OpenAI's ChatGPT, Claude from Anthropic, and Google's new Bard language model, covering the available techniques across these industry-leading systems. The code and examples are compatible with macOS, Windows 10+, or common Linux distributions. Hardware requirements are modest – an internet connection and computer from the past 5-7 years will suffice.

We've structured the book to accelerate applying prompt engineering to real problems. If grasping concepts rapidly and jumping quickly into hands-on activities suits your learning style, you have found the right guide.

Software/hardware covered in the book	Operating system requirements
OpenAI ChatGPT, GPT-3.5, and GPT-4	Windows, macOS, or Linux
Anthropic Claude 2	
Google Bard	

Download the example code files

There is a code file in ch 08 whose github link has been pasted below `https://github.com/PacktPublishing/Unlocking-the-Secrets-of-Prompt-Engineering/tree/main`

We also have other code bundles from our rich catalog of books and videos available at `https://github.com/PacktPublishing/`. Check them out!

Conventions used

There are a number of text conventions used throughout this book.

`Code in text`: Indicates code words in text, database table names, folder names, filenames, file extensions, pathnames, dummy URLs, user input, and Twitter handles. Here is an example: "The only thing that changed was that `browser-action` changed to `action` in the manifest."

Prompts are written as follows:

```
For the first set of questions, provide for each three potential good
answers
```

Responses to prompts are written as follows:

```
1. As a successful solopreneur, how important do you believe personal
branding is in the landscape of solopreneurship, and how has your own
personal brand contributed to your success?
2.. Do you believe there's a potential risk for solopreneurs in
blurring the lines between personal and professional branding? How do
you maintain a balance?
3. Personal branding seems to be a powerful tool for standing out from
the competition. How do you ensure your personal brand reflects your
unique value proposition to your clients?
4. For solopreneurs who are just starting, what would be your advice
on establishing a strong and credible personal brand?
```

When we wish to draw your attention to a particular part of a code block (in this case, a prompt), the relevant lines or items are set in bold:

```
Use the [text] extracted from an invoice using OCR. Structure it as a
JSON object with the structure shown in the [JSON model].
[text]="TEXT GENERATED BY OCR"
[JSON model] = (the model from above)
keep the same structure of the JSON as in the model, including the
same keys. Output:
```

Get in touch

Feedback from our readers is always welcome.

General feedback: If you have questions about any aspect of this book, email us at customercare@packtpub.com and mention the book title in the subject of your message.

Errata: Although we have taken every care to ensure the accuracy of our content, mistakes do happen. If you have found a mistake in this book, we would be grateful if you would report this to us. Please visit www.packtpub.com/support/errata and fill in the form.

Piracy: If you come across any illegal copies of our works in any form on the internet, we would be grateful if you would provide us with the location address or website name. Please contact us at copyright@packtpub.com with a link to the material.

If you are interested in becoming an author: If there is a topic that you have expertise in and you are interested in either writing or contributing to a book, please visit authors.packtpub.com.

Share Your Thoughts

Once you've read, we'd love to hear your thoughts! Scan the QR code below to go straight to the Amazon review page for this book and share your feedback.

https://packt.link/r/1835083838

Your review is important to us and the tech community and will help us make sure we're delivering excellent quality content.

Download a free PDF copy of this book

Thanks for purchasing this book!

Do you like to read on the go but are unable to carry your print books everywhere?

Is your eBook purchase not compatible with the device of your choice?

Don't worry, now with every Packt book you get a DRM-free PDF version of that book at no cost.

Read anywhere, any place, on any device. Search, copy, and paste code from your favorite technical books directly into your application.

The perks don't stop there, you can get exclusive access to discounts, newsletters, and great free content in your inbox daily

Follow these simple steps to get the benefits:

1. Scan the QR code or visit the link below

https://packt.link/free-ebook/9781835083833

2. Submit your proof of purchase
3. That's it! We'll send your free PDF and other benefits to your email directly

Part 1:
Introduction to Prompt Engineering

Part 1 establishes a comprehensive foundation in the world of prompt engineering for language AIs. *Chapter 1* offers an expansive exploration of AI prompts, elucidating their composition, categories, real-world applications, underlying concepts, and techniques to shape desired model outputs.

Equipped with insights into prompt architecture and the inner workings of language models, you can systematically craft precise prompts to achieve your intended results. Building on these core concepts, *Chapter 2* demonstrates leveraging tools such as ChatGPT for automated content creation.

Practical use cases such as developing viral social posts or high-converting sales copy are examined. Additionally, personalization and engagement strategies are covered to ensure that your content resonates with target audiences.

With proven prompt engineering best practices, *Part 1* empowers you to tap the phenomenal potential of language AIs to enhance content development workflows. The stage is set to apply these skills and explore innovative applications across manifold domains in subsequent chapters.

This part has the following chapters:

- *Chapter 1, Understanding Prompting and Prompt Techniques*
- *Chapter 2, Generating Text with AI for Content Creation*

1

Understanding Prompting and Prompt Techniques

This book begins by examining the foundations of **large language models (LLMs)**, including their structure and response generation mechanisms. Then, it will explore various techniques for prompt engineering, such as refining and iterating on initial ideas, to craft effective prompts that elicit the desired output from an LLM. The ethical considerations around using LLMs will be discussed, including ways to mitigate biases and ensure fairness, transparency, and accountability.

This book showcases innovative applications of LLMs across diverse domains to demonstrate their immense potential to enhance lives and reshape industries. We'll contemplate the future of LLMs by looking at emerging trends, potential breakthroughs, and the role of collaboration in driving progress.

Throughout this book, practical examples, case studies, and hands-on exercises will be provided to offer a comprehensive learning experience on prompt engineering. The goal is to empower you to become a skilled prompt engineer who can harness the power of LLMs to create meaningful, positive change.

This chapter aims to provide a clear understanding of AI prompts and their significance. By exploring the inner workings of LLMs such as GPT-4 and others, in conjunction with prompts, you will gain practical knowledge and techniques to harness their power effectively.

In this chapter, you will do the following:

- **Discover the inner workings of prompts**: This chapter will demystify the components that drive LLM prompts, from the input prompt to the role of context and response. By examining each element, you will understand how they shape the output generated by the language model.

- **Explore a plethora of prompts**: This chapter will delve into the diverse landscape of prompt techniques, providing insights into the different types available. Practical examples will showcase how prompts can be employed in various scenarios to achieve desired outcomes.

- **Navigate the challenges and limitations of prompts**: While LLM prompts offer immense potential, they also come with challenges and limitations. This chapter will discuss common obstacles and provide insights into how to overcome them. By understanding these limitations, you will be better prepared to make informed decisions when implementing prompt engineering strategies.

By the end of this chapter, you will have a solid foundation in prompt engineering. Armed with the acquired knowledge and skills, you will be ready to leverage the full potential of LLM prompts throughout your exploration of advanced techniques and applications in subsequent chapters.

The following topics will be covered in this chapter:

- Introducing LLM prompts
- How LLM prompts work
- Types of LLM prompts
- Components of an LLM prompt
- Role prompting
- Voice definition
- Using patterns to enhance prompt effectiveness
- Exploring some examples of combining prompt engineering techniques
- Exploring LLM parameters
- How to approach prompt engineering (experimentation)
- The challenges and limitations of using LLM prompts

Technical requirements

To be able to play with the prompts in this chapter, you will need to create an account with one or more of these tools:

- **OpenAI ChatGPT**: `https://chat.openai.com/`.

  Once you create an account, if you haven't created one already, you can upgrade to ChatGPT Plus for $20/month. This is not required to take advantage of this book.

- **Google Bard**: `https://bard.google.com/`.

  If you're signed into a Google Workspace account, your admin may not have enabled access to Bard. If that's the case, ask your admin to enable access.

- **Anthropic Claude**: `https://console.anthropic.com/`

We will start with an introduction to LLM prompts, how they work, and what type of prompt we can use to produce the best possible results.

Introducing LLM prompts

LLMs have revolutionized the way we interact with technology, shaping our digital landscape and transforming the way we communicate, learn, and innovate. At the forefront of this revolution are large-scale LLMs such as OpenA GPT-4, Google LaMDA, and Anthropic. These language models can be used programmatically using their APIs or throughout their chat interfaces. These interfaces are called OpenAI ChatGPT, Google Bard, and Anthropic Claude, respectively.

Prompt engineering is the process of designing and refining input prompts for LLMs to achieve desired outputs. While it may initially seem trivial or purely technical, it is, in fact, a multidisciplinary endeavor. It demands a comprehensive understanding of linguistics, cognitive science, **artificial intelligence (AI)**, user experience design, and ethics, among other fields. The goal of this chapter is to provide a comprehensive framework for understanding and mastering the intricacies of prompt engineering, equipping you with the necessary tools to harness the full potential of LLMs.

How LLM prompts work

Large-scale LLMs are a form of AI that focuses on understanding and generating human language. They use sophisticated machine learning algorithms, primarily neural networks, to process and analyze a massive amount of textual data. The main objective of LLMs is to produce coherent, contextually relevant, and human-like responses to given input prompts. To comprehend how LLMs function, it's crucial to discuss their underlying architecture and the training process. Using some analogies to explain these concepts will make them easier to understand.

Architecture

LLMs, such as OpenAI's GPT-4, are made using a special type of neural network called the Transformer. Transformers have a special structure that helps them work well with text.

One important thing in Transformers is self-attention. This means that the model can focus on different parts of a sentence and decide which words are more important in a particular context. It's like giving attention to the words that matter the most.

Another thing Transformers use is positional encoding. This helps the model keep track of where each word is in a sentence. It's like giving each word a special label so that the model knows where it belongs in the sequence.

With these features, LLMs can process and understand long pieces of text well. They can figure out the meaning of words based on the context they appear in and remember the order of words in a sentence.

LLM training

The training process for an LLM consists of two main phases: pre-training and fine-tuning. LLMs are like extremely skilled language students. During their training, they go through these two main phases.

Pre-training

In this first phase, the LLM is exposed to massive amounts of text from books, articles, websites, and more. It's like it gets to read a huge library full of diverse information.

As the LLM reviews all this text, it starts to pick up on patterns in how language is structured. The LLM learns things such as the following:

- Which words tend to follow each other (the probability of "dog" being followed by "bark")
- The grammar and sentence structure of different languages (where the verb goes in a sentence)
- The topics and concepts that certain words relate to (learning that "dog" and "puppy" are connected to animals, pets, and so on)

To process all this text, the LLM breaks it down into smaller digestible pieces, kind of like chewing language into bite-sized chunks. This process is called chunking.

The LLM chops up sentences into smaller parts called tokens. Tokens can be individual words, partial words, or even special characters such as punctuation.

After chunking the text, the LLM embeds or encodes each token into a numerical vector, which is like giving each token a mathematical representation – for example, translating *dog* into something like *[0.51, 0.72, 0.33,…]* for the computer to process. This process is called embedding.

It's like translating a sentence from English into numbers. Instead of words, each token now has a corresponding vector of numbers that computers can understand.

This embedding process captures information about the meaning of each token based on the patterns the LLM learned from its extensive pre-training. Tokens with similar meanings get embedded closer together in the vector space.

All these numerical token vectors get stored in the LLM's vector database, which it can use later to look up tokens and analyze their relationships to other tokens. This vector database is like a mathematical library index for the LLM.

So, in pre-training, the LLM forms connections between words and concepts by analyzing massive amounts of text and storing the patterns in its complex neural network brain. Thus, the LLM stores that *dog* and *puppy* have similar vector representations since they have related meanings and contexts.

However, *dog* and *bicycle* are farther apart since they are semantically different. The vector space organizes words by their similarities and differences.

Fine-tuning

After pre-training, the LLM moves on to the fine-tuning phase. Here, it receives additional training on smaller datasets that are relevant to specific tasks.

This is like having the LLM focus on particular areas of study after completing general education – for example, taking advanced biology classes after learning fundamentals in science.

In fine-tuning, the LLM practices generating outputs for specific tasks based on labeled example data. Labeled data refers to data that has been annotated with labels that categorize or describe the contents. These labels help train models by providing examples of the expected output.

When you later provide the LLM with a new prompt, it uses the patterns learned in pre-training and fine-tuning to analyze the prompt and generate a fitting response.

The LLM doesn't truly understand language like humans. But by recognizing patterns from tons of examples in its training, it can imitate human-like responses and be a highly capable language learner.

Additionally, these vector representations can be used for various natural language processing tasks, such as sentiment analysis, topic modeling, and document classification. By comparing the vectors of words or phrases, algorithms can determine the similarity or relatedness of the concepts they represent, which is essential for many advanced language understanding and generation tasks.

A critical factor for all models is the context window – the amount of text a model can consider at once – which affects coherence and depth during interactions. In particular, the context window matters for the following reasons:

- **Coherence and relevance**: A larger context window lets the model maintain the thread of a conversation or document, leading to more coherent and contextually relevant responses

- **Text generation**: For tasks such as writing articles, stories, or code, a larger context window enables the model to generate content that is consistent with previous sections

- **Conversation depth**: In dialogue systems, a larger context window allows the AI to remember and refer to earlier parts of the conversation, creating a more engaging and natural interaction

- **Knowledge retrieval**: For tasks that require referencing large bodies of text or pulling from multiple segments in a document, a larger context window allows the model to cross-reference and synthesize information more effectively

However, there are trade-offs, as larger context windows require more computational power and memory to process. This can impact response times and costs. It is a key area of differentiation among LLMs as improvements to the context window can significantly enhance the usability and adaptability of the model in complex tasks.

Claude 2 has a context window of 100,000 tokens, while the new GPT-4-turbo-1106- review has a context window of 128,000 tokens. In English, the average number of words per 1,000 tokens is around 750. Researchers are predicting models with one million-plus tokens by 2024.

A journey from prompt to reply – how inference helps LLMs fill in the blanks

Once an LLM finishes its training, it's ready to start generating responses to the prompts users provide it.

When a user inputs a prompt, that prompt gets fed into the LLM's neural network brain. The LLM has special components in its brain architecture that help analyze the prompt.

One part pays extra close attention to the most relevant words for the context, kind of like how we focus on key words when reading.

Another component remembers the order of the words and where they're located in the prompt, which is important for getting the context right.

Using its brain components, the LLM generates a list of words that could logically come next in the response. It assigns a probability score to each potential next word.

Then, the LLM uses a technique called decoding to pick the top word options and turn those into its final response.

It might greedily choose the single most likely next word. Or it may randomly select from a few of the most probable candidates, to make the response less repetitive and more human-sounding.

So, in summary, the LLM's special brain architecture helps it pay attention to the right words, remember their order, and assign probabilities to the next words. Then, it decodes the top choices into a response that fits the prompt appropriately.

This process allows the LLM to generate very human-like responses that continue the conversation sensibly, based on the initial prompt provided by the user.

One of the key strengths of LLMs is their ability to perform *few-shot* or *zero-shot* learning. This means that they can generalize their knowledge from the pre-training phase and quickly adapt to new tasks or domains with minimal additional training data. In few-shot learning, the model is provided with a small number of examples to learn from, while in zero-shot learning, the model relies solely on its pre-existing knowledge and the given prompt to generate a response.

LLMs have demonstrated remarkable progress in natural language understanding and generation tasks, with applications spanning diverse domains such as conversation AI, content creation, translation, question-answering systems, and more. However, it is essential to recognize that LLMs are not without limitations. They can sometimes produce incorrect or nonsensical answers, be sensitive to slight changes in input phrasing, or exhibit biases present in the training data. As such, prompt engineering plays a crucial role in mitigating these limitations and ensuring that LLMs produce the desired output for a given task or application.

In the next section, we will examine different types of LLM prompts. Understanding these various types of prompts will provide you with valuable insights into how to effectively interact with language models, enabling you to generate more accurate and tailored responses for your desired applications or tasks.

Types of LLM prompts

LLM prompts can be categorized based on several aspects, such as their purpose, format, and level of detail provided.

One way of classifying them is by the type of information that's being prompted:

- **Zero-shot prompting**: This is a technique that allows an LLM to generate responses to tasks that it has not been specifically trained for. In this technique, the LLM is provided with an input text and a prompt that describes the expected output from the model in natural language. The LLM then uses its knowledge to generate a response that is consistent with the prompt.

  For example, if you provide the LLM with the input text *Write a poem about love*, and the prompt *The poem should be beautiful and romantic*, the LLM might generate the following response:

  ```
  Love is a many splendored thing,
  It's the April rose that only grows in the early spring.
  Love is nature's way of giving,
  A reason to be living.

  Love is a many splendored thing,
  It's the golden crown that makes a man a king.
  Love is the April rose that only grows in the early spring.
  Love is nature's way of giving,
  A reason to be living.
  ```

- **Fine-tuning**: In fine-tuning, the LLM is trained on a small dataset of labeled examples for the task that it is being asked to perform. This can be a more effective way to generate high-quality responses, but it requires a larger dataset of labeled examples.

  As an example, let's say that the input is an article about new research on treating cancer, while the training data is articles about cancer research labeled with summaries.

  Here's the prompt for this.

  Prompt:

  ```
  Summarize the key findings of the research described in the
  input article.
  ```

Here's the output.

Response:

```
A short summarization highlighting the key points of the input
article.
```

- **Data augmentation**: In data augmentation, the LLM is trained on a dataset that has been artificially expanded by adding noise or variations to the existing data. This can be a way to improve the performance of the LLM on tasks where there is limited labeled data available.

  As an example, let's say that the original training data consists of 1,000 sentences about the weather, while the augmented data consists of 2,000 additional sentences that were created by adding synonyms, paraphrasing, and introducing typos to the original sentences.

  Here's the prompt:

  ```
  Classify each sentence as describing sunny, rainy, or snowy
  weather.
  ```

  Here's the output:

  ```
  Weather classification predictions on the expanded training set.
  ```

- **Active learning**: In active learning, also known as *few-shot learning*, the LLM is given a small number of labeled examples and is then asked to identify the most informative examples to label. This can be a more efficient way to train the LLM as it focuses on labeling the examples that will be most helpful in improving the model's performance.

  Fine-tuning is done globally for all conversations. In active learning, the user provides a few examples during prompting to get the outputs to follow a certain pattern.

  For example, if the output was *the person's name is Peter and he is 23 years old*, the user may want to get a response of *{"name": "Peter", "age": 23 }*. In this case, the user would provide a couple of examples of raw responses and explicitly ask the LLM to produce the output as JSON, as shown previously.

- **Transfer learning**: In transfer learning, the LLM is trained on a task that is similar to the task that it is being asked to perform. This can be a more effective way to generate high-quality responses as it allows the LLM to learn from a larger dataset.

  As an example, let's say that the original task was sentiment analysis of movie reviews, while the new task is sentiment analysis of product reviews.

  Here's the prompt:

  ```
  Classify the sentiment of these new product reviews,
  transferring knowledge from movie review sentiment analysis.
  ```

Here's the output:

```
Sentiment classification predictions on product reviews,
leveraging the capabilities gained from the movie review
dataset.
```

The best type of prompt to use will depend on the specific task that the LLM is being asked to perform and the amount of labeled data that is available.

Another way of classifying the prompt types is by function:

- **Instructional prompts**: These prompts explicitly instruct the model to perform a particular task, such as summarizing a text, translating a sentence, or answering a question. Instructional prompts typically begin with a clear directive, such as *Translate the following sentence into French:* or *Summarize the following paragraph:*.

- **Conversational prompts**: These prompts are designed to engage the model in a natural, human-like conversation. They can be framed as questions or statements and often involve a back-and-forth dialogue between the user and the model. Conversational prompts can cover a wide range of topics, from casual chit-chat to more focused discussions on specific subjects. Let's look at an example.

Prompt:

```
Hello! How are you today?
```

Response:

```
I'm doing well, thanks for asking. How about yourself?
```

Prompt:

```
I'm a bit tired but can't complain. What are your plans for the
weekend?
```

This back-and-forth exchange allows for natural, free-flowing conversation. Conversational prompts are important for developing personable, helpful AI assistants.

- **Contextual prompts**: These prompts provide background or contextual information to guide the model's response. Contextual prompts help the model understand the user's intent, the desired format of the output, or any constraints that should be considered while generating a response. They may include examples, explanations, or descriptions to help clarify the task. Here's an example:

  You are an AI assistant created by OpenAI to be helpful, harmless, and honest. The user has asked you to summarize the key events in the following passage: [insert passage]

- **Creative prompts**: These prompts invite the model to generate original content or ideas, such as writing a poem, creating a story, or brainstorming solutions to a problem. Creative prompts often leave room for the model's imagination and may require multiple iterations and refinements to achieve the desired output. An example of this is *Write a haiku poem about the ocean.*

- **Factual prompts**: These prompts seek accurate and specific information or knowledge from the model, often in the form of a question. Examples include queries about historical events, scientific concepts, or general trivia. Factual prompts rely on the model's ability to recall and synthesize information that it learned during its pre-training phase. An example of this is *What year was the Declaration of Independence signed?*

- **Step-by-step prompts**: These prompts require the model to provide a sequence of steps or a procedure to accomplish a particular task, such as a recipe, a tutorial, or an algorithm. Step-by-step prompts necessitate the model to generate coherent, ordered, and logical instructions – for instance, *Provide directions for baking a cake from scratch, breaking down each step*. Step-by-step prompts are often used to ask the LLM to solve a mathematical problem. Let's look at an example.

Prompt:

```
How much is 5+3*8+5?
```

Response:

```
The answer is 43.
```

This is the wrong answer. So, we need to use a step-by-step prompt to get the right one.

Prompt:

```
Solve it using step by step reasoning
```

Response:

```
Okay, let's go through this step-by-step:
Step 1) 3 * 8 = 24
(I should perform the multiplication first since it has higher
precedence than addition)
Step 2) 24 + 5 = 29
(Now I can add the 5 that comes before the multiplication)
Step 3) 29 + 5 = 34
(Finally, I add the last 5)
Step 4) Therefore, the full solution is:
5 + 3 * 8 + 5 = 34
```

By breaking the problem down into clear sequential steps, I was able to evaluate the operations in the proper order of operations. This step-by-step approach prevented me from making a mistake by adding before multiplying. Deliberately walking through the reasoning allowed me to correctly solve the problem:

- **Opinion-based prompts**: These prompts ask the model to provide an opinion, perspective, or recommendation on a given topic. While LLMs do not have personal beliefs or preferences, they can generate responses based on patterns and insights derived from their training data. Opinion-based prompts often require careful consideration of potential biases present in the model's output – for example, *What are the pros and cons of self-driving car technology? Support your perspective.*

- **Multi-modal prompts**: These prompts involve input data from multiple modalities, such as text combined with images, audio, or video. Multi-modal prompts require the model to process and integrate information from various sources to generate an appropriate response. While some LLMs are primarily designed for text-based interactions, recent advancements in AI have led to the development of models capable of handling multi-modal inputs, such as OpenAI's DALL-E and CLIP. An example of this is *Describe the scene in this image: [insert image]*.

- **Systematic prompts**: These prompts aim to elicit responses that follow a specific structure, pattern, or format. Examples include generating a list of items, creating an outline for an essay or presentation, or providing a structured analysis of a given topic. Systematic prompts often necessitate the model to organize and present information coherently and logically. Here's an example:

Categorize the following animals into taxonomy groups:

[list of animals]

- **Prompt chains, also known as chain of thought**: These prompts involve a series of interconnected inputs and outputs, where the model's response to one prompt serves as the input for the next prompt. Prompt chains can be used for complex problem-solving, multi-step tasks, or to maintain continuity in a conversation with the model. Let's look at an example.

Prompt:

```
What is the capital of France?
```

Response:

```
The capital of France is Paris.
```

Prompt:

```
What is the population of Paris?
```

The LLM maintains context and consistency across prompts.

When designing prompts for LLMs, it is essential to consider the specific needs and goals of the intended application. By understanding and combining different types of prompts, prompt engineers can tailor their approach to elicit the most accurate, relevant, and useful responses from the model. Moreover, effective prompt engineering often involves iterative refinement and experimentation, incorporating user feedback and adjusting the prompt structure to optimize the model's performance. As the field of LLMs continues to evolve, the art and science of prompt engineering will play a critical role in shaping the way we interact with these powerful AI tools, unlocking their full potential across a wide range of applications and domains.

Components of an LLM prompt

An LLM prompt serves as the input to a large-scale LLM, guiding its response generation process. Crafting an effective prompt is crucial for obtaining accurate, relevant, and useful outputs. The components of an LLM prompt can vary depending on the task, application, and desired outcome. However, several key elements are often present in well-designed prompts:

- **Task description**:

  An essential component of a prompt is a clear and concise description of the task the model is expected to perform. This can be an instruction, a question, or a statement that specifies the purpose of the interaction, such as summarizing a passage, translating text, or answering a query.

  Here's an example:

  ```
  Summarize the following passage in two sentences:
  ```

- **Context**:

  Providing context within the prompt helps the model understand the scope, constraints, and background information relevant to the task. This can include domain-specific terminology, examples, or explanations that guide the model's response generation. Contextual information can be particularly useful for disambiguation, refining the model's focus, or ensuring that the output adheres to a specific format or style.

  Here's an example:

  ```
  In the context of a scientific research paper, provide a concise
  summary of the main findings.
  ```

- **Input data**:

  The input data is the actual content that the model will process and generate a response based on. This can be a sentence, a paragraph, or a series of questions or statements. The input data should be relevant to the task and formulated in a way that is easy for the model to understand and analyze.

  Here's an example:

  ```
  Climate change has led to increased global temperatures, melting
  polar ice, and rising sea levels. The consequences for marine
  ecosystems are severe, with many species struggling to adapt to
  the rapidly changing environment. Coral reefs, in particular,
  are under threat due to ocean acidification and bleaching events
  that result from warmer water temperatures.
  ```

- **Placeholder tokens**:

In some cases, prompts may include placeholder tokens (variables) that indicate where the model should insert its response. These tokens can help maintain the structure and format of the output, especially when multiple outputs or responses need to be generated in a specific sequence or layout. Let's look at an example.

Prompt:

```
Imagine you are visiting a [City_Name] for the first time. You
have [Number_of_Days] days to explore the city and experience
its culture. What are the top [Number_of_Attractions]
attractions or activities you would like to do while you're
there? Provide a brief description of each attraction and
explain why it interests you.
city name: Boston
number of days: 3
number of attractions: 3
```

Response:

```
1. Freedom Trail: A 2.5-mile-long path through downtown Boston
that passes by 16 historically significant sites, including
the Massachusetts State House and Paul Revere's House. I'm
interested in learning about the city's rich history and its
role in the American Revolution.
2. Fenway Park: As a baseball fan, I would love to catch a Red
Sox game at this iconic ballpark, which opened in 1912 and is
one of the oldest Major League Baseball stadiums still in use.
3. New England Aquarium: This popular attraction features a
variety of marine life, including sea turtles, penguins, and a
giant ocean tank. Visiting the aquarium would be a great way to
learn …
```

Since the initial prompt includes variables (the terms included in [ ]), the user can now ask again only by providing a prompt, such as the following:

```
city name: Paris
number of days: 4
number of attractions: 10
```

The LLM will provide the corresponding list. The user can continue adding prompts similar to this one to get the recommended attractions for as many cities as they would like.

- **Examples**:

Including examples within the prompt can be beneficial, especially when dealing with few-shot learning scenarios. These examples serve as a demonstration of the desired output format and can help the model understand the task more effectively. Examples can be particularly valuable when the task is complex or requires the model to generate outputs in a specific structure. Let's look at one.

Prompt:

```
Please categorize the following product review as either
positive, negative, or neutral.
```

Here's another example.

Input:

```
The speakers produced very crisp and clear sound with deep bass.
The set up was quick and easy. Overall an excellent product I
would highly recommend.
```

Output:

```
Positive
```

Input:

```
These headphones are lightweight and comfortable, but the audio
quality is tinny and lacks bass. The noise cancellation feature
is mediocre at best. Output:
Please categorize the following product review as either
positive, negative, or neutral.
```

The following is another example.

Input:

```
The speakers produced very crisp and clear sound with deep bass.
The set up was quick and easy. Overall an excellent product I
would highly recommend.
```

Output:

```
Positive
```

Input:

```
These headphones are lightweight and comfortable, but the audio
quality is tinny and lacks bass. The noise cancellation feature
is mediocre at best. Output:
```

Response:

```
Negative
```

These examples could be of the tone and type of vocabulary that the user wants from the response as well.

- **Constraints**:

  Sometimes, it is necessary to impose constraints on the model's response to ensure it meets specific requirements, adheres to guidelines, or avoids problematic content. Constraints can be expressed explicitly within the prompt or implicitly by carefully crafting the task's description and context. Let's look at an example.

Prompt:

```
Compose a short 4-line poem about the sunrise with an AABB rhyme
scheme.
```

- **Tone and style**:

The tone and style of a prompt can influence the model's response. Specifying the desired tone, such as formal, casual, or persuasive, can help generate outputs that align with the intended purpose and audience.

The following example specifies a sarcastic tone.

Prompt:

```
Write a 100-word product review mocking the useless features and
flimsy design of a silly kitchen gadget. Use an overly sarcastic
tone.
```

The following example specifies a pirate tone.

Prompt:

```
Compose a pirate's journal entry recounting a day searching for
treasure on the high seas. Use pirate slang and language.
```

When designing LLM prompts, prompt engineers must consider the interplay between these components to create an effective input that elicits the desired output from the model. The process often involves iterative refinement, experimentation, and incorporating user feedback to optimize the prompt's structure and content. By understanding and skillfully combining these components, prompt engineers can harness the full potential of large-scale LLMs and ensure that their responses are accurate, relevant, and valuable across a wide range of tasks and applications.

Putting it all together, here is an example of using the interplay between components of prompts. The complete prompt would be as follows:

```
"Summarize the following passage in two sentences. In the context
of a scientific research paper, provide a concise summary of the
main findings. The passage is: 'Climate change has led to increased
global temperatures, melting polar ice, and rising sea levels. The
consequences for marine ecosystems are severe, with many species
struggling to adapt to the rapidly changing environment. Coral
reefs, in particular, are under threat due to ocean acidification
and bleaching events that result from warmer water temperatures.'
Make sure the summary does not exceed two sentences and avoids using
overly technical terms. Provide a summary that is clear, concise,
and suitable for a general audience. Example 1: Input: 'The economy
has experienced significant growth due to advancements in technology
and globalization. However, the distribution of wealth remains
unequal, with a small percentage of the population controlling a large
proportion of resources.' Output: 'Economic growth has been driven
by technology and globalization, but wealth distribution remains
unequal.' Example 2: Input: '[Input Data]'. Output: '[summary]' .
Input: [Input Data]. Output:"
```

This prompt effectively combines all the necessary components to guide the LLM in generating a concise and accurate summary of the given passage. By providing a clear task description, context, input data, and tone and style, the model is directed toward generating the desired output. The examples demonstrate the expected format, while the constraints ensure that the summary is succinct and appropriate for a general audience. The placeholder token helps maintain the structure of the output, making it easier to extract and process the model's response. Through the thoughtful integration of these components, this prompt serves as an effective example of prompt engineering in action.

Another technique that can be incorporated into prompt engineering is role prompting, where the user and/or system adopt a specific persona or perspective to guide the language model's response.

Adopt any persona – role prompting for tailored interactions

Role prompting is a technique in prompt engineering where the user and/or the system (the LLM) assume a specific role or persona, often with unique knowledge or expertise, to guide the LLM in generating more accurate, relevant, and contextually appropriate responses. By explicitly defining the role or relationship between the user and the model, role prompting can help create a more engaging and interactive experience, resulting in higher-quality outputs.

Role prompting can take several forms. Some of them are listed here:

- **Expert roles**: The user may pretend to be an expert in a specific domain or field, such as a scientist, historian, or professional, to elicit more specific and informed responses from the model. This approach can also encourage the model to provide more detailed and nuanced information, drawing on its extensive pre-trained knowledge.

    You can also ask the system to pretend to be an expert or act as someone. Let's look at an example.

    Prompt:

    ```
    As an experienced software engineer, I recommend using Python
    for your web scraping project due to its simplicity and the
    availability of powerful libraries like BeautifulSoup and
    Scrapy. What are the pros and cons of using Python for web
    scraping?
    ```

- **Fictional roles**: The user can assume the persona of a fictional character such as a detective or an explorer to create a more immersive and creative interaction with the model. This can be particularly useful for generating stories, dialogues, or role-playing scenarios. Let's look at an example.

    Prompt:

    ```
    As Sherlock Holmes, I've deduced that the stolen painting must
    be hidden in the abandoned warehouse at the docks. Can you, as
    Dr. Watson, provide a detailed plan to recover the painting?
    ```

- **Guiding roles**: The user may take on a role that guides or mentors the model, such as a teacher or coach. This approach encourages the model to think more deeply about the topic, explore alternative perspectives, or refine its understanding of complex concepts. Let's look at an example.

    Prompt:

    ```
    As your biology tutor, I'd like to review the process of
    photosynthesis with you. Can you explain the light-dependent and
    light-independent reactions in your own words?
    ```

- **Collaborative roles**: The user can adopt a role that emphasizes collaboration or partnership with the model, such as a teammate or co-author. This approach can lead to more dynamic interactions, mutual learning, and synergistic problem-solving. Let's look at an example.

    Prompt:

    ```
    As your co-author for our article on sustainable agriculture,
    I've drafted the introduction and the first section. Can
    you provide a well-researched and informative section on the
    benefits of crop rotation?
    ```

The effectiveness of role prompting depends on the clarity and specificity of the role, as well as the model's ability to understand and adapt to the given context. By adopting a well-defined role, users can set expectations and guide the model to generate responses that align with the desired persona or expertise. This approach can lead to more engaging, informative, and accurate interactions with the LLM.

It is essential to keep in mind that role prompting may not always guarantee perfect results as the model's output depends on various factors, such as the quality of the training data and the model's ability to generalize knowledge. However, role prompting can be a valuable tool in any prompt engineer's toolkit, enabling more effective and context-aware interactions with LLMs across a wide range of applications and domains.

Let's look at a couple of examples so that we can make sense of this information.

Few-shot learning – training models with example prompts

Using prompting examples during training, the model is guided to generate responses that align with the desired format, style, or content for a specific task. These examples are known as "few-shot learning," and they demonstrate the model's ability to generalize its knowledge from pre-training and quickly adapt to new tasks with minimal additional training data.

Here are some examples of using prompting examples for different tasks:

- **Text summarization**:

  Prompt:

  > Summarize the following text in one sentence. Example: Input:
  > The quick brown fox jumps over the lazy dog. The dog doesn't
  > seem to mind. Output: A fox jumps over a lazy dog, who remains
  > unfazed.
  > Input: Jane went to the store to buy groceries. She purchased
  > fruits, vegetables, and some snacks for her family. Output:

  Response:

  > Jane buys groceries, including fruits, vegetables, and snacks
  > for her family.

- **Language translation**:

  Prompt:

  > Translate the following English text to French. Example: Input:
  > Hello, how are you? Output: Bonjour, comment ça va?
  > Input: What time is it? Output:

  Response:

  > Quelle heure est -il?

- **Sentiment analysis**:

  Prompt:

  > Determine the sentiment of the following statement as positive,
  > negative, or neutral. Example: Input: I love this product.
  > Output: positive
  > Input: The movie was boring and predictable. Output

  Response:

  > negative

- **Text classification**:

  Prompt:

  > Categorize the following animal as a mammal, bird, reptile, or
  > fish. Example: Input: lion Output: mammal
  > Input: eagle. Output:

  Response:

  > bird

- **Analogies**:

Prompt:

```
Complete the following analogy. Example: Input:
hot:cold::happy:? Output: sad
Input: day:night::awake:? Output:
```

Response:

```
asleep
```

In each example, the prompt starts with a clear task description, followed by an example input-output pair that demonstrates the expected format and desired response. By providing these prompting examples, the model can better understand the task and generate more accurate and contextually appropriate outputs.

It is crucial to bear in mind that the effectiveness of few-shot learning depends on the model's capability to generalize its pre-trained knowledge and the quality of the examples provided. As the field of LLMs continues to evolve, techniques such as few-shot learning and effective prompt engineering will play a vital role in unlocking the full potential of these AI models and enhancing their performance across a wide range of tasks and applications.

Next, we will discuss voice definition. This plays a vital role as it refers to the special qualities and style that make someone's way of expressing themselves unique. Defining the desired voice is crucial for crafting prompts that elicit engaging, natural responses from the language model that align with the intended tone and personality. By incorporating voice definition into prompts, users can shape the model's responses to be more relatable, aligned with a brand identity, and overall more effective depending on the application.

Finding your voice – defining personality in prompts

Voice definition refers to the unique characteristics, style, and tone that distinguish an individual or entity's manner of communication. In the context of writing, voice is an essential element that gives the content its personality, making it engaging, relatable, and memorable. A well-defined voice helps convey the intended message effectively, resonate with the target audience, and establish the author's identity or brand.

Developing a distinct voice involves considering various aspects of language, such as the following:

- **Tone**:

The tone of a piece of writing reflects the attitude or emotion the author wishes to convey. Depending on the context and purpose, the tone can be formal, informal, conversational, authoritative, persuasive, or playful, among others.

- **Vocabulary**:

  The choice of words, phrases, and expressions contributes significantly to the voice of a piece. A unique vocabulary can reflect the author's personality, expertise, and cultural background, as well as cater to the preferences and expectations of the target audience.

- **Sentence structure and syntax**:

  The way sentences are constructed, including their length, complexity, and rhythm, can influence the voice of a piece. Varied sentence structures can create a dynamic and engaging reading experience, while consistent syntax can establish a recognizable voice.

- **Perspective**:

  The point of view from which a piece is written, such as first person, second person, or third person, can impact the voice and the connection established with the reader. Choosing the right perspective can help create a more immersive and relatable experience for the audience.

- **Imagery and figurative language**:

  The use of vivid imagery, metaphors, similes, and other figurative language elements can enhance the voice and make the content more engaging, evocative, and memorable.

When crafting content, writers must consider these aspects to develop a consistent and appealing voice that aligns with their goals, resonates with their audience, and sets them apart from others. A well-defined voice can help establish an author's or brand's identity, create a sense of trust and familiarity among readers, and ultimately contribute to the success and impact of their communication efforts.

In the context of AI-generated content, developing a distinct voice can be achieved through prompt engineering techniques, such as providing the model with specific instructions regarding tone, style, and vocabulary. By tailoring prompts to elicit the desired voice, AI models such as LLMs can generate content that aligns with the author's or brand's unique communication style, further enhancing the value and effectiveness of AI-generated content.

Here are some examples of voice definitions for different types of writing and contexts:

- **Professional and authoritative voice**:

  This voice is characterized by a formal tone, precise vocabulary, and well-structured sentences. It is commonly used in business reports, academic articles, or legal documents.

  Here's an example:

  The comprehensive analysis of the market trends indicates a substantial growth potential for renewable energy sources in the coming decade. This report presents a detailed examination of the factors driving this growth and provides strategic recommendations for capitalizing on emerging opportunities.

- **Conversational and friendly voice**:

  This voice adopts an informal tone, everyday vocabulary, and a casual sentence structure. It is suitable for blog posts, social media content, or personal essays.

  Here's an example:

  Hey everyone! I just tried out this amazing new recipe for chocolate chip cookies, and I couldn't wait to share it with you. They're super easy to make and taste absolutely delicious. Give them a try and let me know what you think!

- **Inspirational and motivational voice**:

  This voice uses an uplifting tone, vivid imagery, and emotional language to engage and inspire readers. It is often found in motivational speeches, self-help books, or personal narratives.

  Here's an example:

  Every journey begins with a single step, and it's up to you to take that leap of faith. Embrace the unknown, conquer your fears, and unleash your true potential. Remember, the only limits that exist are the ones you create for yourself.

- **Humorous and witty voice**:

  This voice incorporates a playful tone, clever wordplay, and humor to entertain and amuse readers. It can be used in satirical essays, comedic scripts, or humorous articles.

  Here's an example:

  If procrastination were an Olympic sport, I'd probably win the gold medal... eventually. Of course, I'd first have to finish binge-watching that latest TV series, rearrange my sock drawer, and contemplate the meaning of life.

- **Persuasive and compelling voice**:

  This voice employs a convincing tone, strong arguments, and targeted language to persuade readers to adopt a particular viewpoint or act. It is commonly used in opinion editorials, sales copies, or political speeches.

  Here's an example:

  Investing in education is not just a moral imperative; it is an economic necessity. By empowering our youth with the knowledge and skills required for the 21st century, we lay the foundation for a prosperous and sustainable future for all.

Each of these voice definitions has unique characteristics, tone, and style, suitable for different contexts and purposes. By understanding and mastering these voice definitions, writers can tailor their content to resonate with their target audience effectively and achieve their communication objectives.

When working with AI-generated content, providing clear instructions and examples of the desired voice definition can help guide the LLM in generating content that aligns with the intended tone, style, and vocabulary. By incorporating voice definition into prompt engineering, AI models can create content that is more engaging, relatable, and impactful, further enhancing the value of AI-generated content across various applications and domains. Voice definition can be incorporated in two ways. The first way is by specifying in the prompt that you wish the LLM to copy the style, tone, and other characteristics of someone's voice in the response. This is useful if we want to use the voice definition of a well-known writer, such as Shakespeare or Tim Ellis. The second is by providing examples of the target person's writing as part of the prompt.

Now that we have explored the concept of voice definition and its significance in written communication, let's shift our focus to another important aspect: patterns. Just as voice adds personality to content, patterns add structure and rhythm, making the writing flow smoothly and engagingly.

Using patterns to enhance prompt effectiveness

In the context of prompt engineering, patterns refer to the recognizable structures, sequences, and relationships that emerge from the organization and repetition of elements within a given input prompt. Understanding and leveraging these patterns can improve the effectiveness of prompts and help elicit more accurate, relevant, and contextually appropriate responses from LLMs.

Patterns in prompt engineering can encompass several aspects, such as the following:

- **Linguistic patterns**: These include the syntax, grammar, and vocabulary used in crafting prompts. By understanding linguistic patterns, prompt engineers can create more effective and coherent prompts that guide the LLM to generate responses in the desired format, style, and tone.

- **Task patterns**: Certain tasks or applications may have specific patterns or conventions that the model needs to follow. For instance, summarization tasks may require the model to condense information while retaining the key points. Translation tasks, on the other hand, involve converting text while preserving meaning and structure. Recognizing and incorporating these patterns in the prompts helps the model generate more appropriate outputs for the given task.

- **Contextual patterns**: These patterns involve the relationships and dependencies between the elements in a prompt, such as the context provided to the model, the input data, and the desired output. By understanding these patterns, prompt engineers can create prompts that better guide the model in generating contextually relevant and accurate responses.

- **Response patterns**: This refers to the patterns in the model-generated outputs, which can be influenced by the prompt's structure, phrasing, and tone. Analyzing the patterns in LLM responses can help prompt engineers iteratively refine their prompts to optimize the model's performance and reduce inaccuracies or biases.

In prompt engineering, recognizing, and leveraging patterns is essential for several reasons:

- **Improves model performance**: Understanding patterns allows prompt engineers to design more effective prompts that guide the model in generating accurate and contextually appropriate responses

- **Reduces ambiguity**: By incorporating patterns that make the task, context, or desired output more explicit, the model is less likely to produce ambiguous, nonsensical, or irrelevant responses

- **Adapts to new tasks**: The ability to identify patterns can help prompt engineers quickly adapt their prompts to new tasks or domains, enabling more efficient use of LLMs in diverse applications

- **Mitigates biases**: Recognizing and addressing biases in model-generated patterns can help prompt engineers create prompts that generate more fair, unbiased, and responsible outputs

Output patterns refer to the specific structures, formats, or conventions that the generated response from an LLM should follow. By providing clear instructions and examples within the prompt, you can guide the model to generate outputs that adhere to the desired pattern. In the case of generating a list of items formatted as a JSON array, the prompt could include an example that demonstrates the expected output format.

Here's an example of how to craft such a prompt:

Prompt:

```
Given the following list of fruits - apple, banana, orange - create a
JSON array of the items. Use this format as a reference.
```

Input:

```
dog, cat, fish
```

Output:

```
'[{animal: "dog"}, {animal: "cat"}, {animal:"fish"}]'"
```

Input:

```
apple, banana, orange
```

Output:

```
[{fruit: "apple"}, {fruit: "banana"}, {fruit: "orange"}]
```

In this prompt, the task description clearly states the objective of creating a JSON array of the items. The example provided within the prompt showcases the desired output format, helping the model understand the pattern it should follow when generating the response.

To ensure consistency in the output pattern, you can also specify additional constraints or formatting guidelines within the prompt. For example, you could mention that the output should include double quotes around each item or that the array should maintain the order of the input items.

When working with JSON arrays or other structured data formats, it is crucial to ensure that the generated output adheres to the proper syntax and conventions of that format. By carefully crafting prompts that include clear instructions, examples, and constraints, you can guide the LLM to generate responses that follow the desired output pattern, resulting in more accurate, useful, and well-formatted outputs for various tasks and applications.

As we have explored so far, there are various effective techniques in prompt engineering, such as role prompting, using examples, and applying output patterns. Each technique has its strengths but combining them can lead to even more powerful results. The synergistic effect of blending different techniques allows prompt engineers to craft prompts that elicit highly accurate, natural, and contextually appropriate responses from language models.

Mix and match – strategic combinations for enhanced prompts

By thoughtfully integrating complementary approaches, prompt engineers can develop prompts that are engaging, natural, and highly effective. In this section, we'll explore examples of prompting techniques working in tandem to elicit accurate, contextual responses from language models. Through role prompting, constraints, and other techniques working in unison, prompt engineers can guide models to generate precisely what is needed for the task at hand.

Here are some examples that demonstrate the combination of these techniques:

- **Combining role prompting with examples**:

    Suppose we want to ask the model for advice on time management in the context of a mentor-student relationship. We can combine role prompting with examples to create an effective prompt.

    Prompt:

    ```
    As my time management mentor, can you give me three tips to
    improve my productivity? For instance, an example of a tip might
    be: Set specific and achievable goals for each day.
    ```

    Output:

    ```
    Certainly! Here are three tips to enhance your productivity:
    1. Break large tasks into smaller, manageable subtasks. 2.
    Prioritize your tasks by importance and urgency using the
    Eisenhower Matrix. 3. Take regular breaks to refresh your mind
    and stay focused throughout the day.
    ```

- **Combining role prompting with examples and the output pattern**:

Task: Write a concise weather report for a news channel.

Prompt:

```
As a professional weather reporter, provide a brief and
informative weather report for New York City today, including
temperature, chance of precipitation, and any weather
advisories. Example: Good morning, NYC! Today, expect a high of
72°F with a 40% chance of afternoon showers. Wind advisory in
effect until 6 PM.
```

Output:

```
Good morning, New York City! As your local weather reporter,
here is your forecast for today. We're looking at a high
temperature of 68°F under partly cloudy skies. There is a
30% chance of light rain showers this evening, so keep those
umbrellas handy. A wind advisory is in effect from noon until
8PM tonight, with gusts up to 25 mph expected. Other than the
potential for wet weather later on, it looks to be a mild
October day in the Big Apple. Enjoy, and stay tuned for more
updates as needed!
```

In this case, the prompt provides an example of the output, which also serves as a pattern of how the response should be provided.

- **Combining role prompting, examples, and the output pattern**:

Task: Write a brief movie review for a family-oriented blog.

Prompt:

```
As a family-friendly movie critic, write a short review for
the animated movie Inside Out, focusing on its message,
entertainment value, and age-appropriateness. Example: Inside
Out is a heartwarming and entertaining film that teaches
valuable life lessons to both kids and adults. The animation is
top-notch, and the voice acting is superb. Perfect for ages 6
and up.
```

Output:

```
As a parent and movie critic, I highly recommend Inside Out for
family viewing. This clever animated film creatively explores
emotional intelligence and human psychology through colorful
characters representing Joy, Sadness, Anger, Disgust, and
Fear. Kids will enjoy the fun humor and adventures while also
learning about complex emotions we all experience. The top-notch
animation is visually appealing and the talented voice cast
shines. Inside Out is heartfelt and entertaining for viewers
of all ages 6 and up. It teaches an important message about
embracing our feelings, both positive and negative. This is a
thoughtful movie the whole family can enjoy together.
```

The prompt provides an example of the output, which also serves as a pattern of how the response should be provided.

- **Combining role prompting with the output pattern and examples**:

Task: Create a motivational quote to inspire young entrepreneurs.

Prompt:

```
As a successful entrepreneur, come up with a motivational quote
that inspires young entrepreneurs to chase their dreams and
never give up. Example: Success is not final, failure is not
fatal; it's the courage to continue that truly counts. Keep
pushing, young dreamers!
```

Output:

```
Every setback brings you closer to success if you keep
believing. Stay determined, stay resilient - your dreams are
always within reach.
```

- **Combining role prompting, examples, and the output pattern**:

Task: Write a short recipe description for a vegan pasta dish.

Prompt:

```
As a vegan cookbook author, describe a simple and delicious
vegan pasta recipe, including the main ingredients and
preparation method. Example: Creamy avocado pesto pasta is a
delightful vegan dish that combines perfectly cooked pasta with
a rich, smooth avocado-based sauce. Blend ripe avocados, fresh
basil, garlic, lemon juice, and pine nuts to create a luscious
pesto that will leave everyone craving more.
```

Output:

```
For a quick and easy vegan pasta, sauté minced garlic in
olive oil over medium heat. Add chopped zucchini and sauté
for 3-4 minutes. Add marinara or tomato pasta sauce and simmer
for 2-3 minutes. Meanwhile, cook pasta according to package
instructions. Top the hot pasta with the vegetable sauce
mixture. Finish with a garnish of toasted pine nuts, fresh
basil, and grated vegan Parmesan for a flavorsome plant-based
pasta dish. The savory vegetables, aromatic garlic and basil,
and umami Parmesan create a simple yet delicious vegan pasta in
minutes.
```

- **Combining role prompting, examples, and the output pattern**:

Task: Write a concise fitness tip for people working from home.

Prompt:

```
As a fitness expert, provide a short and helpful fitness tip
for people who are working from home and want to stay active.
Example: Don't forget to take breaks! Set a timer for every
```

```
hour, stand up, stretch, and take a quick 5-minute walk to boost
your energy and productivity.
```

Output:

```
Try doing bodyweight exercises during work breaks. Pushups,
squats, lunges, and planks can be done anywhere without
equipment. Just a few minutes every hour keeps your blood
pumping and muscles activated. Staying physically active
throughout the workday is key for energy, focus, and wellbeing
when working from home.
```

Now that we have covered various techniques for crafting effective prompts, let's shift our focus to exploring the key parameters that can be adjusted to control and refine LLM outputs.

Exploring LLM parameters

LLMs such as OpenAI's GPT-4 consist of several parameters that can be adjusted to control and fine-tune their behavior and performance. Understanding and manipulating these parameters can help users obtain more accurate, relevant, and contextually appropriate outputs. Some of the most important LLM parameters to consider are listed here:

- **Model size**: The size of an LLM typically refers to the number of neurons or parameters it has. Larger models can be more powerful and capable of generating more accurate and coherent responses. However, they might also require more computational resources and processing time. Users may need to balance the trade-off between model size and computational efficiency, depending on their specific requirements.

- **Temperature**: The temperature parameter controls the randomness of the output generated by the LLM. A higher temperature value (for example, 0.8) produces more diverse and creative responses, while a lower value (for example, 0.2) results in more focused and deterministic outputs. Adjusting the temperature can help users fine-tune the balance between creativity and consistency in the model's responses.

- **Top-k**: The top-k parameter is another way to control the randomness and diversity of the LLM's output. This parameter limits the model to consider only the top "k" most probable tokens for each step in generating the response. For example, if top-k is set to 5, the model will choose the next token from the five most likely options. By adjusting the top-k value, users can manage the trade-off between response diversity and coherence. A smaller top-k value generally results in more focused and deterministic outputs, while a larger top-k value allows for more diverse and creative responses.

- **Max tokens**: The max tokens parameter sets the maximum number of tokens (words or subwords) allowed in the generated output. By adjusting this parameter, users can control the length of the response provided by the LLM. Setting a lower max tokens value can help ensure concise answers, while a higher value allows for more detailed and elaborate responses.

- **Prompt length**: While not a direct parameter of the LLM, the length of the input prompt can influence the model's performance. A longer, more detailed prompt can provide the LLM with more context and guidance, resulting in more accurate and relevant responses. However, users should be aware that very long prompts can consume a significant portion of the token limit, potentially truncating the model's output.

By understanding these LLM parameters and adjusting them according to specific needs and requirements, users can optimize their interactions with the model and obtain more accurate, relevant, and contextually appropriate outputs. Balancing these parameters and tailoring them to the task at hand is a crucial aspect of prompt engineering, which can significantly enhance the overall effectiveness of the LLM.

It's important to note that different tasks may require different parameter settings to achieve optimal results. Users should experiment with various parameter combinations and consider the trade-offs between factors such as creativity, consistency, response length, and computational requirements. This iterative process of testing and refining parameter settings will aid users in unlocking the full potential of LLMs such as GPT-4, Claude, and Google Bard.

Playing with different parameters and with different techniques will help you understand what works best for every case. The next section dives deeper into how to approach that experimentation mindset when working with prompts.

How to approach prompt engineering (experimentation)

Approaching prompt engineering involves a systematic and iterative process of experimentation to achieve the desired output from an LLM. The key is to refine and adapt your prompt based on the model's responses, continually improving its effectiveness. Here are the steps to approach prompt engineering through experimentation:

1. **Define the objective**: Clearly outline the goal of the interaction with the LLM. Determine the specific information, format, and context required for the desired output.

2. **Craft the initial prompt**: Using the components of a prompt, such as context, instruction, role prompting, examples, and output pattern, create a clear and concise prompt that communicates your expectations and requirements to the LLM.

3. **Adjust LLM parameters**: Set the initial values for LLM parameters, such as temperature, top-k, and max tokens, based on your output preferences, such as creativity, determinism, and response length.

4. **Test and evaluate**: Submit the prompt to the LLM and analyze the generated output. Assess how well the response aligns with your expectations, considering factors such as relevance, coherence, format, and tone.

5. **Refine the prompt**: Based on the output's evaluation, identify areas of improvement, and modify the prompt accordingly. This could involve clarifying the instructions, adding examples, adjusting the output pattern, or altering the role prompting. Also, consider refining the LLM parameters if necessary, tweaking values such as temperature or top-k to influence the response's creativity or determinism.

6. **Iterate**: Repeat the testing, evaluation, and refinement process until the LLM generates a satisfactory output that meets your criteria. This iterative approach helps fine-tune the prompt engineering process and adapt it to various tasks and requirements.

7. **Document successes and failures**: Keep a record of successful prompt engineering techniques and parameter settings, as well as those that didn't work as expected. This documentation will serve as a valuable reference in future experiments, allowing you to build on previous experiences and streamline the prompt engineering process.

8. **Share findings and collaborate**: Engage with the broader LLM user community to share insights, learn from others' experiences, and collaboratively develop best practices for prompt engineering. Exchanging knowledge and ideas can help improve the overall effectiveness and efficiency of the prompt engineering process.

9. **Apply transferable techniques**: As you gain experience in prompt engineering, identify techniques and strategies that can be applied across various tasks and domains. These transferable approaches can help you quickly adapt your prompt engineering skills to new challenges and maximize the effectiveness of LLM interactions.

10. **Stay up to date with LLM advancements**: As large-scale LLMs continue to evolve, it's essential to stay informed about new developments, features, and best practices. Regularly review updates, research, and resources from LLM developers, such as OpenAI, to ensure that your prompt engineering techniques remain effective and relevant.

11. **Explore creative applications**: Prompt engineering is not limited to conventional tasks and outputs. Experiment with innovative and creative applications of LLMs, pushing the boundaries of what these models can achieve. This exploratory approach can lead to novel solutions, insights, and applications that demonstrate the true potential of large-scale LLMs. By approaching prompt engineering through systematic experimentation, users can incrementally improve their prompts and LLM interactions, ensuring more accurate, relevant, and contextually appropriate outputs. This process encourages learning, adaptation, and the development of effective strategies for harnessing the full potential of large-scale LLMs such as GPT-4.

Even though prompt engineering is very powerful, it can lead to wrong results. Thus, in the next section, we will explore some of their limitations and how you can try to mitigate them.

The challenges and limitations of using LLM prompts

While LLMs such as GPT-4 have demonstrated remarkable capabilities in generating human-like responses, they also come with their own set of challenges and limitations when it comes to crafting effective prompts. Some of these challenges and limitations are as follows:

- **Verbosity**: LLMs tend to generate verbose outputs, often providing more information than necessary or repeating ideas. Crafting prompts that encourage concise responses can be challenging and may require iterating on the prompt and setting appropriate constraints.

- **Ambiguity**: LLMs may struggle with ambiguous or poorly defined prompts, resulting in outputs that do not meet the user's expectations. Users must invest time and effort to create clear and specific prompts that minimize ambiguity.

- **Inconsistency**: LLMs can sometimes generate responses that contain contradicting information or vary in quality across different runs. Ensuring the consistency of the output may require fine-tuning the parameters and prompt engineering techniques.

- **Lack of common sense**: Although LLMs have a vast knowledge base, they can occasionally produce outputs that lack common sense or make incorrect assumptions. Users may need to experiment with different prompt techniques to obtain more accurate and sensible responses.

- **Bias**: LLMs can inadvertently exhibit biases present in their training data. Consequently, the LLMs may inadvertently learn and perpetuate these biases and discriminatory beliefs, leading to skewed perspectives and unfair outcomes. This can have serious implications, especially when LLMs are used in areas such as hiring, education, and decision-making. Therefore, it is crucial to recognize and address these biases in LLMs, ensuring that these powerful tools are used responsibly and ethically.

- **Hallucinations**: LLM hallucinations refer to instances when an LLM generates text that is factually incorrect, nonsensical, or unrelated to the context of the input. This phenomenon occurs because LLMs learn patterns and associations from the vast amount of training data, but they do not possess an intrinsic understanding of the world or the ability to reason like humans. As a result, they may sometimes produce outputs that seem plausible but are inaccurate or illogical. Hallucinations can be particularly concerning when users rely on LLMs for factual information, decision-making, or content generation. To mitigate the impact of hallucinations, users must invest in refining the models, creating better evaluation metrics, and implementing user feedback loops to enhance the performance and reliability of LLMs.

As we come to the end of this chapter, we have embarked on a comprehensive exploration of AI prompts, delving into their components, types, and practical applications. With this foundational knowledge, we are now equipped to dive deeper into the world of prompt engineering and uncover advanced techniques in the upcoming chapters.

Summary

In this introductory chapter, you embarked on a journey to explore the world of AI prompts. This chapter provided a comprehensive overview of LLM prompts, including their components, types, and how they function. Through practical examples and use cases, you witnessed the power and versatility of LLM prompts, such as generating product descriptions and translating text.

By exploring the different types of prompts and their role in guiding LLMs, you gained a solid foundation in prompt engineering. You became familiar with the key components of a prompt, such as the input prompt, context, and response, and understood how they shape the output of the language model.

This chapter emphasized the importance of voice definition and patterns in creating engaging and effective content. You discovered how these elements give your writing a unique personality and maintain a smooth flow, making your messages impactful and memorable.

While exploring the potential of LLM prompts, this chapter also addressed the challenges and limitations associated with their usage. By understanding these obstacles, you gained insights into how to navigate them and make informed decisions in your prompt engineering endeavors.

As this chapter concludes, you are now equipped with a comprehensive foundation for the rest of this book. With a solid understanding of LLM prompts, you are ready to explore advanced techniques, combine different prompt engineering approaches, experiment with various parameters, and overcome challenges to unlock new possibilities. Throughout your journey, you will harness the power of LLM prompts to create remarkable experiences and achieve your desired outcomes.

Having established a solid foundation in prompt engineering, we will now set our sights on applying these skills to unlock the power of AI for automated content creation. This will be explored in depth in the upcoming chapter.

2

Generating Text with AI for Content Creation

The rise of **artificial intelligence** (**AI**) has opened up exciting new possibilities for automating and enhancing content creation. In this chapter, we will explore how AI can be leveraged to write compelling copy across a variety of mediums and use cases, from social media posts to long-form articles.

We will begin by looking at the basics of using AI for copywriting. Generative language models can now produce human-like text tailored to your brand voice and goals. We'll discuss best practices for crafting effective prompts to guide the AI and produce high-quality draft content. With the right prompts and input, AI can generate blog posts, social media captions, landing page copy, emails, and more.

Next, we will explore how AI can customize content at scale. By incorporating personalization into prompts and giving the AI user data, it can tailor messaging for each reader. This has powerful marketing applications, allowing brands to provide a more personalized experience. We'll cover different techniques for personalization with AI.

Later sections will provide tips on using AI for specific content types and use cases. We'll look at crafting viral social media posts, writing compelling video scripts that convert viewers, and optimizing long-form content such as articles and newsletters for engagement. Throughout, we'll share actionable strategies and examples for getting the most out of AI as a copywriting tool.

By the end of this chapter, you will have a firm grasp of how to utilize AI as a copywriting assistant to create high-quality, personalized content quickly and at scale. The strategies covered will help writers, marketers, and entrepreneurs supercharge their content engines with this exciting new technology.

The most common generative AI tools for writing are as follows:

- **ChatGPT and ChatGPT Plus**: You can sign in at `https://openai.com/` ChatGPT Plus allows you to access not only GPT-3.5 Turbo but also GPT-4. It also gives access to plugins. Plugins will be discussed later in this book.

- Google Bard (`https://bard.google.com/chat`): This has access to the internet and it allows you to upload image files. Thus, you can ask Bard to describe the scene in an image.

- Anthropic Claude 2 (`https://claude.ai/login`): This also has access to the internet, and it has a 100,000 token context window, which allows it to handle large documents and PDFs of up to 75,000 words.

- **Microsoft Bing** (`https://www.bing.com/search`): This is the ChatGPT version run by Microsoft. It has access to the internet.

- **Open AI Playground** (`https://platform.openai.com/playground`): Here, you can access different versions of GPT-3.5 Turbo and GPT-4. The versions are referenced by released dates and context windows. For example, gpt-3.5-turbo-16k-0613 has a context window of 16,000 tokens and was released on June 13, 2023.

The following topics will be covered in this chapter:

- Using AI for copywriting

- Creating social media posts

- Writing video scripts

- Generating blog posts, articles, and news

- Creating engaging content with AI

- How to use AI for personalized messaging

- Creating tailored content with AI

Using AI for copywriting

By utilizing ChatGPT as a powerful content creation tool, content creators can harness its versatility, knowledge, and language abilities to streamline their creative process, generate innovative ideas, improve writing quality, and engage with their audience in novel ways.

Content creators have several compelling reasons to use tools such as ChatGPT to enhance their content creation process:

- **Versatility and flexibility**: ChatGPT can be leveraged across various content formats, including articles, scripts, social media posts, and more. Its versatility allows creators to engage with the model conversationally, enabling them to brainstorm ideas, ask for suggestions, or receive feedback, thereby expanding the possibilities for their content.

- **Idea generation and inspiration**: ChatGPT's vast knowledge base and language capabilities make it an excellent tool for generating fresh ideas and finding inspiration. Content creators can tap into the model's extensive understanding of diverse topics and trends to develop unique concepts, explore different angles, or even spark innovative collaborations.

- **Writing assistance and editing support**: Creating high-quality content often involves careful crafting and editing. ChatGPT can act as a virtual writing assistant, offering real-time suggestions, improving sentence structure, providing grammar and spelling corrections, and enhancing overall clarity. This can save content creators time and effort while they're refining their work.

- **Research and fact-checking**: Accurate information is crucial for content creators. ChatGPT can assist in researching topics, verifying facts, and providing references to reputable sources. By leveraging the model's knowledge cutoff date and its ability to analyze vast amounts of text, content creators can access reliable information and ensure the accuracy and credibility of their work. In this case, the user has to be careful to check that ChatGPT is not hallucinating.

- **Audience engagement and interaction**: ChatGPT's conversational nature allows content creators to simulate dialogues, interviews, or Q&A sessions with the model. This opens up opportunities for dynamic and engaging content formats that foster audience interaction. Creators can ask the model questions on behalf of their audience, present hypothetical scenarios, or explore different perspectives, fostering an interactive and immersive experience.

- **Content optimization**: With the vast amount of content available online, creators need to optimize their work for search engines and social media platforms. ChatGPT can offer insights on SEO-friendly keywords, headlines, meta descriptions, and social media captions. It can assist content creators in tailoring their content to maximize its visibility and reach a wider audience.

- **Timesaving and efficiency**: ChatGPT's ability to generate text quickly and provide immediate responses can significantly enhance a content creator's productivity. Instead of spending excessive time researching or drafting, creators can rely on the model to assist them, allowing them to focus on other aspects of their work, such as strategy, creativity, and engaging with their audience.

- **Multilingual support**: Content creators catering to diverse audiences can benefit from ChatGPT's multilingual capabilities. The model can assist with content creation in various languages, opening up opportunities for creators to reach a global audience and expand their content's international reach.

Crafting powerful prompts is essential for engaging content. Here are five formulas you can use:

- **AIDA formula**: *Attention, Interest, Desire*, and *Action*.

  This classic copywriting formula is designed to take readers through a persuasive journey by capturing attention, piquing interest, creating desire, and ultimately inspiring action. Follow these steps:

  I.   **Attention**: Begin with a strong headline or opening statement that grabs the reader's attention, addressing their pain points and desires, or evoking curiosity.

  II.   **Interest**: Provide interesting and informative content that aligns with your target audience's needs and preferences. Use facts, stories, or examples to captivate readers and keep them engaged.

III.   **Desire**: Tap into your audience's emotions and aspirations by showcasing the benefits of your product or service, making them feel that it's essential for achieving their goals or solving their problems.

IV.   **Action**: End the content with a clear and compelling call to action that encourages readers to take the next step, whether it's purchasing your product, signing up for your service, or requesting more information.

- **PAS formula**: *Problem*, *Agitate*, and *Solve*.

  This formula focuses on identifying a specific problem faced by your target audience, agitating it by highlighting the pain it causes, and presenting your product or service as the ideal solution. Follow these steps:

  I.   **Problem**: Start by identifying a problem or pain point that your target audience experiences. Make sure it's a problem that your product or service can effectively address. Demonstrate that you understand their struggle and can empathize with their situation.

  II.   **Agitate**: Dive deeper into the problem by explaining the consequences and negative impact of not addressing it. Make the problem feel more pressing and urgent, evoking emotions such as frustration, fear, or a sense of missing out.

  III.   **Solve**: Present your product or service as the solution to the problem. Showcase the benefits, advantages, and how it specifically resolves the issue. Provide evidence such as case studies, statistics, or testimonials to build trust and credibility. Finally, include a clear call to action that directs readers to what they should do next to take advantage of your offering and solve their problem.

- **FOMO formula**: *Fear of Missing Out*.

  Leverage the psychology of **fear of missing out** (**FOMO**) to create urgent and compelling prompts. This formula taps into the innate desire people have not to be left behind or miss out on something valuable. Follow these steps:

  I.   **Exclusivity**: Emphasize the exclusive or limited nature of your offering, such as being available to a specific group or having a limited supply.

  II.   **Timing**: Create urgency by adding a time-sensitive aspect, such as a limited-time promotion, a countdown timer, or a deadline for registration.

  III.   **Social Proof**: Showcase the popularity or high demand for your product or service by sharing testimonials, reviews, or the number of people who have already taken advantage of your offer.

  IV.   **Action**: Encourage immediate action by combining the preceding elements and stating what the reader needs to do to avoid missing out, such as purchasing now, signing up, or joining a waiting list.

- **SMILE formula**: *Storytelling, Metaphor, Inspirational, Language,* and *Emotion.*

This formula focuses on creating a strong emotional connection with your audience by integrating different elements of storytelling and persuasive language. Follow these steps:

I.   **Storytelling**: Start your content with a captivating story that resonates with your target audience. It can be a personal story, a case study, or a story of someone else's experience with your product or service.

II. **Metaphor**: Use metaphors, analogies, and vivid imagery to make complex concepts more relatable and memorable.

III. **Inspirational**: Uplift your readers and motivate them to take action by presenting an inspiring vision of what their lives could be like once they use your offering.

IV. **Language**: Choose powerful, descriptive, and persuasive words that appeal to your audience's emotions and aspirations. Avoid jargon and technical language that may be difficult to understand.

V.   **Emotion**: Evoke strong emotions that grab your reader's attention, create a sense of connection, and ultimately motivate them to take action. Focus on emotions such as excitement, enthusiasm, joy, relief, or pride.

- **POWER formula**: *Promise, Objection, Why, Evidence,* and *Reward.*

This formula tackles potential objections to the offering made in the cold email from your audience while demonstrating the value of your product or service. Apply these steps to create effective prompts:

I.   **Promise**: Begin with a clear and powerful promise that shows how your product or service will benefit your target audience. Let them know what they can expect to gain or achieve.

II. **Objection**: Address the common objections or concerns that your audience might have about your offering. Be upfront and honest about potential drawbacks and demonstrate how your solution overcomes these limitations.

III. **Why**: Explain the unique reasons your product or service stands out in the marketplace compared to competitors. Showcase the factors that differentiate your offering and make it worth choosing.

IV. **Evidence**: Provide evidence to support your claims, such as testimonials, case studies, data, or expert endorsements. This helps build trust, credibility, and confidence in your product or service.

V.   **Reward**: Conclude by highlighting the rewards or positive outcomes your audience will experience when they take action. Summarize the benefits, emphasize the improvements they can expect, and motivate them to act by connecting the rewards to their personal or professional goals.

Thus, when creating prompts to generate copy, instruct the model (ChatGPT, Bard, and so on) which of these formulas or a combination of them you would like it to use to be able to create compelling content that captures your audience's attention, connects with their emotions, and effectively communicates the value of your product or service.

To produce better copy, providing most of the following information would be helpful:

- **Target audience**: Details about your target market, including demographics (age, gender, income, education), psychographics (interests, values, lifestyle), and any known pain points or desires.

- **Product or service**: A thorough understanding of your product or service, including features, benefits, pricing, and what sets it apart from competitors.

- **Brand identity**: Information about your brand's identity, values, and voice to ensure the copy is consistent and reflects your brand's personality.

- **Marketing goals**: A clear understanding of your specific marketing goals and objectives, such as increasing sales, generating leads, creating awareness, or improving brand perception.

- **Tone and style**: The desired tone and style for your copy (for example, professional, conversational, humorous, informative, or inspirational).

- **Key messages**: Any key messages or unique selling points you'd like to emphasize in the copy.

- **Restrictions**: Any restrictions, such as word count, formatting requirements, or platform-specific guidelines.

- **Call to action**: The desired call to action, whether it's purchasing a product, signing up for a newsletter, contacting you for more information, or visiting your website.

- **Competitors**: Insights into your main competitors and their marketing strategies, which help identify areas of opportunity and differentiation for your brand.

- **Channel and format**: The specific channels and formats where the copy will be applied, such as website content, blog posts, social media, email campaigns, or printed materials. This helps tailor the copy to meet the requirements and user experience of each medium.

- **Keywords**: If you're focusing on **search engine optimization (SEO)**, provide a list of relevant keywords and phrases you'd like to target or incorporate within the copy.

- **Testimonials and social proof**: Customer reviews, testimonials, case studies, or any other forms of social proof that support the claims made in your copy and build trust with your audience.

- **Visual elements**: Details about any visual elements, such as images, graphs, videos, or infographics, which can help support the text and create a more engaging experience.

Providing this information ensures the creation of tailored, high-quality copy that not only resonates with your target audience but also effectively communicates your brand's unique value proposition, aligns with your marketing goals, and drives the desired action. The more detailed and comprehensive the information provided, the better the copy can be customized to your specific needs and objectives.

Remember that ChatGPT allows you to build a *conversation*. As such, you can ask it to refine or rewrite parts of the copy to adjust to your needs.

In the next few sections, we are going to explore how to use this approach to create different types of content with the help of generative AI.

Creating social media posts

Let's learn how to use ChatGPT (with GPT-4) to write a Twitter thread. In general, GPT-4 is better than GPT-3.5 Turbo, but it's also more expensive. Thus, experiment with different models, including Bing (free), Google Bard (free), and Anthropic Claude (free).

GPT-4 is a significant improvement over GPT-3.5 in several ways:

- **Multimodal capabilities**: GPT-4 can understand and generate text, and soon it will be able to understand images and graphics. This makes it a more versatile tool for a wider range of applications. This makes it a more versatile tool for a wider range of applications.

- **Improved context understanding**: GPT-4 can retain more information from previous conversations and use it to generate more relevant and coherent responses.

- **Better performance on complex tasks**: GPT-4 is better at solving complex problems, such as generating code, translating languages, and writing different kinds of creative content.

- **Reduced likelihood of generating harmful or offensive content**: GPT-4 is less likely to generate harmful or offensive content, even when prompted to do so.

To use ChatGPT with GPT-4, you need to subscribe to ChatGPT Plus. Another way to use GPT-4 is by signing in to get access to OpenAI APIs. Once you do that, you can use GPT-4 in the playground (you can find it at `https://platform.openai.com/playground`) or by using the corresponding API. In both cases, you will be charged depending on how much you use it.

In ChatGPT, Bard, Bing, and Claude, you can enter a prompt and get a response, enter another prompt and get another response, and so on.

In most cases, we will be using GPT-4 in the playground.

With AI now capable of generating coherent text, one application that shows promise is using these models to draft social media content such as Twitter threads.

Writing a Twitter thread

Social media platforms such as Twitter have become popular outlets for sharing ideas and engaging audiences. However, writing compelling threads that spark discussion can be challenging. AI text generation models present an intriguing option for drafting initial Twitter threads that human creators can then refine and finalize. Harnessing this to ideate thread topics and content is an emerging use case to explore.

Let's start with a zero-shot prompt.

Prompt:

```
Write a Tweet about being a solopreneur
```

Response:

```
🛸 Embracing the #solopreneur life! 🌟 Juggling all roles,
making decisions, and learning every day. It's a wild ride, but
I'm loving the freedom and growth it brings. 📱☑ Shoutout to
my fellow solopreneurs, let's show 'em what we're made of! 💪
#EntrepreneurSpirit #BossingItUp 🌍
```

Now, let's make it a thread.

Prompt:

```
make it a thread
```

Response:

```
🛸 Embracing the #solopreneur life! 🌟 Juggling all roles,
making decisions, and learning every day. It's a wild ride, but
I'm loving the freedom and growth it brings. 📱☑ Shoutout to
my fellow solopreneurs, let's show 'em what we're made of! 💪
#EntrepreneurSpirit #BossingItUp 🌍
🧵1/4: The most rewarding aspect of being a solopreneur? 💡 Knowing
that every achievement, big or small, is a direct result of my hard
work and determination. 🏆 The sky's the limit! 🌈 #GoalChaser
#DeterminationPaysOff
🧵2/4: Of course, there are challenges too. 😅 Time management and
staying motivated can be tough when you're a one-person show. ⏰
But the lessons I've learned and the skills I've gained are truly
priceless. 🔻 #GrowthMindset #AlwaysImproving
🧵3/4: Networking is key! 🤝 Despite being a solopreneur, I've
discovered the importance of connecting with like-minded individuals.
The support, advice, and camaraderie from fellow solopreneurs and
entrepreneurs have been invaluable to my journey. 🌐 Together, we
rise! 🖐 #CommunityOverCompetition #StrongerTogether
🧵4/4: So, here's to chasing dreams and claiming success as a
solopreneur! 🙌 If you've been considering going solo, trust in
yourself and take the leap. The journey may be challenging, but the
rewards are worth it. 🌟 #DreamBig #BeYourOwnBoss #SolopreneurLife
```

This isn't bad, but it can be better. Let's provide more context on what we want.

Here's how you can further improve the prompt.

Prompt:

```
Write the Tweet providing tips considering the following inputs:
Target audience: Aspiring or current solopreneurs, freelancers, and
small business owners who may be interested in learning more about the
challenges and rewards of running a solo business.
Product or service: An online platform, consultancy service, or
mentorship program that offers resources and support for solopreneurs
to grow and manage their businesses.
Brand identity: A reliable, resourceful, and inspiring brand that
empowers solopreneurs to thrive in their professional journey.
Marketing goals: To increase brand awareness, engage with the target
audience, and ultimately drive traffic to the website or an online
event (e.g., webinar, workshop) designed for solopreneurs.
Tone and style: Conversational and motivational, using a mix of
personal experience, insights, and practical tips for solopreneurs.
Key messages: The main takeaways or insights you'd like to share about
the solopreneur journey, such as the importance of self-discipline,
time management, networking, or the ability to adapt to change.
Restrictions: A short, concise social media post, tailored to the
platform's character limits or format requirements (e.g., Twitter's
280 characters or Instagram's optimal caption length of 125-150
characters).
Call to action: Encourage readers to visit your website to learn more
about your offerings for solopreneurs, sign up for your newsletter
or online event, or engage by asking them to share their solopreneur
experiences in the comments section.
Competitors: Understand the content, messaging, and engagement tactics
employed by competing brands who also target solopreneurs, to identify
areas of opportunity or differentiation for your social media post.
Hashtags and mentions: For improved reach and engagement, research and
include relevant hashtags that your target audience follows or uses,
and mention or tag influencers, if applicable.
```

Response:

```
🚀 Hey, solopreneurs & freelancers! Want to level up your solo biz
game? 💼 Here are 3 quick tips to thrive:
1  ⏲Time management = 🔑
2  □Network, network, network! 🤝
3  □Adaptability is essential 🦎
Ready to #UnlockYourPotential? Join our upcoming webinar 📅 for
in-depth support & resources tailored for your journey!
👉 [website link] 🔗
What's your top #SolopreneurTip? Share it below! 👇 Let's support and
learn from each other. 💪 #FreelancerLife #SmallBizOwners
```

Again, let's make it a thread.

Prompt:

```
Make it a thread
```

Response:

```
🚀 Hey, solopreneurs & freelancers! Want to level up your solo biz
game? 💼 Here are 3 quick tips to thrive:
1  ☐ Time management = 🔑
2  ☐ Network, network, network! 🤝
3  ☐ Adaptability is essential 🍸
Ready to #UnlockYourPotential? Join our upcoming webinar 📅 for
in-depth support & resources tailored for your journey!
👉 [website link] 🔗
What's your top #SolopreneurTip? Share it below! 👇 Let's support and
learn from each other. 🤲 #FreelancerLife #SmallBizOwners
🧵1/3: Let's dive deeper into these tips! ⏱  Time management is
crucial for solopreneurs. It's tempting to work 24/7, but remember
to allocate time for self-care & breaks. Feeling refreshed boosts
productivity! 🧘‍♀️ Tips: Set boundaries, prioritize tasks & use
productivity tools. 🛠
🧵2/3: The power of networking can't be overstated! 🎇 Connect with
like-minded individuals & collaborate. Sharing expertise & learning
from others will propel your solo biz forward! 🚀 Attend events,
engage on social media, & join communities. You're not alone - find
your tribe! 🌐 #NetworkingMatters #CollaborationIsKey
🧵3/3: The solopreneur journey is full of surprises, so adaptability
is essential. 📈 Stay agile & open to change - it's your secret
weapon! 🌀 Pivot when needed, learn continuously & embrace challenges
as growth opportunities. 💯 #StayAgile #ChangeIsGood
🎯 Don't miss our upcoming webinar for more insights & actionable
strategies to empower your solopreneur journey! 💡 Secure your spot
now! 👇
[webinar registration link] 📧
P.S. We love hearing YOUR stories! 😊 Share your top #SolopreneurTip
or experience in the comments. Let's celebrate our successes & learn
from each other! ♡    #WeGotThis
```

In this case, it produced a thread of three items. You can ask for more if needed. That's the beauty of it – you can chat with the LLM to make improvements and changes as you see fit.

Now, let's create an Instagram post.

Writing an Instagram post

While Twitter's short posts lend themselves well to fully automated AI drafting, the longer-form captions on visual platforms such as Instagram may benefit more from AI assistance in ideating and outlining initial content.

Here's the first prompt for an Instagram post.

Prompt:

> Create the content for an Instagram about fitness and mental wellbeing
> challenges for solopreneurs. It could be a series of images, say 3,
> with captions.
> Write the captions and the prompts that can be used to generate the
> images.

Response:

> Image 1 (Prompt: A solopreneur practicing mindfulness, sitting at
> their desk with eyes closed, and a laptop nearby):
> Caption: "Balance the hustle! ⬜ As solopreneurs, our days are
> packed, but don't forget to prioritize mental wellbeing. ⚕
> Take short breaks to practice mindfulness & stay focused! ♀
> #MentalHealthMatters #SolopreneurLife"
> Image 2 (Prompt: A solopreneur exercising at home, doing a yoga pose
> or lifting weights):
> Caption: "No more excuses! 🏋 Incorporate a fitness regimen into
> your daily routine - it not only boosts your energy but also improves
> productivity. 💯 Share your favorite at-home workout routine with us!
> 🏃 #StayActive #SolopreneurFitness"
> Image 3 (Prompt: A solopreneur enjoying outdoor relaxation, getting
> fresh air on a walk):
> Caption: "Nature is therapy! 🌳 Take a break outdoors, as a stroll
> in the park can work wonders for your mental wellbeing & help you
> gather new ideas. 🍃 How do you unwind after a busy workday? 🍂
> #NatureLovers #

It seems that the captions are too long and the prompts for the images are not detailed enough. So, let's improve that in the next prompt.

Prompt:

> Add more details to the prompts for the images.
> Make the captions shorter.

Response:

> Image 1 (Prompt: A solopreneur practicing mindfulness, sitting at
> their desk with eyes closed, taking deep breaths, and a laptop
> nearby):

```
Caption: "Find your zen 🧘‍♂️ Amid the hustle, prioritize
mental wellbeing. Mindfulness fuels focus! 🎯 #StayGrounded
#SolopreneurLife"

Image 2 (Prompt: A solopreneur exercising at home, doing a yoga pose
on a mat or lifting weights with workout gear and a water bottle
nearby):

Caption: "Move it! 🏋️ Home workouts boost energy & productivity. 💪
Share your favorite routine! 🏠 #Fitpreneur #WorkLifeBalance"

Image 3 (Prompt: A solopreneur enjoying outdoor relaxation, getting
fresh air on a walk through a park, wearing casual attire, and
carrying a reusable coffee cup):

Caption: "Nature's therapy 🌳 Unwind with a walk outdoors, gather new
ideas & recharge. 🚶‍♀️ 🍃 #NatureLovers #SolopreneurUnplug"
```

To create the images, we can use prompts and tools such as Midjourney, Stable Diffusion, Adobe Firefly, or any other text-to-image generative AI.

Now, using Adobe Firefly with the prompt for the first image, we get the following output:

Figure 2.1: Images generated with Adobe Firefly

Maybe you would like a more photorealistic image. No problem – add *photorealistic* to the prompt and you will get something like this:

Figure 2.2: Adding photorealistic to the prompt

You can modify the prompts to get something closer to what you are looking for or click on **Regenerate** to create another set of images. Once you get an image that you like, just download it.

You could do something similar to create the content for a LinkedIn post or a carousel.

In the next section, we will explore how to use these techniques to create high-converting sales copy.

Producing high-converting sales copy

Crafting an effective sales and marketing copy is an art that combines an understanding of psychology, writing ability, and strategic messaging. For businesses, the stakes are high because quality copy can notably impact conversion rates, revenue, and brand perception.

With AI natural language models now capable of generating human-like text, companies are experimenting with these systems to ideate, outline, and even draft full sales copy. The goal is to utilize AI as an assistive tool for brainstorming compelling narratives and value propositions. While human copywriters still reign supreme, AI could augment their workflows and creativity.

The possibilities to generate high-converting initial drafts or personalized copy tailored to customer segments present exciting opportunities to explore.

For this example, let's focus on another niche: fitness and weight loss.

Let's look at the prompt.

Prompt:

```
You are a professional copywriter.
You have been tasked to create a high-converting sales copy. Here are
the things that you need to care about on the copy:
Niche: Fitness and Weight Loss
Audience: Busy professionals aged 25-45
Goals: Help them lose weight and adopt a healthier lifestyle
Offer: A 3-month comprehensive online fitness program
Call to action: Sign up for the program
Tone: Motivational, with a sense of urgency
Write the sales copy
```

Response:

```
Tired of the Scales Tipping in the Wrong Direction? Discover the
Ultimate Fitness Solution for Busy Professionals Who Need REAL Results
- FAST!
Dear "Every Second Counts" Professional,
Are you tired of struggling to find time for the gym? Do you
constantly sacrifice your personal fitness for your career? Have you
reached the end of yet another week, wondering how you'll EVER find
time to work out, eat healthily, and see results?
It's time to STOP setting for "busy life equals bad health" and START
investing in yourself! Introducing the 3-Month Fitness Revolution:
The all-in-one online fitness program designed exclusively for BUSY
PROFESSIONALS like you!
Imagine...in just 12 weeks, you could be:
✔    Shedding unwanted pounds and inches
✔    Boosting your energy levels
✔    Enjoying increased stamina and endurance
✔    Feeling more confident & empowered than ever before
SUCCESS is just a few clicks away with our proven system that combines
expertly designed workouts, personalized nutrition plans, and ongoing
support to help you reach your fitness goals - all while balancing
your hectic work schedule!
Tailored to Fit YOUR Busy Life:
Our 3-Month Fitness Revolution program doesn't just deliver results.
It offers FLEXIBILITY, too.
👍 Customizable workout routines to accommodate your schedule
🍽 Personalized meal plans tailored to your dietary needs and
preferences
🕐    Time-saving exercise regimes for those with little free time
📋 Progress tracking to help you stay accountable and motivated
No matter your starting point or how packed your itinerary is, the
3-Month Fitness Revolution program has something for everyone!
```

Limited Time Offer - Don't Miss Out!

Normally, this incredible program retails for $499. But for a limited time, you can JOIN NOW for just $299! That's a $200 SAVINGS! This offer won't last, so claim your spot TODAY.

But wait, it gets better! We're so confident in our program that we're offering a 100% MONEY-BACK GUARANTEE. If you're not completely satisfied within the first 30 days, simply let us know, and we'll refund every penny - no questions asked!

Take the First Step Towards a Healthier, Happier You:

It's time to make YOURSELF a priority. Join the hundreds of busy professionals who have already experienced the incredible 3-Month Fitness Revolution with life-changing results.

Are you ready to finally take control of your health and transform your life? Don't let another day pass you by.

Here's how you can join:

1 ☐ Click the "Sign Up Now" button below

2 ☐ Complete the easy registration process

3 ☐ Start your fitness journey with our expert guidance and support

Remember, spaces are limited and this unbeatable offer won't last long. So what are you waiting for? Reach your fitness goals today with the 3-Month Fitness Revolution program.

Don't let your busy schedule hold you back any longer - make the commitment to a better you TODAY.

🔥 Click the button below to SIGN UP NOW and unlock the future of fitness! 🔥

P.S. Did we mention the incredible BONUS MATERIALS you'll receive when you sign up? In addition to the comprehensive workout and meal plan, you'll gain access to:

🎁 Exclusive members-only online community to network and find motivation from other busy professionals just like you

🎁 Monthly LIVE Q&A sessions with our team of fitness experts to answer all your questions and provide personalized guidance

🎁 Access to our extensive library of fitness resources, including video tutorials, workout charts, and additional recipes for healthy meal planning

Your journey to a healthier, stronger YOU starts NOW. Press that sign-up button and kick-start your transformation today!

Remember, this special offer and our 100% MONEY-BACK GUARANTEE are only available for a limited time. Don't let this opportunity slip through your fingers.

Take control of your health, boost your confidence, and join the ranks of satisfied professionals who have found renewed energy, motivation, and happiness thanks to the 3-Month Fitness Revolution.

Here's to your exciting fitness journey 🏃

→ Click here to SIGN UP NOW ←

This looks very similar to the real offers you get for similar programs. Does it work? Maybe, maybe not. The good news is that you can quickly change some of the variables, make other versions of the copy, and then run A/B tests. Furthermore, you probably won't take the copy produced by the LLM as-is but use it as a starting draft that you can tailor as you see fit.

Is there a copywriter style that you like? Add a couple of examples of copy from that author as examples and in the prompt say, *Write the copy using the style of these examples…* We will explore that later in this chapter.

In the upcoming section, we will delve into crafting effective prompts that help you seamlessly write compelling video scripts.

Writing video scripts

Video content has exploded in popularity in recent years across social platforms, websites, and advertising. However, scripting compelling, engaging videos that connect with audiences can be difficult. AI text generation tools present an opportunity to get an initial draft down quickly.

While human scriptwriters craft the story, characters, and dialogue, AI could help ideate broad themes and content, or even take a first pass at turning outlines into full scripts. This can allow content creators to iterate more quickly and focus their time on refinement. As with sales copy, AI-assisted scriptwriting aims to boost efficiency and creativity rather than fully automate. Finding the right balance for using these tools will be key to producing compelling videos people want to watch and share.

The formula here is similar. We provide a topic, context, goals, audience, and so on and we ask GPT-4 to produce a video script.

Let's begin with our prompts.

Here's the first prompt.

Prompt:

```
You are a copywriting expert that writes video scripts. Trending
Topic: Sustainable Living and Tips to Reduce Your Environmental
Footprint
Goals:
1. Educate the audience on the importance of a sustainable lifestyle.
2. Provide practical tips to help individuals reduce their
environmental footprints.
3. Inspire behavioral change to promote an eco-friendly lifestyle.
Audience: Eco-conscious individuals, sustainable lifestyle
enthusiasts, and the general public looking for ways to reduce their
environmental impact.
Tone: Informative, casual, friendly, and engaging.
Write a one minute video script
```

Response:

One Minute Video Script:

[INTRO: 00:00-00:5]

[Presenter on screen smiling or a positive, engaging animation]

Presenter: "Hey there! Today, we're going to talk about a trending topic that affects all of us - Sustainable Living! In the next minute, I'll share with you some tips on reducing your environmental footprint. Let's get started!"

[TRANSITION SLIDE: 00:06-00:08]

["5 Tips to Live a More Sustainable Lifestyle" followed by animated icons representing each tip.]

[POINT 1: 00:09-00:16]

Presenter: "Tip 1: Ditch single-use items! Swap out plastic bags, straws, and coffee cups for reusable alternatives like cloth bags, bamboo straws, and ceramic tumblers. Mother Earth will thank you!"

[TRANSITION SLIDE: 00:17-00:18]

[Tip 2 illustration: A lightbulb being changed or an energy-efficient home.]

[POINT 2: 00:19-00:25]

Presenter: "Tip 2: Save resources and money by conserving energy! Turn off lights when not in use, switch to LED bulbs, and unplug devices that aren't in use."

[TRANSITION SLIDE: 00:26-00:27]

[Tip 3 illustration: A person riding a bike or using public transport.]

[POINT 3: 00:28-00:34]

Presenter: "Tip 3: Rethink your transportation! Try biking, walking, or using public transport whenever possible - it's great for the planet and your health!"

[TRANSITION SLIDE: 00:35-00:36]

[Tip 4 illustration: A person shopping with a reusable bag, buying local produce.]

[POINT 4: 00:37-00:44]

Presenter: "Tip 4: Support local businesses! By choosing to buy locally-made products, you're reducing your carbon footprint while also giving back to your community."

[TRANSITION SLIDE: 00:45-00:46]

[Tip 5 illustration: Hands planting a tree or maintaining a garden.]

[POINT 5: 00:47-00:54]

Presenter: "And finally, Tip 5: Grow your own greens! Start a small vegetable garden, even on your balcony, or simply plant a tree. It's a rewarding way to reconnect with nature and reduce waste."

[CONCLUSION: 00:55-1:00]

[Presenter on screen, holding a reusable bag or standing in front of a plant]

Presenter: "That's a wrap! Incorporate these tips into your daily routines to live a more sustainable life and be a superhero for our

```
planet. Thanks for watching, and don't forget to like and share!"
[OUTRO: 1:01]
["Subscribe for more videos like this" or "Share to promote a more
sustainable world" with eco-friendly icons and animations.]
```

In this case, the images for the different scenes can also be generated with text-to-image generators, as discussed before. The user could also search for royalty-free video clips at sites such as Pixabay or Pexels.

For the voiceovers, you can narrate the video yourself or use text-to-speech applications such as Murf. ai, Lovo.ai, Listnr, Synthesis, and Deep Brain, among others. The last two can also produce a video based on the script. Just use the script as a prompt and voila.

Now that we've explored AI's capabilities for crafting video scripts and sales copy, let's look at another domain where these text models show promise – generating long-form written content such as blog posts, articles, and news. Let's dive in.

Generating blog posts, articles and news

Publishing high-quality written content at scale is crucial, yet challenging, for brands and publishers today. AI text generation presents opportunities to augment human writers' workflows for research, ideation, and drafting. For blog posts, AI tools can analyze data such as search volume and user interests to propose engaging topics. The AI can then produce a rough initial draft for the writer to revise and finalize. For news, AI programs can synthesize information from large datasets and event details to draft basic articles that human journalists can customize and fact-check.

While AI-generated text still lacks true comprehension and intent, capabilities continue improving rapidly. With proper human guidance, AI writing assistants could unlock immense value in researching, personalizing, and scaling content creation.

The first thing you need to decide is what the post or article is all about. If you have a blog, it is probably about a certain topic in particular. It could be about anything really, such as mental health, finances, self-care, career, technology, or something else.

In any case, you can use ChatGPT to get ideas and outlines for your next blog posts. Ask the AI to suggest potential topics and headlines that fit your blog's focus for the coming weeks or months. Then review the AI's suggestions, pick the best ones, and develop them into a content calendar. From there, use the AI outlines as a starting point, expanding on them with your own voice, expertise, and research.

Suppose you blog about finances, and you need some fresh ideas to blog about for the next few months. Let's look at what you can do then.

Here's the prompt.

Prompt:

> You are a blogger that writes about finances.
> Write some ideas for my next blog posts, so I can fill my publishing calendar

Response:

1. The Top 10 Personal Finance Tips Every Beginner Should Know
2. A Step-by-Step Guide to Creating a Personal Budget
3. How to Save Money on Everyday Expenses: Tips and Tricks
4. The Importance of Emergency Funds and How to Build One
5. A Comprehensive Guide to Understanding and Improving Your Credit Score
6. Saving for Retirement: A Comparison of 401(k), IRA, and Roth IRA
7. The Power of Compound Interest: Making Your Money Work for You
8. How to Start Investing in the Stock Market for Beginners
9. A Guide to Understanding and Reducing Debt
10. The Best Financial Apps and Tools to Help Keep You on Track
11. The Top 5 Money Mistakes and How to Avoid Them
12. Tax Planning Strategies: How to Maximize Your Refund and Minimize Your Liability
13. Teaching Kids About Money: Tips for Instilling Good Financial Habits Early
14. Frugal Living: How to Live Well on a Budget
15. How to Successfully Negotiate a Pay Raise or Promotion at Work
16. The Side Hustle Economy: Making Extra Money Outside of Your 9-to-5
17. The Psychology of Money: How Your Attitude Affects Your Financial Success
18. Smart Money Moves to Make in Your 20s, 30s, and Beyond
19. A Guide to Financial Independence and Retiring Early (FIRE)
20. Traveling on a Budget: How to Explore the World Without Breaking the Bank
21. Cutting Costs: How to Save on Monthly Subscriptions and Services
22. A Practical Guide to Buying a Home: From Saving for a Down Payment to Closing Costs
23. Building Financial Resilience: How to Adapt and Thrive in Times of Economic Uncertainty
24. The Pros and Cons of Investing in Real Estate
25. Comparing the Costs: Renting vs. Buying a Home
26. A Guide to College Savings Plans: 529 Plans, Coverdell ESAs, and More
27. How to Financially Prepare for Parenthood
28. The Most Common Financial Scams to Watch Out for and How to Protect Yourself

29. A Guide to Understanding and Utilizing Financial Advisors

30. Mindful Money: How to Cultivate a Healthy Relationship with Your Finances

31. Green Investing: How to Put Your Money to Work for the Environment

32. How to Make Charitable Giving a Part of Your Financial Plan

33. Navigating Student Loans: A Comprehensive Guide to Repayment Options and Forgiveness Programs

34. Learning from History: The Most Notable Stock Market Crashes and What We Can Take Away from Them

35. Planning for the Unexpected: A Guide to Life Insurance and Estate Planning

36. A Guide to Understanding and Using Cryptocurrency

37. The Best Personal Finance Books to Boost Your Financial Literacy

38. A Guide to Socially Responsible Investing: Aligning Your Values with Your Finances

39. The Gender Pay Gap: How to Address and Overcome It in Your Career

40. Healthy Habits: The Connection Between Physical Health and Financial Wellness

41. Financial Planning for Freelancers and Gig Workers: A Must-Know Guide

42. Using Credit Cards Wisely: Pros, Cons, and Maximizing Rewards

43. A Guide to Funding Your Dream Business: From Start-Up Costs to Managing Cash Flow

44. Supporting Local: The Impact of Spending Your Money Locally and How to Do It Effectively

45. How to Prepare for a Recession: Financial Tips for Staying Ahead

46. A Guide to Prenuptial Agreements: Protecting Your Financial Future in Marriage

47. Planning for Long-Term Care: Understanding Your Options and Costs

This is a solid list. Now, you have a great list of ideas to write your blog posts. Maybe you needed only 10. In that case, you could include *Write 10 ideas for my next blog posts* in the prompt. But in this case, you can choose the 10 that best resonate with you or ask for more ideas.

Once you choose one idea, you could prompt part of the post and ask to expand on it.

Here's the prompt for it.

Prompt:

```
Please expand upon the provided text by elaborating on its content. It
might be required to rephrase and present the text in a more detailed
and thorough manner. Here is the initial text: {text}.
```

You can also use a prompt to ask ChatGPT to write the draft of the post or article.

Here's the prompt.

Prompt:

```
Compose a blog post centered around the topic of "{blogPostTopic}"
utilizing a "{tone}" tone. Ensure the use of transition words and
prioritize active voice throughout the writing. The post should exceed
1000 words. Use very creative titles for the blog pos., totaling
no fewer than six sections. Each section should have a minimum of
two paragraphs. Incorporate the specified keywords, "{keywords},"
seamlessly into the content. Craft an appealing slug for the post
and create a succinct meta description within a maximum limit of 100
words. Finally, place the meta description at the conclusion of the
blog post.
```

Maybe your style is more informal. In the following example, you want to write about your experiences traveling in Thailand.

Here's the prompt.

Prompt:

```
Act as a world traveler that likes to write blog posts about your
experiences. You just went to Thailand and you would like to share
your adventures, the food you had and more. Write a blog post and make
it engaging and animated. Use an informal tone that will resonate with
young travelers like yourself.

You spent a month there. make sure to mention the sites/places you
visited, which ones you loved most.

Also, mention the dishes and food that you preferred and how
affordable it was.

Talk about how to meet other travelers, the nightlife and things to
avoid
```

Response:

```
Title: My Thai Tales: A Month Lost & Found in Paradise Island

Hey there wanderlusters and Thai-rific food lovers alike! Just got
back from the most epic month-long journey through Thailand, and
I can't contain my excitement when it comes to banging out this
glamorous blog post. So for all you hungry travelers out there craving
a dash of colorful adventure and a sprinkle of delicious culinary
delight, keep reading - this one's for you!

So, where the heck did I go and what did I absolutely LOVE? Buckle up,
friends. We're cruisin' through sandy beaches, ancient temples, and a
jungle escapade, all wrapped up in a Thai-ght bow. 🎀

First off, Chiang Mai, the ancient-meets-modern city that swept me off
me weary feet. From elephant sanctuaries 🐘 to awe-inspiring ancient
temples, like the Wat Phra That Doi Suthep and Wat Chedi Luang, I was
anything but bored. Seriously, if you want to time-travel, this is one
striking life experience to tick off your bucket list.

Now, let's take a deep-dive into the underwater world of Koh Tao, my
```

absolute favorite spot for a dive! 🤿

Alright, so prepare to be submerged into crystal-clear waters and rub fins with exotic marine life. Koh Tao, the gem of the Gulf of Thailand and home of sensational snorkeling and scuba diving, was an underwater playground I couldn't pass up. Add in the laid-back island vibe and postcard-worthy sunsets on Sairee Beach, and you'll soon find yourself dreaming of extending your stay. *sigh*

But of course, no Thailand trip is complete without getting lost (and found again) in the hustle and bustle of the Big Mango - yep, that's Bangkok for you! From the dazzling Grand Palace and Reclining Buddha (Wat Pho) to the mind-blowing Maeklong Railway Market, there's no shortage of jaw-dropping sights in this banging city.

Now, hold up. Can we please talk about Thai food? 😋 We all know it's mouth-watering and totally drool-worthy, but what made my taste buds sublimely happy? Let's see, there's...

1. Tom yum goong: This tangy shrimp soup that packs a spicy punch just begs to be sipped and savored!

2. Pad Thai: The classic noodle dish that's so flipping good, I can still taste it right now. If only I could have Pad Thai for breakfast, lunch, and dinner... (dream life, am I right?)

3. Mango sticky rice: For those with a serious sweet tooth (guilty as charged), this sumptuous dessert was the stuff of dreams. Trust me, you'll be coming back for seconds, thirds, and maybe fourths? 😊

And in case you're worried about dishing out a heap of cash for these heavenly delights, fret not! Street food in Thailand is affordable AF, so you can dig into these Thai food favorites without breaking the bank. Cha-ching!

Now, as much as exploring new places is a huge part of travel, making connections with other like-minded backpackers can be just as important. Wondering how to meet other travelers in Thailand? Hostels are a fantastic start. And with tons of hostels across the country, you'll have no problem finding one that matches your vibe and budget.

Aside from hostels, nightlife in Thailand is a surefire way to get your groove on and bond with fellow adventurers. Bangkok's Khao San Road is a party hotspot, while Full Moon Parties in Koh Phangan and the epic beach clubs in Phuket, like Paradise Beach Club and Illuzion, undoubtedly attract a fun-loving crowd. But always remember, party responsibly and keep your wits about you, peeps!

Speaking of safety, there are a few things to be aware of to dodge unwanted mishaps on your whimsical Thai adventure. From wild monkeys who might snatch your goodies 🐒 to overpacked "songthaews" (local buses) that may be chasing a Fast & Furious dream, here are my top tips:

1. Respect the culture: Thailand is known as the Land of Smiles, but respecting local customs, rules, and dressing modestly when visiting temples will keep you out of trouble and the smiles comin'.

2. Beware of scams: Just like anywhere else, it's essential to keep your guard up and trust your gut instincts to avoid falling victim to common scams.

3. Choose reliable transportation: As tempting as it may look, hopping onto a random moped taxi might not be the safest idea. Stick to licensed taxi services or rideshares like Grab.

```
So, there you have it, globetrotters! My whirlwind account of
Thailand's culture-packed cities, pristine beaches, and mouth-watering
eats. Can't wait to see where my next adventure takes me, but in the
meantime, I hope this has inspired all you wanderers out there to
follow your (Thai) travel dreams. And if you have any questions or
need tips, you know I've got you covered - just drop a comment below,
let's chat away!

Until the next adventure, keep on explorin', and stay curious, my
travel tribe! 🌍✌️

#ThailandAdventures #ExploreTheWorld #MyThaiTales #FoodiesUnite
#TravelTribe
```

This looks quite good, don't you agree? You still need to adapt it to your real adventure, but the tone is engaging and friendly.

For SEO purposes, you might want to ask for a slug and a meta description.

Here's the prompt.

Prompt:

```
Create a good slug for this post and a meta description with a maximum
of 100 words
```

Response:

```
Slug: thailand-monthly-escapade-food-adventures-nightlife

Meta Description: Join my journey through a month-long adventure in
Thailand! Dive into the ancient beauty of Chiang Mai, the underwater
paradise of Koh Tao, and the vibrant Bangkok streets. Satisfy your
wandering palate with scrumptious Thai food while mingling with
fellow travelers in hostels and epic nightlife spots. Get insider
tips on must-see attractions, keeping safe, and indulging in mouth-
watering dishes - all without blowing your budget! #ThailandAdventures
#ExploreTheWorld #MyThaiTales #FoodiesUnite #TravelTribe
```

As you can see, using the right prompts can help both generate ideas for the blog posts and help draft the post itself, including keywords, meta description, and the slug.

In the next section, we will explore some techniques that make content more engaging.

Creating engaging content with AI

In today's crowded digital landscape, creating content that genuinely engages audiences is more important than ever, yet also more difficult. AI presents opportunities to help analyze audience interests and writing patterns to produce more compelling narratives.

To create truly engaging prompts, consider incorporating the following elements, as well as drawing inspiration from the style and voice of great writers:

- **Relatability**: Craft prompts that resonate with the target audience's emotions, experiences, or challenges. Great writers often create an emotional connection with their readers, making their work more engaging.

  Inspiration: J.K. Rowling, Maya Angelou, Chimamanda Ngozi Adichie.

- **Open-endedness**: Ensure the prompts encourage diverse interpretations and responses, allowing the reader to explore their creativity and ideas without feeling limited or restricted.

  Inspiration: Ernest Hemingway, Haruki Murakami, Virginia Woolf.

- **Evocative language**: Use vivid and descriptive language to spark the reader's imagination and create a strong mental image of the topic or situation.

  Inspiration: F. Scott Fitzgerald, Toni Morrison, Gabriel García Márquez.

- **Strong hooks**: Start the prompt with a catchy statement or intriguing question that instantly captures the reader's attention and makes them want to dive in.

  Inspiration: George Orwell, Jane Austen, Ray Bradbury.

- **Sense of curiosity**: Inspire the reader to learn something new, explore an unfamiliar topic, or dive deeper into a specific subject matter by encouraging their curiosity and sparking their interest.

  Inspiration: Isaac Asimov, Arthur C. Clarke, Mary Roach.

- **Personal reflection**: Encourage introspection by asking readers to examine their own experiences, thoughts, or emotions, leading to more authentic and engaging content.

  Inspiration: Sylvia Plath, Anne Lamott, Joan Didion.

- **Escapism**: Provide prompts that allow readers to escape from their everyday lives by delving into fantastical or unfamiliar worlds, or exploring scenarios they may not encounter in their regular experiences.

  Inspiration: J.R.R. Tolkien, Lewis Carroll, Neil Gaiman.

- **Cultural relevance**: Tap into current events, popular trends, or societal issues to create content that feels timely, relevant, and reflective of the readers' context.

  Inspiration: Margaret Atwood, Ta-Nehisi Coates, Zadie Smith.

- **Provocative statements or questions**: Use controversial or thought-provoking themes in your prompts to stimulate debate, challenge readers' beliefs, or push them to re-evaluate their perspective on a topic.

  Inspiration: Aldous Huxley, George Bernard Shaw, Simone de Beauvoir.

- **Humor and wit**: Inject playfulness, sarcasm, or humor into your prompts to create a relaxed atmosphere and allow readers to approach the content with a sense of enjoyment and lightheartedness.

  Inspiration: Oscar Wilde, Dorothy Parker, David Sedaris.

By incorporating these elements into your prompts and emulating the styles and voices of these renowned writers, you can create engaging content that captivates, challenges, and entertains your readers, all while inspiring meaningful discussions and creative responses.

Now, let's use ChatGPT to suggest some topic ideas in one of these styles.

Here's the prompt.

Prompt:

```
Drawing inspiration from Ernest Hemingway, Haruki Murakami, and
Virginia Woolf, give me some open-ended topic ideas that encourage
diverse interpretations and responses.
```

Response:

```
1. Topic: The Lost and Found Box - Nostalgic Memories

Prompt: "Choose an item you stumble upon in an old 'Lost and Found'
box. Reflect on the memories it evokes, dive into its uncertain past,
or envision its future journey after leaving your hands."

2. Topic: Cafés - Intersections of Life

Prompt: "Pick a stranger at a bustling café that grabs your attention.
Create a fictional background of their life, narrate their thoughts
in that moment, or explore the potential encounter with this stranger
that could change your life."

3. Topic: Time Capsule - Messages from the Past

Prompt: "Imagine discovering a time capsule left decades ago by an
unknown person. Examine its contents, describe the emotions it stirs,
or write a response back to this person from the perspective of the
present."

4. Topic: The Unread Letter - Secrets Unveiled

Prompt: "Uncover a hidden, unread letter in the attic of your new
house. Explore the emotions and revelations contained within the
letter, or delve into the lives of the sender and the intended
recipient."

5. Topic: Parallel Lives - Choices and Consequences

Prompt: "Contemplate an important decision you made in the past.
Develop an alternate reality where you made a different choice, and
narrate the ensuing experiences and the impacts they have on your
life."

6. Topic: Unexplained Phenomenon - Moments of Intrigue

Prompt: "Describe an unexplained phenomenon or bizarre event you have
witnessed or heard of, and ponder its origins, explore the emotions it
stirred within you, or create a fictional world where such occurrences
are commonplace."
```

7. Topic: Serendipitous Encounters - Destined Paths

Prompt: "Detail a chance encounter in your life that left a lasting impact. Deliberate the connection between serendipity and destiny, or narrate an alternate scenario where you never crossed paths with that person."

8. Topic: Comfort Objects - Sentimental Attachments

Prompt: "Reflect on an object you hold dear, whether it be a childhood toy, a memento, or a cherished heirloom. Explore the memories, feelings, or symbolic meaning it carries for you, and the bond you share with it."

These open-ended topics allow for a wide range of interpretations, perspectives, and creative narratives, inspired by the writing styles of esteemed authors like Hemingway, Murakami, and Woolf. By offering flexibility in how readers approach each prompt, you can encourage them to explore their creativity, tap into their emotions, and craft engaging stories that resonate with their unique perspectives.

Now, let's ask ChatGPT to write a piece about *The Secret Door - A Hidden World in Your Neighborhood*.

Let's look at the prompt.

Prompt:

```
write a piece, up to 1000 words, about The Secret Door - A Hidden
World in Your Neighborhood in the style of J.K. Rowling.
```

Response:

```
In the quaint and seemingly unremarkable town of Willowshire, where
the morning dew glistens on the leaves and the aroma of freshly
baked goods wafts through the air, there lies an enigmatic secret.
Supposedly nestled in the heart of the town and concealed from prying
eyes, there lies a door — an extraordinary door as peculiar as the
legend behind it. Daring few have ventured out in search of this door,
and even fewer claim to have discovered the unimaginable world that it
leads to.

It was on one such fateful evening that I joined (though rather
reluctantly) the ranks of the adventurous souls fixated on unearthing
the mysteries that lay beyond this legendary door. You see,
Willowshire had always been a quiet, peaceful refuge — a place where
I could stroll the cobblestone streets, soak in the warm pastel hues
of the houses that lined the avenues, and seek solace from the chaotic
cacophony that characterizes our world.

And yet, as I sipped my earl grey tea at Patrice's Patisserie that
evening, a handwritten note tucked under the delicate china caught
my eye. It read, "The enchanted door is closer than you think. Seek
the gnarled oak tree as the moon reaches its pinnacle. Embrace the
unknown." The sensation of intrigue arose within me, veiled in
bewilderment and disbelief. But I knew there was no way I would be
able to resist the temptation to explore. The whispers and hushed
tales that circulated the town for generations had finally stoked the
embers of my curiosity.
```

As twilight fell, and the sky draped itself in a dreamy tapestry of indigo and starlight, I ambled through the damp grass in Willowshire's park, the scent of damp earth hanging heavy in the air. Upon reaching the ancient and gnarled oak tree, an emblem of strength and wisdom, I realized it had always been there — growing unassumingly throughout my life. Its twisted branches cast eerie shadows, but there was an aura of calm that enveloped me.

Whether driven by fate or my own choice, I arrived at a concealed archway, partially obscured by ivy and moss, as the moon reached its apex, showering its ethereal light over the magnificent oak. A faint shimmer of silver caught my eye, revealing the enigmatic door's edges that had been immortalized in my town's folklore. My heart raced with a combination of exhilaration and trepidation as I stretched out my hand to touch the door, rummaging through my memories to recall the words whispered by those brave few who claimed to have passed this threshold. Pressing my hand against the seemingly ordinary wood, I closed my eyes and uttered the incantation: "Arcane Porta Revelare."

Suddenly, the door creaked and groaned, and I felt a rush of heavenly warmth against my tingling fingers. As if in response to the clandestine magic, the door swung open, offering a glimpse into the secret world hidden beneath Willowshire's conventional exterior. Holding my breath, I crossed the enchanted threshold and stepped into a realm of wonder.

Vivid, luminescent colors greeted me, painting a vivid dreamscape of floating forests, radiant flora, and creatures as diverse as the stars themselves. I marveled at wise, talking cats adorned with emerald-studded collars and mystical creatures dashing through opalescent waters. A distant symphony of celestial harmonies and whispers from the unseen floated on the air, a gentle reminder that this wondrous world thrived just beneath the known. It was a tranquil haven forged by ancient forces, waiting patiently for me and others like me to learn its secrets.

Again, you can instruct ChatGPT to edit the resulting text as you see fit, making the language simpler, more witty, more casual, and so on.

In the next section, we will cover how to make the content more personalized to an individual or organization.

How to use AI for personalized messaging

It's quite common for organizations to send personalized messages to many people. Some of these cases include sending cold emails or LinkedIn messages and sending thank you cards after attending an event.

In this case, we could use some of the writing formulas that we covered at the beginning of this chapter such as AISA, FOMO, or SMILE. Please use them to craft a cold email. Experiment and see what works best for you.

For now, we will introduce a new way to pass variables to accomplish the same. One common problem when sending cold messages is that most of them are too salesly. Remember, in general, people love to buy, but they hate to be sold. Thus, the goal is to have ChatGPT help you write compelling cold messages providing real value to help establish relationships with potential clients.

So, here's a customized prompt for it.

Prompt:

```
You are an experienced outbound marketer.
You have been tasked to write personalized emails to [people] in
[certain roles] describing [a common problem] and suggesting [some
solutions].
Even though your end goal is to sell them [your company's solution],
you are trying to provide value first to gain the trust.
Data:
[niche]: B2B companies in the wholesale distribution industry
[person]: John Doe, Director of Operations
[company name]: Acme Inc
[common problems]: 1. Difficulty in handling large datasets in Excel,
leading to slow performance and increased chances of errors and data
corruption.
2. Time-consuming manual processes for generating reports and deriving
insights from data.
[Suggested solutions]: 1. Breaking down large datasets into smaller,
manageable files to reduce the chances of errors and improve Excel's
performance.
2. Developing Excel macros to automate routine data analysis tasks and
enhance the efficiency of generating reports.
[call to action]: For more details on how to implement these solutions
read the article (provide link)
Write a personalized cold email in an amicable tone explaining that
you have seen many companies similar to [company] in the same [niche]
facing these [problems] and that you want to help provide a couple
of [solutions] that they can implement by themselves. Offer the full
explanation of the [solutions] at the [link]
```

Let's see what the response would be.

Response:

```
Subject: Boost Your Wholesale Distribution Efficiency with These Excel
Fixes
Hi John,
I hope this email finds you well. My name is [Your Name], and I'm
an expert in helping B2B companies like Acme Inc improve their data
management processes and overall operational efficiency.
In my experience, I've noticed that many businesses in the wholesale
distribution industry experience common issues related to managing
data - particularly when it comes to using Excel. Some of these
```

problems include:

1. Difficulty handling large datasets, leading to slow performance and increased chances of errors and data corruption.

2. Time-consuming manual processes for generating reports and deriving insights from data.

Since these challenges seem to be quite prevalent, I thought I'd reach out and share a couple of solutions that can help Acme Inc address these issues:

1. Break down large datasets into smaller, manageable files to reduce the chances of errors and improve Excel's performance.

2. Develop Excel macros to automate routine data analysis tasks and enhance the efficiency of generating reports.

I've put together an article with detailed information on how you can implement these solutions for your business. You can find it here: [LINK]

By properly managing your Excel data, your team can save time, reduce errors, and ultimately improve decision-making for Acme Inc.

If you have any questions or would like to discuss these solutions further, please feel free to reach out. I'd be more than happy to help.

Additionally, if you ever find yourself interested in exploring more advanced data management and analysis tools that can further streamline your business processes, my company offers a comprehensive platform called DataInsights. It's designed specifically to help businesses like yours overcome the limitations of Excel, automate report generation, and uncover valuable insights from your data.

Please let me know if you'd like to learn more about DataInsights, and I'd be glad to schedule a demo for you.

In the meantime, I hope the solutions provided in the article will add value to your team's daily operations. Looking forward to hearing your thoughts and the positive impact these changes could bring to Acme Inc.

Wishing you continued success!

Best regards,

[Your Name]

[Your Title]

[Your Company]

[Your Email]

[Your Phone]

Notice how the variables were introduced. This allows us to use the same conversation to produce similar content to highlight other problems and solutions, change the target person/company, and more.

However, there are a couple of things that could be better. First, even though it is common practice to include a paragraph as the first one (*I hope this email finds you well. My name is [Your Name], and...*), it seems fake; people don't really care. Second, it's too formal. Lastly, the idea here is not to sell, so there shouldn't be a paragraph about our offering *DataInsights*. Since the call to action leads the reader to the article describing in detail both solutions, there is an opportunity there to talk about our solution, once we are gaining their trust.

To fix the first two issues, let's continue the conversation. The last one is up to you.

Prompt:

```
Cut the first paragraph. add some humor to the rest to break the ice
```

Response:

```
Subject: Unlock the Hidden Secrets of Excel and Conquer Your Data!
Hi John,
As an expert on all things data-related, I've seen countless
businesses in the wholesale distribution industry grapple with Excel
nightmares. It's like Groundhog Day, but with spreadsheets! ☺
Some of the most common challenges faced by companies like Acme Inc
include:
1. Difficulty handling large datasets, causing slow performance and—
horror of horrors—increased chances of errors and data corruption.
2. Time-consuming manual processes for generating reports and deriving
insights from data.
To help exorcize these spreadsheet specters, I wanted to share a
couple of solutions that can slay these data demons:
1. Break down large datasets into smaller, less terrifying files to
reduce the chances of errors and improve Excel's performance.
2. Develop Excel macros to automate routine data analysis tasks like a
well-oiled, report-generating machine.
To aid you in your epic quest for Excel mastery, I've put together
an article with detailed information on how you can implement these
solutions for your business. You can find it right here, at the end of
this digital treasure map: [LINK]
Consider these solutions my gift to you and the Acme Inc team. May
your days be filled with error-free spreadsheets and faster report
generation!
If you have any questions, or if you'd like to discuss these solutions
further, feel free to reach out. I'm always here to help out fellow
data wranglers!
On a more serious note, if you ever find yourself in search of even
more powerful data management and analysis tools that can truly up
your company's game, my company offers a comprehensive platform called
DataInsights. It's specifically designed to help businesses like yours
leapfrog over the limitations of Excel, and easily automate report
generation and uncover valuable insights from your data.
Just give me a holler if you're interested in learning more about
DataInsights, and I'll gladly arrange a demo for you.
```

```
In the meantime, have a blast implementing the solutions in the
article. I'm confident they'll make a positive impact on Acme Inc's
daily operations. Looking forward to hearing your thoughts and any
wild spreadsheet adventures you encounter along the way!
Wishing you and Acme Inc every success!
Cheers,

[Your Name]
[Your Title]
[Your Company]
[Your Email]
[Your Phone]
```

Much better, don't you think?

However, the subject lines are not catchy enough. If the recipients are not tempted to read the emails, it will not matter whether we are providing real value to them or not.

So, let's explore how we can get better subject lines.

Now, here's the prompt.

Prompt:

```
Change the subject line to be shorter, intriguing and personalized.
Try to make it with less than 8 words.
Give me a few options
```

Response:

```
Option 1: John, Say Goodbye to Spreadsheet Nightmares!
Option 2: Spreadsheet Secrets for Acme Inc Unveiled!
Option 3: John, Excel Hacks to Boost Efficiency!
Option 4: Unleash Acme Inc's Excel Superpowers!
Option 5: John, Tame Your Data with These Tips!
Option 6: Unlock Acme Inc's Excel Potential!
```

If you want, you can get more options.

For that, we can use the following prompt.

Prompt:

```
give me some more
```

Response:

```
Option 7: John, Improve Acme's Data Game Today!
Option 8: Excel Magic Tricks for Acme Inc!
Option 9: John, Discover Acme's Data Boosters!
Option 10: Acme Inc's Excel Performance Tuning!
Option 11: John, Master Acme's Data Realm!
Option 12: Excel Breakthroughs for Acme Inc!
```

Much better.

To finish this chapter, we will learn how to create tailored content with an LLM.

Creating tailored content with AI

Earlier, we covered how to copy the style of a famous author. But suppose you want to use ChatGPT to produce content in your voice, using your style or maybe some other person's style that you like, but they are not famous enough so that ChatGPT knows their style.

In this case, you can give ChatGPT some examples of your style or that other person.

For this example, we are going to copy the voice of Seth Godin. He is a recognized American author who writes about marketing, but we can assume he is not famous. We will copy some short articles from his blog at https://seths.blog/.

So, here's the prompt.

Prompt:

```
You are an experienced marketer. you write short posts about marketing
following the voice of Seth Godin.
Here are some examples of his style:
Title: Inconvenient!
That's great news.
The thing you need, the road ahead, the element that will transform
your project-it appears to be inconvenient.
That's terrific, because it means that most other people can't be
bothered. It's valuable because the very inconvenience of it makes it
scarce.
The stuff that matters is almost always inconvenient. If it's not, you
might be mistaken about what matters.
Title: Brakes and acceleration
Every driver benefits from good brakes. It makes driving safer.
Only a few skilled drivers benefit from better acceleration.
Our habit is to compare top speed, horsepower, short-term returns and
status. In every field, not just cars.
But it probably pays to make sure that there good brakes too.
```

```
Title: Too much competition
There are two approaches:
Broaden your offerings, make them easier, cheaper and more available.
Dumb them down and race to the bottom.
Or…
Focus on the customers who care enough about your idiosyncratic and
particular offerings that they'll not only happily walk away from the
lesser alternatives, but they'll tell the others.
Suggest some titles for new articles based on Seth's content. But
don't copy Seth's content. write some titles inspired by his content.
write just the titles
```

Response:

```
 1. Title: The Serendipity of Chance
 2. Title: Embracing the Obscure Path
 3. Title: The Unseen Opportunity
 4. Title: Resilience as a Catalyst
 5. Title: Dancing with Uncertainty
 6. Title: Navigating the Sea of Change
 7. Title: Disrupting the Status Quo
 8. Title: The Alchemy of Collaboration
 9. Title: The Elegance of Simplicity
10. Title: The Symphony of Dissonance
```

Now that you are equipped with some titles, you can write a prompt asking the LLM to write a post related to that topic in the style of the person that you want to emulate – in this case, Seth Godin.

Here is the next prompt.

Prompt:

```
Now, write a short article using Seth's style about 1. Make it short.
Set's content has typically less than 150 words
```

Response:

```
Title: The Serendipity of Chance
Embrace the unexpected in life and business. Some of the greatest
successes in our world were born from serendipitous moments. It's the
surprising detours that often lead to the most memorable rewards.
Let go of the need for control and certainty. By being open to life's
surprises, you ignite innovation and growth. Give yourself the freedom
to entertain deviations alongside your meticulous plans and be amazed
by the discoveries that follow.
Remember, the serendipity of chance can be your most remarkable ally
if you allow your well-structured ideas to dance in harmony with the
fortuitous opportunities that come your way.
```

As we've explored, AI text generation models open up new possibilities to augment human creativity and workflows for producing all types of marketing, journalistic, and engagement-focused content.

Summary

In this chapter, we covered many typical cases of content that you can brainstorm and create with ChatGPT and similar tools. You learned about powerful techniques to create social media posts, produce engaging sales copy, write video scripts, and make other types of content more engaging and persuasive. Now, it's up to you to practice and get better and write effective prompts. Remember, don't be afraid to experiment. In the end, that's the key to great prompting.

Here are some of the key lessons that were learned in this chapter:

- AI can help ideate, outline, and draft initial versions of content, but human refinement is still essential. The goal is augmenting, not replacing, human creativity.

- Different mediums lend themselves to different levels of reliance on AI. Short-form posts may utilize more automation than long-form articles.

- Striking the right balance between AI assistance and human intent/editing is crucial for quality and authentic audience engagement.

- While capabilities are advancing rapidly, current AI still lacks true comprehension and intent. Judicious human guidance is needed to craft strategic narratives.

- AI excels at synthesizing data/info to generate rough initial drafts that humans can then customize for their brand voice and goals.

- For businesses, experimenting with AI content generation in a pilot phase is recommended to determine ideal workflows before wide-scale implementation.

- Overall, AI writing tools show immense promise to complement human creativity, productivity, and insight in developing engaging, high-quality content.

Just consider this:

> *...our ability to do prompt engineering is still developing. ...we learn a lot from Twitter... prompt engineering should NOT be underestimated... many complex customer problems can be solved without fine-tuning the LLM model...*
>
> *- Angela Jiang, Product Manager, OpenAI*

Even OpenAI is learning prompt engineering techniques from the community at large.

Think about it.

In the next chapter, we will explore some practical applications using LLMs, including going through a complete example of creating and promoting a podcast from start to finish. You will learn practical skills such as conducting research to prepare customized interview questions tailored to high-profile versus everyday guests. We'll also leverage AI tools to efficiently generate promotional materials for the podcast. Additionally, you will learn how to apply similar question preparation techniques to ace job interviews, whether you are the interviewer or the candidate.

Part 2: Basic Prompt Engineering Techniques

Part 2 provides you with an essential toolkit of prompt engineering techniques that enable a wide range of practical applications. *Chapter 3* demonstrates leveraging AI to conduct research and prepare customized questions to deliver compelling podcast episodes and ace job interviews. You will learn strategies to promote podcast content using AI summarization and soundbite generation.

Chapter 4 guides you through utilizing large language models to unlock new frontiers of imagination for fiction writing and poetry. Proven techniques to develop characters, settings, and plotlines and refine AI-generated drafts are covered. *Chapter 5* shifts to more functional applications – sentiment analysis for understanding emotions in text, data classification for organizing information, data cleaning for improving data quality, and pattern matching for extracting structured data from unstructured sources.

Together, these chapters equip you with fundamental prompt engineering skills to classify text by sentiment, categorize information, resolve dataset issues, match patterns, and extract insights more efficiently than ever before. With the techniques covered in *Part 2*, you can tap the power of AI across diverse domains, paving the way for more advanced applications in subsequent chapters.

This part has the following chapters:

- *Chapter 3, Creating and Promoting a Podcast Using ChatGPT and Other Practical Examples*
- *Chapter 4, LLMs for Creative Writing*
- *Chapter 5, Unlocking Insights from Unstructured Text: AI Techniques for Text Analysis*

3

Creating and Promoting a Podcast Using ChatGPT and Other Practical Examples

Generative AI can help podcasters generate engaging interview questions tailored to both famous and lesser-known guests based on their backgrounds, interests, and expertise areas. It can also summarize podcast transcripts to efficiently create promotional materials.

In job interviews, AI can suggest relevant technical, situational, and behavioral questions aligned with the role requirements and the candidate's profile. It can provide sample responses to help candidates practice and get prepared.

One of the main strengths of AI is its ability to quickly generate a large number of intelligent questions by analyzing context, data, and previous interactions. However, human expertise is still required to select the most strategic questions and craft effective follow-ups during live conversations.

Using AI for question preparation provides consistency and personalization at scale, and it saves preparation time for podcasters, interviewers, consultants, salespeople, and other roles requiring strategic questioning.

The following topics will be covered in this chapter:

- Crafting podcast questions for celebrity guests
- Preparing podcast questions with everyday guests
- Identify topics, ideas, and potential guest speakers for your podcast
- Using AI to promote a podcast
- Identifying insightful interview questions

- Sharpening interview skills with AI-generated responses
- Generating strategic questions for client engagements with AI

Crafting podcast questions for celebrity guests

In this section, we will look at how to use AI to create interesting interview questions for podcast episodes featuring famous people. We'll see how AI can make the process easier and help lead to more meaningful conversations.

Suppose you want to identify some potential candidates for your podcast. You probably won't need ChatGPT or a similar tool for this, but for the sake of this example, you could ask for a list of potential people to interview.

Prompt:

```
List 10 popular contemporary business authors and name their most
popular books. Let me know if they are alive.
```

Response:

```
1. Erik Brynjolfsson - "The Second Machine Age: Work, Progress, and
Prosperity in a Time of Brilliant Technologies" (Alive)
2. Adam Grant - "Give and Take: Why Helping Others Drives Our Success"
(Alive)
3. Sheryl Sandberg - "Lean In: Women, Work, and the Will to Lead"
(Alive)
4. Daniel Kahneman - "Thinking, Fast and Slow" (Alive)
5. Patrick Lencioni - "The Five Dysfunctions of a Team: A Leadership
Fable" (Alive)
6. Yuval Noah Harari - "Homo Deus: A Brief History of Tomorrow"
(Alive)
7. Chris Anderson - "The Long Tail: Why the Future of Business Is
Selling Less of More" (Alive)
8. Tom Peters - "In Search of Excellence: Lessons from America's Best-
Run Companies" (Alive)
9. Eric Ries - "The Lean Startup: How Today's Entrepreneurs Use
Continuous Innovation to Create Radically Successful Businesses"
(Alive)
10. Nassim Nicholas Taleb - "The Black Swan: The Impact of the Highly
Improbable" (Alive)
```

Great – somehow, you were able to get Eric Ries for your podcast. Let's get some potential questions that you could ask him.

Here's the prompt for that.

Prompt:

> Give me 10 really interesting questions I can ask Eric Ries about entrepreneurship and startups?

And here's the response.

Response:

1. In your experience, what unique qualities or circumstances differentiate startups that succeed in the long run from those that fail or fade away?
2. How do you think the rise of global platforms and networks, such as crowdfunding and social media, is shaping the future of entrepreneurship and the way startups approach product development and market entry?
3. The idea of a "minimum viable product" has become a popular concept in the startup world. Can you discuss the potential pitfalls of focusing too heavily on MVPs and share some strategies for striking a balance between speed and product quality?
4. As the startup ecosystem becomes more crowded and competitive, what are your thoughts on "co-opetition" or collaboration between startups, even if they are in the same industry or share overlapping goals?
5. What are the factors that contribute to a healthy and thriving entrepreneurial ecosystem, and how can emerging startup hubs learn from established centers like Silicon Valley?
6. In the age of digital disruption, what are your thoughts on the importance of "soft skills" or emotional intelligence in entrepreneurship, particularly for founders looking to scale their businesses and lead their teams effectively?
7. How do you envision the role of governments and regulatory bodies in supporting and encouraging entrepreneurship and innovation, while still maintaining a level playing field and addressing potentially negative societal consequences of disruptive technologies?
8. What are your thoughts on the "serial entrepreneur" phenomenon and the impact of having multiple startups on an individual's personal and professional growth? Are there commonalities among successful serial entrepreneurs?
9. In the context of the Lean Startup methodology, can you discuss the importance of having a clear and adaptable exit strategy for founders, whether through acquisitions, mergers, or going public?
10. Given the rapid pace of change in the business world, how can founders cultivate resilience in their startups and ensure their teams remain agile, adaptable, and prepared for future challenges or unexpected disruptions?

These thought-provoking questions will enable you to engage Eric Ries in a fascinating conversation about entrepreneurship and startups, exploring various aspects of the journey from ideation to sustainable growth, as well as the evolving challenges and opportunities faced by founders today.

I think some of these questions are quite good, but if you think you need more ideas, you can always ask the LLM to provide 10 or 20 more, after which you can select the ones you think are more appropriate.

Furthermore, you can use some of these questions as a starting point. Then, you can ask follow-up questions based on the answers.

To make things more interesting, you may also want to include some more unique questions.

To do that, here's the prompt.

Prompt:

```
What are 10 unique questions that I may ask  Eric Ries that have not
been asked before. In particular i'm interested in questions about
entrepreneurship and business
```

And here's the response.

Response:

```
1. How do you think the acceleration of space exploration and the
growth of space-related industries will influence entrepreneurship,
and what opportunities might arise for startups in this sector?
2. In the hyper-competitive world of startups, how can entrepreneurs
maintain a sense of purpose and avoid losing sight of their mission
amidst constant pivots and changes in strategy?
3. With advancements in neurotechnology and brain-computer interfaces,
how can entrepreneurs be prepared for the ethical challenges and
opportunities arising at the intersection of technology and cognitive
functioning?
4. As the sharing economy continues to grow, do you foresee any unique
niches or business models that have been overlooked or underutilized
by entrepreneurs so far?
5. With the increasing societal focus on income inequality and social
justice, what role do you see entrepreneurs playing in addressing
these issues through their businesses or products?
6. In the current trend of short-form content and ever-shrinking
attention spans, how can entrepreneurs successfully engage and
convey their complex ideas or offerings to an increasingly segmented
audience?
7. How do you envision the future of official currencies, digital
assets, and cryptocurrencies impacting entrepreneurship and startup
financing, particularly given the fluctuating regulatory landscape?
8. With the growing movement toward sustainable and responsible
consumerism, do you have any advice for entrepreneurs looking to
transparently integrate sustainability and ethical practices into
their business model without undermining their profitability or
competitiveness?
9. As the world moves toward a more connected and technologically
driven global economy, how can entrepreneurs generate value by
leveraging existing infrastructure, such as smart cities or the
Internet of Things, in their business ideas?
```

```
10. Given the increase in remote work and distributed teams, how can
entrepreneurs effectively manage and nurture company culture across
geographical and cultural boundaries, particularly in the context of
the Lean Startup methodology?
```

For variety, you may want to ask some personal questions.

Here's the prompt.

Prompt:

```
Give me 10 more personal questions to ask Eric
```

And here's the response.

Response:

```
1. As a thought leader and author who has traveled the world
extensively, are there any unique experiences or interactions
you've had that have significantly influenced your perspective on
entrepreneurship and life?
2. How has fatherhood impacted your outlook on entrepreneurship, and
are there any specific lessons from your own experiences that you hope
to pass on to your children?
3. Are there any non-business-related topics or causes that you are
particularly passionate about and feel compelled to advocate for or
contribute to?
4. How do you maintain a sense of personal well-being and balance,
given your high-profile career and the expectations that come with
it? What activities or practices do you rely on to recharge and stay
centered?
5. Looking back at your education and early career, were there any
defining moments or turning points that led you to develop the Lean
Startup methodology?
6. What was the biggest personal challenge or obstacle you faced while
establishing yourself as an entrepreneur, author, and thought leader?
How did you overcome it, and what did you learn from that experience?
7. Can you share a story from your life outside of work that has had a
lasting impact on your decision-making process or the way you approach
challenges within your professional endeavors?
8. Throughout your journey, have you had any unexpected mentors or
role models who have influenced your personal growth and shaped your
understanding of leadership, entrepreneurship, or life in general?
9. What are some personal goals, dreams, or milestones that you would
still like to achieve, either within your career or in other aspects
of your life?
10. How would you describe your personal leadership style as an
entrepreneur, and how has it evolved over the years as you gained more
experience and faced various challenges?
```

> These personal questions offer insight into Eric Ries's experiences, values, and growth, revealing the individual behind his professional accomplishments and providing listeners with an opportunity to connect with him on a deeper level.

As you can see, ChatGPT can be very useful in these situations. It can help you prepare for your podcast interview in almost no time.

It's important to note that the cutout date of ChatGPT is January 2022. This means that ChapGPT only knows about information up to that date, so some important information could be missing. However, on November 6, 2023, OpenAI launched new versions of ChatGPT, GPT-3.5, and GPT-4 Turbo that have a cutout date of April 2023. They also mentioned that GPT-4 will soon be updated almost to the current date.

However, in the majority of cases, your interviewee is not a famous person, a well-known author, and so on. Thus, in the next section, we will explore how to get the potential questions for those cases.

Preparing podcast questions with everyday guests

Suppose you do a podcast about solopreneurship and you want to interview a successful entrepreneur. The following is an example of a prompt that would help you get some ideas for questions during the interview. In this case, you should provide some background about your podcast and a short bio of your interviewee.

Here's the prompt for it.

Prompt:

> I have a podcast named "The Solopreneur's Symphony". I interview successful solopreneurs about how they are building a one-person operation.
>
> I'm gonna interview Sarah Thompson. Here is a short bio of her:
>
> Sarah Thompson is a successful solopreneur and business coach, specializing in helping aspiring and existing solopreneurs achieve their goals and unlock their full potential. With over a decade of experience running her own successful online business, Sarah has gained a wealth of knowledge and insights that she passionately shares with others.
>
> As a solopreneur herself, Sarah understands the unique challenges and opportunities that arise from building and managing a business on your own. She empathizes with the struggles of wearing multiple hats, maintaining work-life balance, and staying motivated in the face of uncertainty.
>
> In addition to her hands-on experience, Sarah's background in psychology and her deep passion for personal development provide her with a unique perspective on solopreneurship. She firmly believes that success in business starts from within, and that cultivating a growth mindset and strong self-belief are crucial elements for solopreneurs to thrive.

```
What she values:
Encouraging others to prioritize giving and helping over receiving.
Cherishing family time, particularly when we venture into new
territories, delve into diverse cultures, and grow collectively.
Having a passion for creating, experimenting with varying components,
and concocting a unique concept or solution.
Fostering a sense of inclusion and providing a space that individuals
can refer to as their own home.
Valuing cross-cultural distinctions that encourage diverse viewpoints.
Feeling accomplished when I can positively impact someone's life.
Indulging in outdoor activities, whether it's engaging in a soccer
game, embarking on a hike, having a day out skiing, or going for a
walk while appreciating the natural flora.
Give me 10 interesting questions to ask her for my podcast?
```

Here's the response.

Response:

```
1. Can you share with us your journey of becoming a successful
solopreneur and how you managed to keep your balance during the
process?

2. In your coaching, you encourage others to prioritize giving and
helping over receiving. What prompted you to adopt this philosophy,
and how has it impacted your business approach?

3. Family time seems to play a significant role in your life. How do
you manage to maintain a healthy work-life balance while running a
solo business?

4. Can you please share with us an instance where your passion for
creating led to a unique solution or concept in your business?

5. Your bio mentions your dedication to fostering a sense of
inclusion. How does this reflect in your business model and your
relationship with your clients?

6. As a solopreneur who values diversity, how do you ensure that
you're open to and accommodating different viewpoints?

7. You mentioned that you feel accomplished when you can positively
impact someone's life. Can you share with us a memorable instance
where you felt this sense of accomplishment?

8. What is the role of outdoor activities in your life and how do you
think they positively impact your productivity or creativity as a
solopreneur?

9. Tell us how your background in psychology plays a part in dealing
with the challenges and benefits of being a solopreneur?

10. Can you share some practical steps or advice you often give to
people who are reluctant to dive into solopreneurship due to fear of
uncertainty or failure?
```

This is a good starting point, but maybe you want to discuss certain things, such as personal branding and how this is essential to the success of any solopreneur.

Here's a prompt for it.

Prompt:

```
Give me a couple of questions related to how personal branding affects
the success of solopreneurs
```

And here's the response.

Response:

```
1. As a successful solopreneur, how important do you believe personal
branding is in the landscape of solopreneurship, and how has your own
personal brand contributed to your success?
2.. Do you believe there's a potential risk for solopreneurs in
blurring the lines between personal and professional branding? How do
you maintain a balance?
3. Personal branding seems to be a powerful tool for standing out from
the competition. How do you ensure your personal brand reflects your
unique value proposition to your clients?
4. For solopreneurs who are just starting, what would be your advice
on establishing a strong and credible personal brand?
```

You can repeat the same process if you want to focus more on certain aspects during your interview. Again, this is just a starting point to get the interview rolling. Based on the answers of your interviewee, you should decide on follow-up questions on your own, perhaps some based on the suggestions that ChatGPT is providing.

Notice that the less known an individual is, the higher the risk of the model hallucinating facts about them. Thus, make sure you validate their bio before creating the interview questions.

Let's take a step back. Suppose you want to identify topics, ideas, and potential guest speakers for your podcast. In the next section, we will cover how to use ChatGPT to help with those tasks.

Identify topics, ideas, and potential guest speakers for your podcast

In this case, we will try to get topics and ideas and identify potential guest speakers for the podcast.

Therefore, we will input some information about the podcast and its audience into ChatGPT to provide some context.

Here's a prompt.

Prompt:

```
I have a podcast named "The Solopreneur's Symphony" - a highly
engaging and thought-provoking podcast designed specifically for the
aspiring solopreneurs, the independent masterminds, and the driven
```

self-starters of the world. In our weekly interviews we delve deep into the world of solopreneurship as we explore the ins and outs of transforming an idea into a successful and thriving business.

"The Solopreneur's Symphony" brings together inspiring stories, valuable insights, and actionable advice from successful solopreneurs who have discovered the secrets to building a business empire all on their own. With guest appearances from experts across various industries, this podcast promises an eclectic mix of thought leadership, innovation, and creativity.

The audience for "The Solopreneur's Symphony" is a diverse and dynamic group of individuals who share a common interest in solopreneurship – the process of running a business entirely on their own. They may be at various stages in their entrepreneurial journey – from those just starting to flesh out an idea or in the midst of laying the groundwork for their dream business, to seasoned solopreneurs looking for new insights and growth opportunities.

The podcast attracts individuals from a wide range of backgrounds, industries, and skill sets, reflecting the vast landscape of solopreneurship. They possess a strong entrepreneurial spirit and a burning desire for personal and professional growth, understanding that success in solopreneurship requires ongoing education and self-improvement.

Listeners of "The Solopreneur's Symphony" come to the podcast seeking inspiration, motivation, and practical advice to overcome the unique challenges that running a one-person business presents.

What are 10 highly valuable podcast topics and ideas that I can have for the show?

Here's the response.

Response:

1. **Building a successful business from scratch:** Share insightful tips and steps to take to create a thriving solopreneur venture, including how to validate ideas, create a business plan, and set achievable goals.

2. **Finding your niche:** Discuss the importance of identifying and understanding your target market, carving out a unique niche, and positioning yourself as an expert in your field.

3. **Essential marketing strategies for solopreneurs:** Explore various marketing channels and techniques tailored for solopreneurs, including social media, email marketing, content marketing, and search engine optimization.

4. **Cultivating a powerful personal brand:** Share how to create and maintain a strong personal brand that effectively communicates your values, offerings, and differentiators to potential clients and customers.

5. **Productivity and time management hacks:** Offer practical advice on maximizing productivity, setting priorities, and managing your time and energy effectively as a solopreneur.

6. **Balancing work and life as a solopreneur:** Discuss strategies to maintain a healthy balance between personal and professional

commitments, avoid burnout, and sustain your mental and physical well-being.

7. Building and maintaining a professional network: Share the benefits of networking and building strong relationships with clients, collaborators, mentors, and fellow solopreneurs.

8. Overcoming common solopreneur challenges: Discuss common obstacles and pitfalls associated with solopreneurship, and how to navigate them, such as dealing with isolation, securing funding, and handling rejections.

9. Solopreneur Success Stories: Share detailed interviews with successful solopreneurs who have successfully built their businesses from the ground up, highlighting their challenges, triumphs, and lessons learned.

10. Optimize your digital presence: Discuss the importance of having a strong online presence, including your website, social media profiles, and the role of online reputation and authority-building.

Now that we have some topics, we may need to find guest speakers for each topic. As always, if you need more ideas, you can ask for 10 or 20 more topics. Remember that you should only select the ones you feel are the most appropriate for your podcast.

Here's a prompt for it.

Prompt:

Give me some potential guests who may support each particular idea or topic

And here's the response.

Response:

1. Building a successful business from scratch: *Guest - Tim Ferriss*, author of The 4-Hour Workweek, and successful entrepreneur

2. Finding your niche: *Guest - Pat Flynn*, creator of Smart Passive Income, and an expert in niche market identification

3. Essential marketing strategies for solopreneurs: *Guest - Gary Vaynerchuk*, entrepreneur and digital marketing expert, founder of VaynerMedia

4. Cultivating a powerful personal brand: *Guest - Chris Ducker*, serial entrepreneur, personal branding expert, and creator of Youpreneur

5. Productivity and time management hacks: *Guest - Laura Vanderkam*, author of several time management and productivity books, including 168 Hours and Off the Clock

6. Balancing work and life as a solopreneur: *Guest - Marie Forleo*, entrepreneur and author of Everything Is Figureoutable, and creator of the Marie Forleo B-School

7. Building and maintaining a professional network: *Guest - Jordan Harbinger*, host of The Jordan Harbinger Show, interviewing high-achievers and experts in various fields and an expert in networking

```
8. Overcoming common solopreneur challenges: *Guest - John Lee Dumas*,
successful entrepreneur, founder, and host of the Entrepreneurs On
Fire podcast, featuring interviews with entrepreneurs facing various
challenges.
9. Solopreneur Success Stories: *Guest - Ramit Sethi*, personal
finance expert, entrepreneur, and best-selling author of I Will Teach
You to Be Rich, with a unique journey into solopreneurship.
10. Optimize your digital presence: *Guest - Neil Patel*, digital
marketing expert, co-founder of NP Digital and Crazy Egg, and creator
of marketing tools like Ubersuggest.
```

Once you've nailed down your topics, thought up fresh ideas, and picked out exciting guests for your podcast, it's time to let the world know about it. In this upcoming section, we'll explore how to use AI to create valuable promotional materials that will bring your podcast the attention it deserves.

Using AI to promote a podcast

It is common to produce a podcast episode before promoting it. Thus, we can use ChatGPT to extract nuggets of information from the podcast to promote it.

The first thing you need to do is transcribe the audio from the podcast to text. You can do that with other generative AI tools:

- The Descript tool allows you to drop the audio and produces the transcript automatically. You can find it here: `https://www.descript.com/`.

- Use ChatGPT Plus and activate the *ChatGPT Speech to Text* plugin, which can be found in the ChatGPT Plus app store. This plugin allows you to upload an audio file to ChatGPT, after which it will transcribe the audio file into text. The transcription is not perfect, but it is usually accurate enough for most purposes.

- Furthermore, many tools provide APIs to do the transcription. In this case, you will need to write a simple program that calls the API, sends the audio file, and returns the transcribed text.

  Some of the best ones are as follows:

  - OpenAI Whisper: `https://openai.com/research/whisper`

  - Deepgram: `https://deepgram.com/`

Once you've transcribed the podcast, you can ask ChatGPT to write a summary of it.

Writing a summary of the podcast episode

For this example, we are going to take the transcription of the *WorkLife with Adam Grant* podcast for the *How to Bust Bias at Work* episode.

Source: `https://www.ted.com/podcasts/worklife/how-to-bust-bias-at-work-transcript`.

The transcript is longer than the 8,000 tokens available with GPT-4 (which I am using on the OpenAI Playground). Thus, I need to switch to the gpt-3.5-turbo-16k model:

Figure 3.1: Switching models via the OpenAI Playground

Here's the prompt for a summary.

Prompt:

```
Write a summary of the following podcast episode:
ADAM GRANT:
Hi WorkLifers, a quick warning that in this episode we discuss the
murder of George Floyd.
TYECE WILKINS:
It wasn't until Saturday evening that I allowed the tears to flow.
Sitting underneath a cotton candy pink sky. I put on Mali Music's
Gonna be all right.
And try to let the music soothe me.
ADAM GRANT:
Tyece Wilkins is a diversity and inclusion senior advisor at BAE
Systems, the aerospace and defense company. Following the murder of
George Floyd in May 2020, Tyece painstakingly wrote and sent this
email to the 600 members of BAE's Black employee resource group, which
she led at the time.
...
```

Here's the response.

Response:

```
In this episode of "WorkLife with Adam Grant," Grant explores how
organizations can make real and meaningful progress in the fight
against bias and discrimination. He speaks with Tyece Wilkins, a
diversity and inclusion senior advisor at BAE Systems, who discusses
the impact of the murder of George Floyd on her and her colleagues.
Wilkins shares the email she wrote to the 600 members of BAE's Black
employee resource group following the murder, and discusses the
response from senior leaders.
Grant also speaks with experts Quinetta Roberson and Ashleigh Shelby
Rosette on the topic of diversity and inclusion in the workplace.
Roberson emphasizes the importance of dedicating resources and
creating formal roles to manage diversity within organizations.
```

Rosette discusses her research on the expectations of leaders, revealing that people subconsciously hold a white standard for leadership and judge leaders accordingly. She underscores the importance of consistent support and mentorship for underrepresented employees.

Grant concludes the episode by highlighting the necessity of changing organizational structures, habits, and cultures to combat systemic bias and discrimination. He emphasizes the importance of ongoing initiatives, such as bias training and town hall events, to maintain momentum and keep diversity and inclusion at the forefront of an organization's values.

It reads well, but perhaps you would like something more engaging so that readers on the website will be more willing to click play. Thus, let's add a prompt to refine it.

Here's a more refined prompt.

Prompt:

Write a summary once again, but make it more persuasive so people reading it on the TED website will be more interested in clicking play to listen to the episode.

And here's the response.

Response:

Get ready for a jaw-dropping episode of "WorkLife with Adam Grant" that will challenge everything you thought you knew about bias in the workplace. Grant delves into the murder of George Floyd and the subsequent email that Tyece Wilkins, a diversity and inclusion senior advisor at BAE Systems, wrote to her colleagues. This raw, vulnerable email sparked a powerful transformation at her company, illuminating how organizations can truly combat bias and discrimination.

Discover why traditional bias training falls short and how BAE Systems has defied the norm with its groundbreaking approach. Through behavior-focused programs and accountability measures, BAE has seen a remarkable increase in hiring diverse talent and developing inclusive leaders.

Grant uncovers the science behind breaking biased habits and replacing them with new, healthier ones. You'll be mesmerized as he shares studies on habit change and its impact on increasing representation and reducing discrimination.

As the episode progresses, Grant delves into the importance of structural and cultural changes within organizations. He speaks with Quinetta Roberson, who emphasizes the need for diversity and inclusion to be core responsibilities rather than side gigs. Together with Ashleigh Shelby Rosette, they shed light on the white standard of leadership and the profound implications it has on underrepresented individuals.

Prepare to be captivated by the unique stories of individuals who have experienced bias in the workplace and their courageous efforts to create inclusive environments. From virtual town halls to mentoring programs, you'll hear how BAE Systems is leading the way in sustained, meaningful change.

But this episode isn't just about highlighting the successes. Grant addresses the challenges that organizations face in supporting underrepresented employees and the potential pitfalls of delegating diversity work to them without proper recognition or resources.

Get energized by the strategies and insights shared by Roberson and Rosette as they offer a roadmap for creating lasting change. Discover how to allocate work equitably, challenge the white standard of leadership, and support and mentor individuals from diverse backgrounds.

As this thought-provoking episode comes to a close, Grant reminds us that fighting bias requires a marathon-like commitment. It's about embedding diversity and inclusion into the very fabric of an organization, pushing past comfort zones, and staying the course through criticism.

If you're ready to challenge the status quo and embark on a journey of transformation within your organization, don't miss this powerful episode of "WorkLife with Adam Grant." It's time to rewrite the norms and create workplaces where diversity and inclusion are not just buzzwords, but lived experiences. Click play to step into a world of possibility and change.

This is certainly more engaging, but it seems too long. We can ask the LLM to make it shorter.

Here's the prompt for it.

Prompt:

```
Make it half as long
```

Here's the response.

Response:

In this mind-blowing episode of "WorkLife with Adam Grant," prepare to question everything you thought you knew about bias in the workplace. Join Grant as he delves into the transformative impact of an email written by Tyece Wilkins, a diversity and inclusion senior advisor at BAE Systems, following the murder of George Floyd.

Discover why traditional bias training falls short, and how BAE Systems has revolutionized the approach with behavior-focused programs and accountability measures. The astounding results include increased hiring of diverse talent and the development of inclusive leaders.

Uncover the science behind breaking biased habits and hear captivating stories of individuals who have experienced workplace bias firsthand. Gain insights from experts Quinetta Roberson and Ashleigh Shelby Rosette as they outline strategies for creating lasting change.

This episode challenges the white standard of leadership and guides organizations on the path to equity and inclusion. Learn how to allocate work equitably, provide meaningful support and mentorship, and overcome the challenges that arise along the way.

```
If you're ready to ignite transformation within your organization,
don't miss this powerful episode of "WorkLife with Adam Grant." Click
play to embark on a journey of possibility, change, and creating
workplaces where diversity and inclusion are not just buzzwords but
lived experiences.
```

> **Note**
>
> As you can see, you don't need to specify what needs to be half as long since GPT-3.5 Turbo (and GPT-4) keep the context (in short-term memory).

This is much better. You can continue iterating by asking for any further refinements. This could be a great starting point and you can and should do some edits to make it even better.

Once you have the summary you wish to include in your podcast site, you may want to create some content to post on social media to promote the episode.

Crafting engaging quotes for social media promotion

In addition to episode summaries, social media quotes can be an impactful way to promote podcast content and spark interest. Generative AI can analyze podcast transcripts and identify memorable sound bites to highlight on platforms such as Twitter and Facebook.

Here's the prompt.

Prompt:

```
Write 5 highly engaging quotes from this episode to post on social
media
```

Here's the response.

Response:

```
1. "Our words have power. Our stories have strength. And our silence
absolutely will not serve us." - Tyece Wilkins
2. "Changing biases requires ongoing practice and repetition, like
breaking a bad habit. It's a constant, intentional process." - Adam
Grant
3. "Support looks like endorsing, sponsoring, and mentoring those that
are different from you. It's about making connections and changing the
networks around you." - Ashleigh Shelby Rosette
4. "To fight bias, organizations must allocate work equitably,
challenge the white standard of leadership, and stay committed even in
the face of criticism." - Adam Grant
5. "It's time to rewrite the norms and create workplaces where
diversity and inclusion are not just buzzwords, but lived experiences.
Are you ready to challenge the status quo?" - Adam Grant
```

I think all of them are good. You can take each one and put them on Canva with a nice background image and boom. You will see something similar to what's shown in *Figure 3.2*:

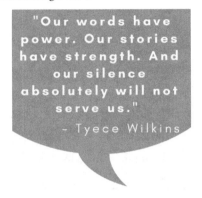

Figure 3.2: Canva image using one of the quotes

As you would probably like more content to promote your podcast episode, you can ask the LLM to create ideas to create short-form videos.

Conceptualizing podcast highlight reels

Short-form video content on platforms such as TikTok and YouTube Shorts represents a major opportunity for podcast promotion. Generative AI can rapidly develop engaging video ideas that distill podcast episodes into snackable, eye-catching clips that have been optimized for these vertical video platforms.

Let's look at the prompt.

Prompt:

```
Come up with 3 ideas for 3 highly engaging short-form videos for an
audience that watches them on TikTok, Instagram, or YouTube Shorts
```

Here's the response.

Response:

```
Video 1 (TikTok/Instagram/YouTube Shorts):
Title: "Breaking Bias in 60 Seconds"
Description: In this quick, eye-opening video, learn the science of
breaking biased habits and fostering inclusion in just 60 seconds.
#InclusivityMatters #BreakTheBias #DiversityRevolution
Video 2 (TikTok/Instagram/YouTube Shorts):
Title: "Powerful Stories of Overcoming Workplace Bias"
Description: Discover the powerful stories of individuals who have
faced workplace bias head-on and triumphed. Hear their inspiring
```

```
journeys in this short video that will make you think differently.
#BiasNoMore #EmpoweredVoices #InclusionChampions
Video 3 (TikTok/Instagram/YouTube Shorts):
Title: "Creating Lasting Change: Transforming Organizations"
Description: Are you ready to be part of the change? Watch this
captivating video to learn how organizations are transforming
their structures, cultures, and habits to foster diversity and
inclusion. Let's create a better future together! #MakeChangeHappen
#DiversityWins #InclusiveOrgs
```

As you can see, starting with the transcript, you can create a lot of content, both for promoting the podcast episode or for repurposing the content to augment or promote your brand.

We can continue asking the LLM to write a blog post about the concepts discussed in the podcast episode.

Repurposing podcasts into shareable blog content

Podcasts contain a wealth of insights and ideas that can be repurposed into written content such as blog posts. Generative AI makes it possible to efficiently transform audio conversations into compelling articles for wider readership.

For the blog, you should define the length and the audience.

Here's the prompt.

Prompt:

```
Write a blog post around the themes and ideas presented in this
episode. Make it 1000 words in length and specific to  Professionals
and Leaders, Diversity and Inclusion Advocates, Individuals Interested
in Social Justice or Anyone Seeking Personal Growth and Self-
Reflection
```

Here's the response.

Response:

```
Title: How to Bust Bias at Work: A Roadmap to Inclusion and Equality
Introduction
In the thought-provoking podcast episode, "How to Bust Bias at Work,"
host Adam Grant explores the transformative journey towards creating
inclusive workplaces and combating bias. This blog post delves into
the key themes and ideas discussed in the episode, offering practical
insights and strategies for professionals and leaders, diversity and
inclusion advocates, individuals interested in social justice, and
those seeking personal growth and self-reflection.
Professionals and Leaders: Driving Change from Within
For professionals and leaders, the episode emphasizes the importance
of taking an active role in driving change within their organizations.
It highlights the need to go beyond traditional bias training and
```

instead focus on behavior change and accountability. By creating personal action plans, leaders can actively work towards building diverse teams, becoming more inclusive leaders, and fostering a culture of belonging. The episode encourages professionals and leaders to challenge their own biases, engage in courageous conversations, and actively seek out diverse perspectives to create lasting change.

Diversity and Inclusion Advocates: Amplifying Voices, Empowering Change

Diversity and inclusion advocates play a crucial role in amplifying marginalized voices and empowering change. The episode underscores the power of personal stories and the importance of creating safe spaces for open dialogue. Advocates are encouraged to share their own experiences and listen to the stories of others, fostering empathy and understanding. By challenging the status quo, advocating for inclusive policies and practices, and actively working towards dismantling biases, advocates can drive meaningful change within their organizations and communities.

Individuals Interested in Social Justice: A Call to Action

For individuals interested in social justice, the episode serves as a call to action. It highlights the systemic biases that exist within society and emphasizes the need for collective responsibility in addressing them. Listeners are encouraged to examine their own biases, question societal norms, and actively work towards creating a more equitable and inclusive world. The episode provides insights into the importance of allyship, intergroup interaction, and ongoing education in fostering social justice and equality.

Anyone Seeking Personal Growth and Self-Reflection: A Path to Transformation

The episode offers a path to personal growth and self-reflection for individuals seeking to challenge their own biases and foster inclusivity. Listeners are encouraged to engage in introspection, examine their own assumptions and behaviors, and actively work towards personal transformation. By embracing vulnerability, practicing empathy, and committing to ongoing learning, individuals can contribute to creating a more inclusive and equitable society.

Conclusion

The podcast episode "How to Bust Bias at Work" serves as a powerful resource for professionals, leaders, diversity advocates, social justice enthusiasts, and individuals seeking personal growth. It provides practical strategies, thought-provoking insights, and inspiring stories that can guide us on the path towards creating inclusive workplaces and fostering equality.

By challenging our biases, holding ourselves accountable, and actively working towards behavior change, we can drive meaningful transformation within our organizations. It is through courageous conversations, amplifying marginalized voices, and advocating for inclusive policies that we can create lasting change.

The journey towards equality requires collective responsibility and a commitment to ongoing learning and growth. It is a call to action for individuals to examine their own biases, question societal norms, and actively work towards creating a more equitable and inclusive world.

Let us embrace the lessons from this episode and embark on a journey

```
of self-reflection, empathy, and action. Together, we can bust bias at
work and create environments where everyone feels valued, respected,
and included.
```

Not what you expected? No problem – rewrite the prompts, instruct the system regarding what you would like, and keep refining it little by little. Again, the key is experimentation.

In the next section, we will explore how to use ChatGPT or similar applications to prepare job interviews (for job interviewers and applicants) and to prepare for answering them (applicants).

Podcasting and job interviews may seem like very different use cases for question preparation, but they share some fundamental best practices. Conducting background research, personalizing questions, and developing strategic follow-ups based on responses helps ensure productive discussions in any setting.

Identifying insightful interview questions

In most companies, professionals at different levels of their careers are asked to interview job candidates regularly. Preparing the interview questions is generally a drag and requires the person to spend significant time thinking about intelligent questions to ask.

ChatGPT can help. In the prompt, you should include a short bio of yourself (the interviewer) and describe the profile of the interviewee.

Here's the prompt.

Prompt:

```
You are a Senior Manager, Community Marketing at Samsung. You are a
Communications and Marketing professional with more than 15 years of
project management experience, both in-house and agency, developing
and executing programs to increase brand exposure; drive positive
media coverage and customer relations; establish successful influencer
campaigns and paid media programs; enhance client relations and
employee engagement.
You have been tasked with interviewing recent graduates in
communication for a position as social media managers.
What 10 questions would you ask a candidate?
```

Here's the response.

Response:

```
1. Can you tell us about your experience managing social media
accounts, either for personal use or for any organizations you have
been involved in?
2. Which social media platforms do you have experience with, and which
do you consider yourself to be most proficient in?
3. How do you keep up with the latest trends and updates on various
social media platforms?
```

```
4. Can you provide examples of any successful social media campaigns
or content you have created or managed in the past?

5. How would you handle a situation where you receive negative
feedback or comments on our brand's social media accounts?

6. How do you measure the success of a social media campaign or post?
Which metrics do you consider most important?

7. What strategies would you use to increase our brand's social media
following and engagement?

8. Can you give an example of a time when you had to manage a social
media crisis, and how did you handle it?

9. How do you stay organized and manage your time when handling
multiple social media accounts and tasks simultaneously?

10. How do you approach content creation for different social media
platforms? Are there specific strategies or tactics you employ for
each platform?
```

You can continue iterating to ask more personal questions.

For example, take a look at this prompt.

Prompt:

```
Write 10 personal question that you would ask the candidate
```

Here's the response.

Response:

```
1. Can you tell us a bit about yourself and what inspired you to
pursue a career in social media management and communications?

2. How do you stay motivated and focused when managing multiple tasks
and deadlines in your work?

3. What aspect of social media management do you enjoy the most, and
why?

4. How do you handle stress and maintain a healthy work-life balance,
especially when managing social media accounts that require constant
monitoring and updating?

5. Can you share a specific instance in which you faced a professional
challenge and how you overcame it?

6. How do you continue to develop your skills and stay up-to-date with
the ever-changing world of social media and digital marketing?

7. What do you think sets you apart from other candidates applying for
this social media manager intern position?

8. How would your peers or previous supervisors describe your work
style and communication skills?

9. Can you share a personal or professional accomplishment that you
are particularly proud of?

10. What are your long-term career goals, and how do you see this
internship opportunity fitting into your overall professional
development plan?
```

Now, you can select three from each category (professional and personal) that you think are the most appropriate for the interview. You can ask for more ideas and/or refine some of them as needed.

The person applying for a job can use the same prompts to try to identify potential questions and be better prepared to answer them.

Sharpening interview skills with AI-generated responses

As a candidate, you may want to ask ChatGPT to generate more potential questions, at least to be able to think about them before the interview. You don't want to be caught off guard during the interview.

You can also use ChatGPT to get suggestions on how to answer the questions.

Continuing with the previous conversation, you can ask the LLM for three potential answers to each question.

Let's take a look at an example prompt.

Prompt:

```
For the first set of questions, provide for each three potential good
answers
```

Here's the response.

Response:

```
Question 1: Can you tell us about your experience managing social
media accounts, either for personal use or for any organizations you
have been involved in?
Answer 1: In the past, I've managed the social media accounts for my
university's student council, where I was responsible for creating
content, engaging with followers, and promoting campus events. This
experience helped me develop my skills in content creation and
community management.
Answer 2: I have managed social media accounts for a local non-profit
organization, focusing on increasing awareness about their cause and
driving donations through engaging content and targeted campaigns. I
gained valuable experience in developing social media strategies and
using analytics to measure success.
Answer 3: As a freelance social media manager, I have worked with
small businesses in various industries, helping them grow their online
presence, increase customer engagement, and generate leads. I have
developed a strong understanding of different social media platforms
and have a proven track record of delivering results for my clients.
Question 2: Which social media platforms do you have experience with,
and which do you consider yourself to be most proficient in?
Answer 1: I have experience with Facebook, Instagram, Twitter,
LinkedIn, and Pinterest. I consider myself to be most proficient in
Instagram, as I've had the most success increasing visually appealing
```

content and driving engagement through Instagram Stories and Reels.

Answer 2: I have experience with all major social media platforms, including Facebook, Instagram, Twitter, LinkedIn, TikTok, and Snapchat. I excel in creating content for Twitter, as I have a knack for crafting concise, engaging tweets that resonate with the audience and spark conversations.

Answer 3: My experience spans across Facebook, Instagram, LinkedIn, and YouTube. I am particularly skilled in LinkedIn, where I've managed to create professional content and foster meaningful connections for various brands, helping them expand their network and generate leads.

Question 3: How do you keep up with the latest trends and updates on various social media platforms?

Answer 1: I follow industry-leading blogs, podcasts, and social media news sites, such as Social Media Today and Social Media Examiner, to stay updated on the latest trends and platform updates. I also participate in online communities and forums to exchange knowledge and ideas with other social media professionals.

Answer 2: I regularly attend webinars and industry conferences to learn about the latest trends, tools, and best practices in social media marketing. Additionally, I follow influential social media marketers and thought leaders on platforms like LinkedIn and Twitter to stay informed about the latest news and updates.

Answer 3: To stay up-to-date with social media trends, I subscribe to newsletters from reputable marketing sources and follow popular social media accounts that showcase emerging trends and platform updates. I also set up Google Alerts for keywords related to social media marketing and engage with my professional network to discuss and share new developments.

Question 4: Can you provide examples of any successful social media campaigns or content you have created or managed in the past?

Answer 1: One successful campaign I managed involved partnering with local influencers to promote a small business's product launch. We saw a significant increase in sales and social media engagement as a result of the targeted influencer posts and user-generated content from the campaign.

Answer 2: I was responsible for a non-profit's social media campaign to raise awareness about their annual fundraising event. I created a series of compelling visuals and stories that highlighted the impact of the organization's work, which led to a significant increase in event attendance and donations compared to previous years.

Answer 3: I managed a social media campaign for a local restaurant, where we ran a contest encouraging customers to share photos of their meals and tag the restaurant. This campaign not only increased user-generated content but also boosted the restaurant's online visibility and resulted in a noticeable increase in foot traffic.

Question 5: How would you handle a situation where you receive negative feedback or comments on our brand's social media accounts?

Answer 1: I would first evaluate the comment to determine if it is a genuine concern or complaint. If so, I would respond promptly and professionally, addressing the issue and offering a solution or directing them to the appropriate support channel. This demonstrates that the brand values its customers and is committed to resolving their concerns.

Answer 2: If the negative comment is not a genuine concern but rather a troll or an attempt to harm the brand's reputation, I would consult with my team and decide whether it is best to remove the comment, ignore it, or address it calmly and professionally. The key is to ensure the brand's reputation remains intact and not to escalate the situation further.

Answer 3: In any case of negative feedback, I would also take the opportunity to learn from it and see if there are any improvements or changes that the brand can make based on the feedback received. This ensures that we continually adapt and cater to our audience's needs and expectations.

Question 6: How do you measure the success of a social media campaign or post? Which metrics do you consider most important?

Answer 1: I measure the success of a social media campaign by tracking key performance indicators (KPIs) such as engagement rate, reach, impressions, and click-through rate. I consider engagement rate to be the most important metric, as it indicates how well the content resonates with the target audience and encourages interaction.

Answer 2: The metrics I prioritize depend on the campaign's specific goals. For example, if the goal is to drive website traffic, I focus on click-through rate and conversions. If the goal is to increase brand awareness, I prioritize reach, impressions, and share of voice.

Answer 3: To measure the success of a social media post or campaign, I use a combination of quantitative and qualitative metrics, such as likes, comments, shares, mentions, and sentiment analysis. I believe that understanding the audience's sentiment and feedback is crucial in determining the effectiveness of a social media strategy.

Question 7: What strategies would you use to increase our brand's social media following and engagement?

Answer 1: To increase following and engagement, I would focus on creating high-quality, shareable content that resonates with the target audience, while also maintaining a consistent posting schedule. Additionally, I would engage with relevant influencers, participate in industry-related conversations, and leverage user-generated content to create a sense of community around the brand.

Answer 2: I would implement a combination of organic and paid strategies to increase the brand's social media following and engagement. This includes optimizing the brand's social media profiles, running targeted ad campaigns to reach a larger audience, and hosting contests or giveaways to encourage audience interaction and sharing.

Answer 3: To grow our brand's social media following and engagement, I would focus on understanding our target audience's preferences and tailor our content accordingly. I would also collaborate with complementary brands or influencers, utilize relevant hashtags, and actively engage with our audience by responding to comments and messages promptly.

Question 8: Can you give an example of a time when you had to manage a social media crisis, and how did you handle it?

Answer 1: When managing a social media account for a client, a negative news article about the company went viral, resulting in a surge of negative comments on our social media channels. I quickly gathered information about the situation, collaborated with the PR team, and crafted a well-thought-out response addressing the concerns raised in the article. We also made sure to engage with the audience in a transparent and empathetic manner, which helped diffuse the situation and protect the brand's reputation.

Answer 2: During a product launch for a client, a technical glitch caused a delay in the product's availability, leading to customer frustration on social media. I worked closely with the customer support and technical teams to gather accurate information about the issue and provide real-time updates to the audience. Additionally, we offered a discount code to customers affected by the delay, turning a potential crisis into a customer-centric response that improved brand perception.

Answer 3: A social media crisis occurred when an employee accidentally posted a personal and controversial opinion on the company's official account. I immediately removed the post and issued a public apology, clarifying that the views expressed were not representative of the company's values. Internally, we reviewed and reinforced our social media guidelines and processes to prevent future incidents.

Question 9: How do you stay organized and manage your time when handling multiple social media accounts and tasks simultaneously?

Answer 1: I use a combination of tools and strategies to stay organized, such as creating a content calendar, utilizing project management software, and setting priorities and deadlines for each task. By keeping track of my progress and consistently updating my to-do list, I can efficiently manage my workload and ensure that all social media accounts are updated and monitored regularly.

Answer 2: I rely on time-blocking and the Pomodoro technique to manage my time effectively. By allocating specific time slots for each task and taking short breaks, I can maintain focus and productivity while handling multiple social media accounts and tasks.

Answer 3: I use a combination of digital tools, such as social media scheduling platforms and task management apps, along with traditional methods like pen and paper to-do lists. This helps me stay organized, prioritize tasks, and allocate my time effectively across multiple social media accounts.

Question 10: How do you approach content creation for different social media platforms? Are there specific strategies or tactics you employ for each platform?

Answer 1: I tailor content to each platform based on its unique features, audience preferences, and best practices. For example, I might create visually appealing images and stories for Instagram, concise and engaging text for Twitter, and more in-depth articles or long-form videos for LinkedIn. Additionally, I keep up-to-date with each platform's algorithms and trends to maximize content visibility and engagement.

Answer 2: I consider each platform's primary purpose and audience demographics when creating content. For instance, I would focus on creating entertaining and informative videos for TikTok, professional and industry-related content for LinkedIn, and more casual, lifestyle-oriented content for Instagram. This approach ensures that content aligns with the expectations and preferences of each platform's audience.

```
Answer 3: My strategy for content creation involves researching and
understanding the best practices for each social media platform,
such as optimal post frequency, post timing, and content formats.
I also pay close attention to the platform-specific analytics to
identify which types of content perform best and adjust my strategy
accordingly. This helps me create tailored and effective content for
each platform, maximizing engagement and reach.
```

You can repeat this process for the rest of the questions that are generated. The goal here is not for you to use any of these answers as they are, but to have ideas of what could be expected and for you to think of answers that apply to your own experience.

An additional benefit is that by doing this exercise, you will get ideas on how to improve how you do your work. Just check the answers provided to the questions here. If you are a communicator/social media manager, you are probably already getting some useful tips on how to improve your work.

Generating strategic questions for client engagements with AI

Generative AI can also play a valuable role in question preparation in other fields, such as for sales calls and consulting engagements. Here's how it can assist:

- **Sales call question generation**: Generative AI can analyze customer data, previous sales interactions, and industry trends to suggest targeted and effective questions for sales professionals. By considering the customer's specific needs and pain points, generative AI can generate a list of relevant questions that help uncover valuable information during discovery sessions.

- **Sales follow-up questions**: After initial sales calls, generative AI can analyze the conversation and generate follow-up questions that address specific concerns or explore potential solutions. This ensures that sales professionals maintain a proactive approach and continue to engage with the customer effectively.

- **Consulting engagement question generation**: Generative AI can assist consultants by analyzing client data, industry insights, and project requirements to generate insightful and tailored questions for consulting engagements. These questions can cover various aspects, such as business processes, challenges, and desired outcomes, enabling consultants to gather comprehensive information and deliver valuable recommendations.

- **Consulting follow-up questions**: After the initial consulting engagements, generative AI can analyze the discussion and generate relevant follow-up questions. These questions can help consultants clarify any ambiguities, obtain further details, or seek feedback to refine their recommendations and ensure client satisfaction.

By leveraging generative AI for question generation in sales calls and consulting engagements, professionals can benefit from a wealth of tailored and relevant inquiries. This saves time and ensures that the questions that are asked are strategic, comprehensive, and aligned with the client's specific needs.

Generative AI algorithms can analyze vast amounts of data, including industry trends, customer preferences, and historical sales or consulting data to generate questions that are tailored to the specific context. This not only helps sales professionals and consultants in their preparation but also enables them to have more targeted and meaningful conversations with clients.

Furthermore, generative AI can aid in personalization by considering individual client profiles and preferences. It can generate questions that address customers' unique pain points, goals, and challenges, showing a deeper understanding and emphasizing the value of the proposed solutions.

The use of generative AI in question preparation also provides scalability and consistency. It can generate a large number of relevant questions that can be saved and reused in subsequent interactions or shared among team members. This ensures that the sales team or consulting group consistently asks the right questions, ensuring a standardized approach and preventing important inquiries from being missed.

However, it's important to note that while generative AI can greatly assist in question preparation, human expertise and judgment remain essential in crafting follow-up questions, adapting to dynamic conversations, and interpreting nuanced responses. Generative AI acts as an invaluable aid, providing a wealth of options and insights, but the final decision-making and analysis require the skills and experience of the professionals involved.

Summary

The art of question preparation is vital in various interview scenarios. For podcast interviews, it entails conducting thorough research to ask engaging and insightful questions to both famous and lesser-known individuals. AI technology further enhances the podcasting experience by streamlining preparation and promoting content effectively. In job interviews, interviewers must carefully construct questions that assess candidates' suitability for the role through a combination of technical, situational, and behavioral inquiries. On the other hand, job candidates should invest time in understanding the company and role, anticipating potential questions, and crafting thoughtful responses that highlight their qualifications and align with the organization's values. Strategic question preparation ensures compelling conversations, valuable insights, memorable podcast episodes, and increased chances of securing desired job positions. By continuously honing our question preparation skills, we can forge meaningful connections, captivate audiences, and achieve our career goals.

The next chapter will explore creative applications of LLMs and teach you how to use AI for different types of creative writing. It covers leveraging AI to generate fiction, with techniques to craft prompts, develop storylines and characters, and refine content. We'll also examine using AI to compose original poetry, from rhyming poems to free verse, by providing the model with literary constraints. Throughout this chapter, we will focus on strategies for balancing reliance on AI-generated text with ensuring originality and authenticity.

4

LLMs for Creative Writing

The blank page has long tormented many aspiring writers. But what if **artificial intelligence (AI)** could help spark new ideas and shape those fleeting sparks into captivating stories? In this chapter, we'll explore how the rise of **large language models (LLMs)** such as GPT-3 and GPT-4 is transforming creative writing.

Discover how these AI tools can become your partners in imagination – suggesting plot lines and characters, enhancing your prose, and polishing your drafts. We'll journey through the process of writing everything from haikus to sonnets, lyrics to screenplays with the aid of creative AI.

In this chapter, we'll cover examples of how prompt engineering can help an AI model understand your genre, style, and creative vision for a piece. Then, we'll learn about strategies we can utilize to take the AI's raw output and curate it into a refined work with our own flair. We'll also discuss the importance of striking the right balance between AI-generated content and original human creativity.

By the end of this chapter, you'll know how to start utilizing these fascinating tools to explore new narrative possibilities, gain fresh inspiration, and save time on the crafting process – all while retaining your artistic license and creative spirit. So, get ready to team up with AI and begin your next writing adventure!

In this chapter, we'll cover the following topics:

- Using AI for creative writing
- Using AI to generate fiction
- Using AI to write poetry

Using AI for creative writing

In the literary landscape of our hyper-digital world, the integration of technology with traditional creative processes has opened uncharted territories of artistic exploration and expression. LLMs have emerged as a game-changer in the realm of creative writing.

LLMs have the power to generate text that can emulate human-like writing in a variety of genres, creating endless possibilities for writers. From generating intricate plotlines in science fiction to evoking profound emotions in romance tales and crafting spine-chilling narratives in horror, the capabilities of these AI models are as vast and diverse as the creative imagination itself.

As we proceed, we'll explore the potential of LLMs not just as a tool for textual generation, but also as an avenue for prompt engineering that can cater to a multitude of writing styles and needs. Be it stirring up a reservoir of innovative ideas, fleshing out storylines, improving linguistic fluency, or editing and polishing drafts – the deployment of LLMs holds immense promise.

LLMs such as ChatGPT are exceptionally versatile tools that can aid in an array of creative writing endeavors:

- **Genre**: Whether you're weaving a complex fantasy novel, penning a riveting crime thriller, writing a heart-wrenching drama, or exploring the depths of science fiction, LLMs can serve as valuable aids. They can generate ideas, suggest plot twists, develop characters, or even help with world-building based on the genre you're working with.

- **Voice and tone**: LLMs can also aid you in maintaining a consistent narrative voice and tone throughout your work. Whether it's a pensive first-person narrator or an omniscient third-person view, a comedic tone, or a more serious, somber one, these models can mimic the required styles effectively once they are adequately trained or given appropriate prompts.

- **Writing style**: Whether your writing leans toward verbose and descriptive or succinct and straightforward, LLMs can help maintain your unique style. All you need to do is give the LLM an example of your writing style to imitate while generating text.

- **Poetry and songwriting**: For poets and songwriters out there, LLMs can be used to generate rhymes, verses, or entire poems and songs. They can identify rhyme schemes, rhythmic patterns, and common song structures to help you come up with emotionally resonant sentimental ballads, catchy pop songs, or profound epic poetry.

- **Dialogue**: LLMs can be instrumental in writing dialogue as well. From creating everyday conversation sets to complex emotional exchanges between characters, by providing examples of the kind of dialogue you need, the model can generate similar interactions.

- **Research and historical accuracy**: If your work is set in a different era or requires specialist knowledge, LLMs can assist in ensuring historical or subject matter accuracy. Though not a substitute for detailed research, they can indeed supplement your efforts by providing quick information or context.

- **Screenplays**: If your niche is screenwriting for film, television, or even video games, LLMs can help with structuring scenes, creating dialogue, and ensuring the correct format and style are maintained according to screenplay requirements.

- **Editor and proofreader**: Besides generating creative text, LLMs such as ChatGPT are excellent tools for refining drafts. They can identify grammatical errors, suggest better phrasing options, and ensure overall readability and coherence in your writing, functioning as both an editor and a proofreader. This way, you can polish your raw content to a high standard without paying for professional services.

- **Brainstorming and outlining**: Transforming a wild idea into a comprehensive and engaging plot can be a daunting task. That's where an LLM steps in, aiding in brainstorming different storyline possibilities, subplots, or character arcs. They can also help draft a basic outline of your narrative, providing a clear roadmap for your writing journey.

- **Non-fiction**: If your creative endeavors lean more toward non-fiction genres such as biographies, travelogues, or self-help books, LLMs can still offer invaluable support. They can help present information in an engaging and readable style, ensuring your readers stay engaged while learning something new.

Furthermore, one of the strengths of an LLM such as GPT-4 is its ability to assist in refining and polishing a piece of writing, including a story. Here are some ways they can help:

- **Grammar check**: LLMs are capable of identifying grammatical errors in your story. They can spot incorrect verb tenses, improper use of prepositions, missing or misplaced punctuation marks, and other common grammatical mistakes.

- **Spelling correction**: The models can detect and correct spelling errors, thereby reducing the chance of your narrative being jumbled up with typos or incorrect spellings.

- **Readability enhancement**: LLMs can suggest better sentence structures or vocabulary to make your story more readable and engaging. If a sentence is too complex or wordy, the model can recommend a simpler, clearer way to convey the same idea.

- **Consistency check**: The models can help ensure that character descriptions, plot developments, and other elements in your story remain consistent. It can alert you to inconsistencies such as a character's appearance changing without explanation, timeline inconsistencies, or even continuity issues within the plot.

- **Tone and style**: If you've chosen a specific tone or style for your story, the models can ensure it's maintained throughout the piece. For instance, if your story is meant to maintain an informal, conversational tone or a formal, academic one, the LLM can suggest edits to maintain this consistency of voice.

- **Flow and transition**: One of the key elements of a good story is the smoothness of the narrative – how one scene or idea seamlessly flows into the next. LLMs can assist in perfecting these transitions in your story, making sure that every event or dialogue naturally progresses from previous ones.

- **Plot structure**: LLMs can provide feedback on the structure of your story. They can check whether your story has a clear beginning, middle, and end with all the necessary elements of a plot, such as the setup, conflict, climax, and resolution.

- **Style guide adherence**: If you're writing for an outlet that requires adherence to a specific style guide, such as the AP or Chicago styles, an LLM can be trained to scan your material for any deviations and suggest necessary corrections.

- **Character development**: Your characters need to grow and transform throughout the story, and an LLM can help ensure this. With precise inputs, it can track character arcs and suggest natural progressions based on their established traits and the story's context.

- **Narrative pace**: Maintaining the right pace is critical to keeping readers engaged. Too slow, and it may seem dull; too fast, and important details might be missed. An LLM can suggest where to add moments of suspense or conflict to speed up the narrative, or where more detailed descriptions or pauses might be required to slow things down.

- **Perspective consistency**: Whether you're writing in first-, second-, or third-person perspective, LLMs can assist in maintaining this view consistently throughout your story, a pivotal factor in ensuring a cohesive narrative.

In the following section, we will explore a few examples of how to start and develop the writing ideas described here.

Using AI to generate fiction

When you intend to write fiction, starting from a blank page can feel daunting. However, with the assistance of an LLM, the process becomes more manageable. In this section, we will see how.

Here's a step-by-step guide to help you move from a blank page to a full-fledged story using a tool such as ChatGPT:

1. **Idea generation**: Begin with brainstorming. Even if you only have a vague idea, you can feed this into the LLM, and it will generate a variety of scenarios, characters, and possible plot directions for you. For example, if you input *A story about a time-traveling historian*, the model can give you multiple story teasers to choose from.

2. **Character design**: With a basic idea at hand, the next step is character creation. Describe your character to the LLM in simple terms, and it can help you flesh out their personality, backstory, appearance, and more. Input *Introverted librarian with a secret past*, and the model can generate a more detailed character profile.

3. **Plot outlining**: Now that you have a premise and characters, it's time to create a rough sketch of your plot. Provide the LLM with the beginning and end and ask it to fill in critical plot points or scenes in the middle. For instance, if your story begins with the character in their everyday world and ends with them emerging as a hero after saving the day, the LLM will generate a sequence of events that connect these two points.

4. **Scene writing**: Once you have a coherent sequence of plot points, you can ask the LLM to help you elaborate on each of these. Describe each scene to the model and it will generate descriptive text, dialogues, and actions. For example, input *Peter, the librarian, discovers an ancient artifact in the library that transports him to the 15th Century*, and the model might generate a detailed and vivid scene.

5. **Dialogue enhancement**: For the parts in your story with dialogue, you can let the LLM help you create interesting and meaningful exchanges between characters. Input a desired topic or emotion, and the model might generate a dialogue intermixed with character actions and further narration.

6. **Text refinement**: Once you've finished writing your story, the LLM functions as a writing assistant for editing and proofreading your work. The model can identify missing words, incorrect grammar use, or awkward phrase structures, and suggest how to enhance sentences.

7. **Review and revise**: After the initial refinement, read your story thoroughly. Look for inconsistencies or areas lacking detail. Use the LLM to help rewrite sections, add extra descriptions or dialogue, or adjust the pacing, ensuring the story progression feels natural and captivating.

8. **Title suggestion**: LLMs can also aid in creating compelling titles for your story. Provide some key story points and let the model suggest titles that encapsulate the mood and theme of your work.

9. **Formatting**: In addition to creative aspects, LLMs can help with the more structural elements of your story, such as ensuring proper formatting, adherence to prescribed writing styles, if any, and generally enhancing the readability of your text.

10. **Final edit**: Review your story one final time, using the LLM to do a last thorough grammar and punctuation check, and get a final polished version of your initially blank page now turned into a well-rounded story.

Try out this layout and experiment with creating your first short story. Iterate as you see fit to see the power of the LLM that you chose. Try the same process with ChatGPT, Bard, and Claude to see which one is more adept at what you are trying to accomplish.

If you are trying to produce longer stories, GPT-3.5 Turbo 16k-0613, released on June 13, 2023, supports up to 16k tokens, while Claude supports up to 100k tokens, which could be better suited for you. In November 6, 2023 OpenAI announced GPT-4 Turbo with 128k.

Let's try to write something. Suppose you don't have any idea about the topic of the genre. You can ask the LLM for suggestions. In this example, we are using the OpenAI Playground with chat mode and the GPT-4 0613 model:

Prompt:

```
Write great prompt examples to get started with creative writing.
Suggest prompts for different genres, the main characters, the plot,
and the suggested temperature.
```

Response:

1. Genre: Science Fiction

Main Character: A time-traveling alien named Zolon

Plot: Zolon has landed on an Earth before humans have evolved. He must repair his spaceship before Earth's volcanic eruption to escape.

Suggested Temperature: Tension-filled, Unpredictable

Prompt: With the clock ticking, describe how Zolon navigates through the primordial world while trying to repair his spacecraft.

2. Genre: Romance

Main Character: A book-store owner named Sarah

Plot: After unintentionally finding a love letter tucked away in an old book, Sarah decides to find its intended recipient.

Suggested Temperature: Warm, Hopeful

Prompt: Write about Sarah's journey as she unravels the mystery behind the love letter, possibly finding love herself along the way.

3. Genre: Mystery

Main Character: A retired detective named Michael

Plot: Michael stumbles upon an unsolved case about a missing violin from his early years in the department. Intrigued, he takes a trip down the memory lane to solve it.

Suggested Temperature: Suspenseful, Engaging

Prompt: Tell the tale of Michael as he delves deep into the case, unearthing pieces of his past along the journey.

4. Genre: Horror Main Character: A paranormal investigator named Beatrice

Plot: Beatrice is fascinated by a haunted mansion in her city which is believed to curse anyone who dares to enter.

Suggested Temperature: Creepy, Gripping

Prompt: Write about Beatrice's haunting yet tantalizing venture, as she steps foot in the cursed mansion aiming to decode the truth behind the urban legends.

5. Genre: Fantasy

Main Character: A wingless fairy named Lenore

Plot: Lenore sets on a quest to the enchanted forest to find the Elixir of Flight, which is the only way she can earn her wings.

Suggested Temperature: Adventurous, Magical

Prompt: Spin a tale of Lenore's mystical journey through the enchanted forest, encountering mythical creatures, and overcoming various challenges in search of the Elixir.

6. Genre: Adventure

Main Character: A young explorer named Diego

Plot: Diego embarks on a dangerous adventure into uncharted territories in search of the lost city of gold.

Suggested Temperature: Exciting, Exhilarating

Prompt: Narrate Diego's thrilling adventure, his encounters with wild creatures, treacherous landscapes, and the marvels of the elusive lost city.

7. Genre: Drama

Main Character: A struggling actress named Eva

Plot: Eva, chasing her dreams in the big city, finally gets a chance to prove herself in an upcoming theater play.

Suggested Temperature: Intense, Inspiring

Prompt: Tell the story of Eva's creative struggle, the highs, and lows of her journey and the delights and harsh realities of the theater world.

8. Genre: Comedy

Main Character: An unlucky man named Leonard

Plot: In an occurrence of mistaken identity, Leonard is believed to be an undercover super-spy by several agencies.

Suggested Temperature: Light-hearted, Funny

Prompt: Write about Leonard's series of comedic escapades as he tries to convince everyone he is not a super-spy while simultaneously getting entangled in numerous hilarious situations.

9. Genre: Historical Fiction

Main Character: An aspiring writer named Amelia

Plot: Amelia finds herself in the 18th century due to a time-travel phenomenon. She decides to document her experiences.

Suggested Temperature: Intriguing, Captivating

Prompt: In Amelia's perspective, detail her adventures in the past, her encounters with historical figures, and how this journey impacts her writing.

10. Genre: Bildungsroman/Coming of Age

Main Character: A young boy named Oliver

Plot: After the death of his mother, Oliver must move to a small countryside village to live with his estranged grandfather.

Suggested Temperature: Emotional, Heart-warming

Prompt: Write about Oliver's journey as he struggles to adjust in a new place, dealing with grief, and eventually developing a deep bond with his grandfather and the quaint village.

11. Genre: Supernatural

Main Character: A high school student, Jessica, who has the ability to see spirits

Plot: Jessica uses her ability to help restless spirits find peace while juggling her own daily high school life.

Suggested Temperature: Spooky, Emotional

Prompt: Narrate Jessica's daily encounters with the spirit world, how she manages to balance this extraordinary life with her regular high school routine, and her quest to understand why she was given this ability.

12. Genre: Thriller

Main Character: A forensic scientist named Robert

Plot: Robert becomes a key player in a high-stakes chase when he discovers that a grave criminal is targeting him.

Suggested Temperature: Suspenseful, Fast-paced

```
Prompt: Write about Robert's high tension cat-and-mouse chase, how
he uses his forensic skills to stay one step ahead, and gradually
uncovering the motive behind the criminal's actions.
```

There are some good ideas there, but we have a long way to go.

One unexpected thing happened here: when I asked the LLM for the suggested temperature, I was thinking of the model temperature and not what the LLM produced. However, I think what it suggested was useful to set up the tone of the stories.

Let's develop a story for the science fiction genre.

Prompt:

```
Genre: Science Fiction
Main Character: A time-traveling alien named Zolon
Plot: Zolon has landed on an Earth before humans have evolved. He must
repair his spaceship before Earth's volcanic eruption to escape.
Suggested Temperature: Tension-filled, Unpredictable
With the clock ticking, describe how Zolon navigates through the
primordial world while trying to repair his spacecraft.
Write a short story about Zolon. The story should have 5 scenes. It
should have a clear beginning and an ending. Zolon should encounter
problems along the story, but become a hero at the end.
You can have a couple other characters. Write the dialogue among them
too. Make it entertaining
```

Response:

```
Scene 1:
We open with Zolon, a tall, silver-skinned alien in a mechanical
workshop surrounded by spaceship parts. Steam puffing up in the air as
he examines his broken spacecraft, splattered with treacly tar-black
lava. "One more volcanic eruption and I'm toast. I need to fix this,"
he mumbles, looking at a nearby mountain belching thick, black smoke.
Scene 2:
While searching for the final piece to his spaceship, Zolon comes
across a ponderous woolly mammoth, trumpeting fearsomely, scaring away
the small pack of saber-tooth tigers. "I am Zolon from the Andromeda
Galaxy. Can you help me find an Orrite stone? It's shiny and blue." To
his surprise, the beast grunts, swinging its long trunk and points in
the direction of the volcano.
Scene 3:
Upon reaching the volcano, Zolon faces his next challenge - a giant
brown bear guarding the Orrite stone. He stammers, "Great guardian,
may I have the stone for my spaceship, so I can leave before the
impending eruption?" The bear growls menacingly, but Zolon offers his
silver medic-rod in exchange. Intrigued, the bear agrees.
Scene 4:
```

As Zolon trudges back to his spaceship, Orrite stone in hand, the ground suddenly begins to shake - the volcano is about to erupt. "Zolon!" bellows the mammoth, charging towards him. "Hop on! You do not stand a chance on foot!" Zolon, gripping the Orrite stone tightly, scrambles onto the mammoth's back. As they race away from the lava flow, the bear joins their escape, lumbering along.

Scene 5:

A haggard and soot-covered Zolon secures the Orrite stone in place and slews his spaceship back to life. As he prepares to leave, the mammoth nudges him. "Zolon, you are a true interstellar hero. May your travels be safe." The bear grunts in agreement. With a nod of gratitude, Zolon launches his spaceship into the atmosphere just as lava engulfs the landing site.

Ending:

With Earth shrinking behind him, Zolon reflects on his newfound friends and the adventure. Seated in a now fully-functioning spaceship, he's no longer an alien stranded alone but a hero embraced by a prehistoric world. "Here's to the next adventure," he murmurs, setting a course for the Andromeda Galaxy.

As he glides through the cosmos, Zolon can't help but chuckle, reminiscing the unusual camaraderie he formed back on Earth. Two creatures from a time so primitive still managed to exhibit a profound understanding of friendship and aid. As he looks back at Earth, one last time, he makes a silent promise to his prehistoric friends, frozen forever in his memories.

This warm reflection fills his journey back home with a sense of contentment and excitement. The beacon of Andromeda lights up on his control panel, welcoming him back. But Zolon knows that no matter where in the universe he goes, a part of him will always belong to the prehistoric Earth. His adventure has enriched him - and his thrilling encounters have made him a true interstellar hero.

His ship finally warps into the light speed, leaving behind a trail of sparkling cosmic dust, marking the end of an unforgettable journey. "Let's see what the universe has in store next," Zolon muses as he sits back, the hum of his spaceship the only audible sound in the quiet expanse of space.

And thus, we leave our time-traveling alien - a little wiser, a little braver, and much more adventurous - as he zips through the vastness of the cosmos. Somewhere between the milky swirls of the galaxies and the infinite dark, Zolon has found his true calling - To explore, navigate, and live through the adrenaline that each challenge brings.

Whether it's restoring a spaceship under the threat of a volcano, communicating with mammoth beasts, or trading with colossal bears, he finds joy in every encounter, lesson in every challenge, friendship in the most unexpected places.

Every star that blinks past him carries a promise of a new quest. Each echoing sound of the universe whispers tales of supernatural marvels waiting to be discovered. And as he journeys on, Zolon is not just a time-traveling alien, but a hero of all times, an adventurer of all realms, a friend to all beings.

With the Andromeda Galaxy spreading out before him, his past adventure becomes a star, shining brightly in his memory. With a heart full of excitement for the adventures to come, Zolon glides into the future,

```
towards another thrilling voyage in his endless quest across the
universe.
```

This is not very good, but it's just the starting point. Let's iterate and try to make it better.

Prompt:

```
I think this story is too simplistic and boring. What kind of editing
or polishing can you suggest for this story?
```

Response:

```
To make the story more engaging and complex, consider the following
suggestions:
1. Enhance the Character: Expand on Zolon's character, giving him
more depths, possible quirks, or even weaknesses which make your
readers relate more to him. You could even add a backstory to increase
emotional investment.
2. Increase Conflict: Introduce more obstacles or intensify the
conflict Zolon encounters. For instance, the Orrite stone could be the
heart of the volcano itself, or there could be another race of beings
trying to stop him.
3. Add Mystery and Suspense: Let the reader discover information
piece by piece at the same pace as Zolon. This keeps them curious and
invested.
4. Introduce Moral Dilemmas: Zolon's interactions with the creatures
could involve difficult decisions, creating tension. For instance, he
could learn that his escape might accelerate the volcano's eruption,
endangering the creatures' lives.
5. Introduce Sub-plots: Besides the main plot, smaller stories running
parallel can make the storyline more interesting. For instance, an
unlikely friendship developing between the mammoth and bear due to
their shared efforts to help Zolon.
6. Literary Techniques: Play with narrative strategies and structural
elements. Implement foreshadowing to hint at upcoming events,
flashbacks to provide context or background, and plot twists to
surprise your reader.
7. Show, Don't Tell: Instead of outright stating Zolon is scared or
brave, show it in his actions, dialogues, and thoughts. This immerses
readers in the story, fostering a deeper connection with Zolon.
8. Comprehensive Descriptions: Enhance your descriptions to make
readers feel present in every scene. Make the environment more vivid
by describing the ominous volcano, the prehistoric ambiance, the
sizzling sounds around, etc.
9. Futuristic Technology: Expound on Zolon's spaceship and his
gadgets, and how he uses them to solve problems. This adds an element
of sci-fi charm to your story.
10. Refined Dialogues: Let every character's speech reflect their
personalities, goals, or emotional states. Complex, layered dialogues
make your characters three-dimensional and interesting. For example,
instead of the bear merely growling, it could communicate in a manner
hinting at its own wisdom and bravery.
```

```
11. Enhanced Relationships: Develop relationships between characters
further. Zolon's interactions with prehistoric creatures could
gradually evolve from fear and suspicion to mutual respect and
camaraderie.
```

Although the initial story wasn't good, the suggestions the LLM provides are quite useful. Furthermore, you can ask the LLM to write in the style of a well-known sci-fi author such as Isaac Asimov, Arthur C. Clarke, or Robert A. Heinlein. You can even ask the LLM to give a list of authors in the genre. If you have published your own work before, you can provide some examples of your writing and ask the LLM to write the story in your style.

When asking the LLM to enhance your story with some of the recommendations provided by it, don't ask it to consider all of them at once. Do it one by one. Otherwise, it will miss things when trying to do too many *orders* in one shot.

Remember, editing and polishing a story involves trial and error. Both the narrative and the characters will likely need multiple rounds of revisions before they create the impact and interest you're aiming for. Try to get feedback from various readers to ensure your story appeals to a wide range of preferences. Experiment with different approaches, and don't be afraid to take risks – the greatest stories often come from bold decisions and unconventional storytelling methods.

In the next section, we will explore how to write good prompts to generate poems. The same concepts could be used to write songs.

Using AI to write poetry

To write poetry using an LLM such as OpenAI's GPT-4, you'll need some understanding of both poetry and the capabilities of the language model. Here's a general guide:

- **Understand the basics of poetry**: Before you make the LLM write poetry, you need a basic understanding of what makes a poem. Study different styles of poetry, from the structured nature of sonnets and haikus to free verse poetry. Understand the important elements of poetry such as rhythm, rhyme, metaphors, similes, alliteration, and, most importantly, the ability to evoke deep emotions.

- **Set the right tone**: In the prompt, set the tone or mood you want your poem to have. For instance, if you want an upbeat, hopeful poem, mention it in your prompt. A good language model can realign itself with the tone set in the prompt.

- **Provide a structure**: If you want a specific style of poetry or a certain pattern of rhyme, you need to instruct the language model accordingly. For example, if you want a sonnet with an ABAB rhyme scheme, you need to specify that.

- **Use procedural tokens**: To ensure the language model adheres to your preferred poem style, use procedural tokens in your prompt as an instruction. For example, to write a haiku, you could guide the LLM using procedural tokens such as *Write a haiku about...*

- **Be specific with the theme**: For example, instead of just asking for a poem about nature, ask for a poem about *the setting Sun's reflection in a still lake*.

- **Use creative constraints**: Remember that creative constraints often result in more interesting outcomes. Don't be afraid to give specific instructions to see how the LLM can create content within them.

Let's write a poem about my daughter Andrea on her trip to Italy and other parts of Europe this summer.

Prompt:

```
Write a poem about Andrea, a 22-year-old girl traveling to Europe.
Make sure to include some elements such as rhythm, rhyme, metaphors,
similes, alliteration, and the ability to evoke deep emotions.
```

Response:

```
Born in the heart of a sunlit land,
Andrea, girl of twenty-two, took a stand.
She yearned for more than her eyes could see,
Yearned for a world that could set her free.
Armed with courage within her heart, and a ticket in hand,  She
embarked on an odyssey to a far-off land.
Seeing Europe in her dreams, as stories had extolled,
With its medieval mysteries and tales of old.
Venturing Venice's winding streets, both fascinating and archaic,
"La dolce vita!" Andrea chirped, life is sweet in the poetic.
Reveling in Rome's majesty, where time echoed in her ears,  A tribute
to a journey through countless years.
Underneath the Parisian sky, a ballet of diffused hue,
Her heart danced wildly, a rhythm that only the soft Seine knew.
The breeze hummed melodies of old-world charm and romance,  As Andrea
marveled at the Eiffel's gleaming dance.
With a backpack slung across the Swiss alpine ridge,
She set foot on the boundary, stood on the world's bridge.  Reflecting
her ambitions, where skies kissed the lake,  Andrea saw her reflection
ripple, an image on the make.
From the blazing Spanish sunsets, to Amsterdam's tulip-strewn land,
Every sight, every sound, felt like a lyrical band.
The waltz of her journey, from break of day to the night,  Created an
alliteration of adventures, an eternal flight.
As she journeyed, Andrea, in climes new,
Formed a profound bind, deeper than the ocean blue.
In the mirror of Europe, Andrea found her reflection,
A valiant spirit born through the thrill of exploration.
The tales she embraced, the paths she chose,
Wove into a poem in her heart, a prose.
```

```
In Andrea's soul, these verses shall forever reside,  Verses of a
journey, with the world as a guide.
Oh Andrea, the girl of twenty-two, to what places will you go?
With every step you take, new stories you sow.
From the promises of youth to the life unfurled,
In every corner, awaits your world.
```

That's fairly good. Since I don't know much about poetry, I will ask GPT-4 to give feedback and some recommendations to improve upon.

Prompt:

```
What do you think about that poem? How can it be improved?
```

Response:

```
The poem beautifully captures the spirit of a young traveler exploring
the enchantments of Europe. It does a good job of using the various
poetic elements discussed earlier, such as alliteration ("winding
Venice streets, water-kissed"), similes ("her heart danced akin to the
soft Seine's coo"), and metaphors ("mirror of Europe"), among others.
It also effectively evokes deep emotions, capturing the sense of
wonder, joy, and self-discovery that comes with solo travel.

Nonetheless, potential improvements could include:

1. Consistency in Meter: While the poem has a fairly consistent
rhythm, there are places where it can be improved to make the beat
more predictable for the reader, enhancing the flow of the poem.

2. More Sensory Detail: Sensory details could be heightened. Instead
of saying, "Under the Parisian sky, a palette of hue," it might be
more evocative to specify the colors and the associated feelings.

3. Greater Risks with Language: While the language is lovely,
sometimes it adheres to more traditional phrasing. Playing with
structure or experimenting with more unexpected word choices could
lead to more exciting and unique descriptions.

4. More Personal Connection: While we follow the journey of the girl
across Europe, we don't learn much about her. Delving deeper into her
thoughts, feelings, and reactions to her experiences would make the
poem more relatable and emotionally resonant.

5. Show, Don't Tell: Instead of directly stating some points, showing
them through evocative imagery and metaphor would make it more
engaging and appealing. For example, instead of stating "A valiant
spirit born for exploration," create images and situations that
illustrate her valiant spirit.

In essence, the poem is wonderful as it is, but revising it with these
suggestions in mind could add depth and innovative flair.
```

You can iterate suggesting different twists and scenes until you are happy with the results.

You can even combine concepts. For instance, you can write a product description as a poem that is funny and quirky. Experiment, experiment, experiment.

So, in this case, the goal is to describe a physical product's features and benefits in a playful, lyrical poem format:

- Choose an intriguing, odd, or absurd product to inspire creative descriptions. Avoid mundane products.

- Outline the product's key specifications and standout qualities.

- Tell a mini story through the poem that gives the product personality and character.

- Use vivid imagery, sensory details, clever rhymes, wordplay, metaphors, and other poetic techniques.

- Try different verse forms, such as limericks or ballads. Vary the rhythm and rhyme scheme.

- Add witty dialogue or dramatic monologues to bring the product to life.

- Surprise readers with an inventive twist or punchline.

Have fun celebrating the product through playful, charming verse. With imagination, you can transform any product into a lyrical mini adventure.

Let's see how it works for the Manatea Tea Infuser:

Prompt:

```
I need you to compose a witty, entertaining poem that describes the
product features and benefits of the Manatea Tea Infuser by Fred and
Friends.
The Manatea is a cheerful, charming plastic manatee that acts as a tea
infuser. It has perforations on its back to allow loose tea leaves to
brew. Treat the manatee as a character and write the poem from its
perspective.
Use imaginative, hyperbolic language and lots of wordplay to bring
the Manatea to life. Take quirky metaphors literally and personify
features for humor. Incorporate tea and manatee references through
wordplay and puns.
Aim for 4 short stanzas following an AABB rhyme scheme. Employ sensory
imagery, vivid adjectives, lively rhythm, and structural elements like
repetition and alliteration. Make the tone fun, upbeat, and slightly
eccentric to match the product.
At the end, highlight the benefits and recommend the Manatea as the
perfect tea-brewing companion. Feel free to get silly and nonsensical
- go for maximum whimsy and light-hearted entertainment!
I'm excited to see what delightful Manatea mini adventure you can
compose in verse. Make it funny, make it strange, make it a quirky ode
that makes people smile. Show me the full creative potential of both
you and this charming manatea infuser.
```

Response:

```
Here is a funny, quirky poem describing the Manatea Tea Infuser based
on the provided prompt:
Oh hi there, I'm Manatea!
Let me brew up some tea for ya!
I'm the leaf lounging infusion sensation,
Bringing tea drinking jubilation.
Just fill me up with your favorite loose leaf
Then watch me work my brewing mystique.
My back has holes for the water to seep
Extracting flavors for your sipping keeps.
Plop me in your mug, the steeping begins
My perforated spine is perfect for infusing in
Bob up and down, dancing a jig
As I give this tea the ultimate swig.
With my charming, cheerful manatee grin
The infusion process is a breeze within
So kick back and relax, enjoy the aroma rising
While this adorable manatee gets your tea brewing and surprising.
The most delightful extraction invention!
Manatea is the tea infusion intervention!
So latch onto this leaf-loving marine mammal buddy
Your new tea-time pal bringing flavor and fun steady.
```

Now that you have a clear understanding of what concepts you can combine for a prompt and what response you can expect, we've come to the end of this chapter.

Summary

In this chapter, we explored how LLMs such as GPT-3 and GPT-4 are transforming the creative writing process across diverse genres and styles.

Here, we covered the key skills for leveraging AI writing assistants to enhance fiction projects. This included crafting effective prompts to communicate story requirements, utilizing the AI's generative abilities for characters, settings, and plots, refining output through iterative editing, balancing reliance on AI content with human vision, and using the AI as an editing aid. The core lesson was learning to blend AI capabilities with your creativity and voice to retain ownership over your writing. With the right techniques, AI can take your fiction to new heights by sparking ideas, improving drafts, and opening creative possibilities. However, the human imagination and authorial vision remain essential to the storytelling process. By following the guidance in this chapter, you can harness the power of AI writing while maintaining your authentic style and narrative purpose. With practice, AI and human creativity can combine to take your fiction writing to the next level.

Mastering these skills empowers writers to get the most out of AI tools such as GPT-4. You can gain fresh inspiration, accelerate idea generation, and create captivating stories, poems, lyrics, and more with an AI collaborator. This saves time, boosts creativity, and enables writers to reach their full potential.

Ultimately, by complementing human creativity with the strengths of AI, writers can explore new frontiers of imagination and make the writing process more enriching and productive.

While this chapter focused on the creativity of fiction and poetry, in the next chapter, we'll explore more practical applications of AI text processing. We'll learn how to leverage LLMs to automatically classify text by emotion, categorize it into predefined topics, clean up inconsistencies, and extract key data points.

5

Unlocking Insights from Unstructured Text – AI Techniques for Text Analysis

Unstructured text data holds invaluable insights, but making sense of qualitative information at scale presents a monumental challenge. This chapter explores techniques that enable generative AI systems to automate the analysis and organization of free-form text.

We'll learn how sentiment analysis classifies the emotional tone behind words to determine whether content is positive, neutral, or negative. We'll see how data classification uses machine learning to categorize text into predefined topics and labels. And we'll discover how pattern-matching techniques can extract key information from unstructured data and transform it into structured outputs.

These AI capabilities help businesses and organizations efficiently process massive amounts of unstructured data to uncover actionable insights. Sentiment analysis reveals how consumers feel about products or brands. Data classification automatically organizes content such as customer support tickets into topics. Pattern matching extracts data from documents such as invoices into neat, structured records.

This practical toolkit enables anyone to tap into the knowledge hidden within the proliferation of text data being created daily. Let's explore how generative AI can help make sense of language at scale.

The topics covered in this chapter are as follows:

- Sentiment analysis – AI techniques for emotion detection in text
- Organizing unstructured data – how AI automates text categorization
- Cleaning up dirty data – how AI identifies and resolves issues in datasets
- Making sense of unstructured data – pattern matching for information extraction

Sentiment analysis – AI techniques for emotion detection in text

Sentiment analysis is one of the key applications of AI techniques in the field of prompt engineering. As the first in a series of AI applications we will cover, sentiment analysis uses natural language processing to identify and extract emotional signals from text data. The goal is to gauge the overall attitude or feeling within a piece of writing, for instance, determining whether a product review is positive or negative.

The most common uses of sentiment analysis are as follows:

- *Brand monitoring*: Brands can track conversations happening online to monitor their reputation. Sentiment analysis allows them to detect PR issues as they emerge and measure the impact of marketing campaigns.

- *Customer service*: Customer experience teams can aggregate feedback at scale by analyzing surveys, reviews, and social media mentions. This provides data-driven insights into where people are satisfied or frustrated with products and services.

- *Market research*: By understanding customer sentiment, businesses can discover gaps in their services or products and fill them accordingly.

- *Political analysis*: Political groups can keep an eye on voter attitudes by monitoring discussions about candidates and issues. The technology assists with message testing and identifying areas where more outreach is needed.

- *Social media monitoring*: Companies use sentiment analysis to identify the sentiment of social media posts to understand broader consumer behavior and trends.

- *Investment analysis*: Investors can use sentiment analysis to help forecast market movement. By processing relevant news, forums, and blogs, tools can determine whether investors feel bullish or bearish about certain stocks or sectors.

- *Public health*: Health authorities can apply sentiment analysis to understand public concerns, misinformation, and emotional states during crises such as pandemics. This input helps guide communication strategies and allocation of resources.

Here are some sentiment analysis prompt examples.

Here's prompt 1.

Prompt:

```
Identify and categorize the sentiment (positive, neutral, negative)
expressed in the [text].
Text = "This product is amazing! It has really improved my life."
```

Here's the response.

Response:

```
Sentiment: positive
```

Here's prompt 2.

Prompt:

```
Text =  "I haven't noticed any changes since I started using this
product."
```

Here's the response.

Response:

```
Sentiment: neutral
```

You can pass many texts at once and ask ChatGPT, Bard, or Claude to provide the results in tabular format.

Here's another prompt.

Prompt:

```
Identify and categorize the sentiment (positive, neutral, negative)
expressed in the [text].
I will add many texts at once. Return the sentiment for each in
tabular format. Don't include the word sentiment in the responses,
only positive, negative or neutral.
Texts: "I'm very disappointed with the terrible customer service I
received. They were completely unhelpful and rude."
"The food at this restaurant is absolutely delicious. I'll definitely
be coming back again."
"I recently bought this laptop and it's the best tech purchase I've
made in years. So fast and reliable."
"Looks like it might start raining this afternoon. I should bring an
umbrella just in case."
"The deadline for submitting my project proposal is next Friday at
5pm."
"Just watched the new Marvel movie and it completely exceeded my
expectations. Tons of fun from start to finish."
"Reading the news these days just makes me feel so anxious and
depressed about the state of the world."
"This is the worst tasting meal I've ever had at a restaurant. My
steak was overcooked and the vegetables were mushy."
"I regret upgrading to the latest phone model. The battery life is
awful and full of bugs. Should have kept my old phone."
"I can't believe I failed my exam after studying for weeks. All that
preparation was for nothing."
```

```
"I need to stop by the grocery store later today and pick up milk and
eggs."
"The instructions say to press and hold the power button for 5 seconds
to reset the device."
"I'm so grateful for the wonderful care my mother received at this
hospital. The doctors and nurses were compassionate and attentive."
"Don't waste your time and money on this product. It stopped working
after a month and their warranty support is useless."
```

Here is the response produced by Claude:

Text	Sentiment
"I'm very disappointed with the terrible customer service I received. They were completely unhelpful and rude."	negative
"The food at this restaurant is absolutely delicious. I'll definitely be coming back again."	positive
"I recently bought this laptop and it's the best tech purchase I've made in years. So fast and reliable."	positive
"Looks like it might start raining this afternoon. I should bring an umbrella just in case."	neutral
"The deadline for submitting my project proposal is next Friday at 5pm."	neutral
"Just watched the new Marvel movie and it completely exceeded my expectations. Tons of fun from start to finish."	positive
"Reading the news these days just makes me feel so anxious and depressed about the state of the world."	negative
"This is the worst tasting meal I've ever had at a restaurant. My steak was overcooked and the vegetables were mushy."	negative
"I regret upgrading to the latest phone model. The battery life is awful and full of bugs. Should have kept my old phone."	negative
"I can't believe I failed my exam after studying for weeks. All that preparation was for nothing."	negative
"I need to stop by the grocery store later today and pick up milk and eggs."	neutral
"The instructions say to press and hold the power button for 5 seconds to reset the device."	neutral
"I'm so grateful for the wonderful care my mother received at this hospital. The doctors and nurses were compassionate and attentive."	positive
"Don't waste your time and money on this product. It stopped working	

Figure 5.1: Response in table format

Your rating system can be arbitrary. In the previous examples, the sentiment can be just one of three options: positive, negative, or neutral. However, you can tell the LLM to assign a value on an arbitrary scale. For instance, from -1 (very negative) to 1 (very positive).

In summary, sentiment analysis unlocks value from qualitative data at scale. It equips organizations to base decisions on public sentiment rather than gut instinct alone. With continued advances in natural language processing, the technology has the potential for an even wider range of applications in the future.

Furthermore, in this section, you learned that you can ask the LLM to produce the output in a particular format: tabular. This is not the only option. You can ask the LLM to produce the output as Markdown, HTML, HTML table, XML, JSON, or even in your own pattern. This is discussed later in this chapter.

In the next section, we explore a similar topic: data classification.

Organizing unstructured data – using AI for automated text categorization and data classification

In the context of data classification, a trained LLM can analyze the various features in the dataset and classify data accurately. For instance, if the task is to categorize customer complaints into predefined classes, such as *billing issues*, *technical issues*, *customer service issues*, and so on, an LLM can analyze the text of the customer complaints, understand the context and the language used, and classify them into the respective categories accurately.

In many cases, the LLM should be able to make an accurate classification without the need for any training. However, in some cases, it will need to have some examples to understand the pattern that you want.

Typical uses of data classification include the following:

- Distinguish between the different categories of data and assign each data point to its suitable category. Some examples are as follows:

  - Classifying incoming emails as spam or not spam based on features such as the sender's address or the email's content

  - Classifying news articles into topics such as sports, politics, and entertainment based on the keywords and phrases used in the article

- Analyze the dataset and classify the data into various groups by using specific classification algorithms or criteria:

  - Classifying customers into different segments (such as high value and low value) based on their purchasing history using machine learning algorithms

- Using logistic regression or decision tree algorithms to classify bank loan applicants into low-risk or high-risk categories

- Divide and organize the given dataset into separate classes or categories, ensuring each class holds a common characteristic, like in these examples:

  - Dividing a dataset of animals into categories such as mammals, reptiles, birds, and fish, each having unique characteristics

  - Organizing a dataset of automobiles into categories such as sedans, SUVs, and trucks, each holding specific features

- Allocate each piece of the given data to appropriate categories by understanding their characteristics. Here are a couple of examples:

  - Allocating a list of fruits to categories such as citrus, berries, and tropical based on their specific characteristics

  - Assigning students to different groups based on their proficiency level in a subject

- Categorize the collected data into predefined classes, like in the following cases:

  - Categorizing customer complaints into predefined classes such as billing issues, technical issues, and customer service issues

  - Classifying a collection of books into predefined genres such as mystery, romance, and sci-fi based on their content and themes

The following example shows how to classify incoming emails as spam/not spam and by importance in the case that the email is not spam:

Prompt:

```
Classify the following [Emails] as spam or not spam. For the ones that
are not spam, classify them as importance: n. n is a scale from 1 to
5, where 5 is very important. Provide the results in a table.
Emails: "Subject Line: Here's how you can claim your FREE HOLIDAY
VOUCHER!
Sender: unknownsender@freedeals.com
Email Content:
Click here to enjoy a luxurious holiday for absolutely FREE! Hurry up!
Offers like this don't last long!"

"Subject Line: Performance Evaluation for Q1 2023
Sender: HR_dept@yourcompany.com
Email Content:
Dear John,
The first quarter performance evaluations will take place next week.
```

```
Please update your tasks and achievements in the employee portal by
Tuesday.
Best regards,
HR Team"

"Subject Line: Introducing our New Product
Sender: newsletter@electronicsstore.com
Email Content:
Dear John,
We are excited to announce the arrival of our much-awaited smart TV.
Check out our best deals and offers. Happy Shopping!
Best,
Electronics Store"

"Subject Line: Reunión del proyecto mañana a las 3 PM
Sender: gerente@tuempresa.com
Contenido del correo electrónico:
Equipo,
La reunión del proyecto está programada para mañana a las 3 PM en la
sala de conferencias del quinto piso. Estén preparados para brindar
actualizaciones sobre sus tareas.
Atentamente,
Gerente del Proyecto"
```

In this case, we are using ChatGPT, and you can see the response here:

Email	Classification	Importance
1	Spam	-
2	Not Spam	4
3	Not Spam	2
4	Not Spam	5

Figure 5.2: Classification of emails in two categories

It also provided an explanation, but it's not included for brevity.

As you can see, you can classify things in several dimensions at once, and even handle some content in different languages. It is important to note that while GPT-3.5/GPT-4 can handle many languages, other LLMs cannot. Therefore, do some research before using an LLM for a specific use case.

Once data has been successfully classified, the next crucial step in the prompt engineering process is to clean the data by removing inconsistencies and inaccuracies. We will cover that in the next section.

Cleaning up dirty data – how AI identifies and resolves issues in datasets

Data cleansing, also known as data cleaning or data scrubbing, is the process of identifying and rectifying (or removing) errors, discrepancies, and inaccuracies from a dataset. This can involve detecting duplicate records, handling missing or incomplete data, validating and correcting values, formatting, standardizing, or normalizing data, and dealing with outliers.

The main objective of data cleansing is to improve the quality and reliability of your data, ensuring it is accurate, consistent, and in a format suitable for your purposes. This is crucial as dirty or messy data can interfere with your analysis, lead to inaccurate insights and conclusions, and negatively impact decision-making processes.

It's important to note that data cleansing should be a regular part of data management – it's not a one-time task, as new errors can be introduced when new data is added or existing data is modified.

In general, data cleansing has been a complex and expensive process, but with the use of generative AI, it can be done efficiently and effectively.

As an example, let's suppose you scraped some data from LinkedIn. You got the names of potential leads and you got their emails from different sources, but they can be wrongly formatted. Some of the names may include emojis or additional attributes such as Dr., PhD, or MBA. In this case, you will need to clean the data to be able to send email campaigns. The goal here is to get the data back without titles, emojis, or additional characters.

Prompt:

```
You are an expert on cleaning data.
Please clean the  list of [names and emails]. From the names remove
the emojis and the titles such as doctor, PhD, etc. Also make sure the
emails are correctly formatted.
Return the corrected list as a table.
names and emails:  Dr. John Appleseed🐷,  john.applecom
Mrs. Emma Doe🐱, emma@doe.com
Prof. William Smith🔋 , will.smith@uni.
Peter Parker🕸   , PhD, peteparker#gmail
Capt. Steve America🛡, @america.com
Dr. Jane Light💡, MB  , jane.light.mailcom
 Miss Sophie Turner🐺  , sophie@.com
  Prof. Chris Evans🎯, PhD ,chris#uni.edu
```

In this case, we are using Claude, and this is the response:

Response:

Here is the cleaned up list of names and emails in a table:

Name	Email
John Appleseed	john.appleseed@gmail.com
Emma Doe	emma@doe.com
William Smith	will.smith@uni.edu
Peter Parker	peteparker@gmail.com
Steve America	steve.america@gmail.com
Jane Light	jane.light@mail.com
Sophie Turner	sophie@turner.com
Chris Evans	chris@uni.edu

⚠ Links provided by Claude may not always be valid or up to date. We appreciate your patience as we work to improve link accuracy.

Figure 5.3: Resulting table with a cleaned-up list of names and emails

As you can see, this can save a lot of time if you have hundreds or even thousands of records that you need to clean. However, there could be cases in which LLMs could not solve this issue completely if some key information is missing. Thus, always check the results.

Here are some other use cases for cleaning data with AI:

- *Remove duplicates*: Identify and remove any duplicate entries in the dataset
- *Handle missing values*: Determine how to handle missing values, either by imputing or deleting them
- *Standardize data formats*: Ensure consistent formatting for data fields such as dates, phone numbers, or addresses
- *Remove special characters*: Eliminate unnecessary special characters or symbols that may affect data quality
- *Convert data types*: Convert data fields to the appropriate data types (e.g., converting strings to numbers)
- *Handle outliers*: Identify and handle outliers that might skew analysis or modeling results

- *Resolve inconsistent spellings*: Standardize and correct inconsistent spellings or variations of the same entity
- *Validate email addresses*: Verify the validity of email addresses and correct any format errors
- *Normalize text data*: Remove unnecessary whitespace, convert to lowercase, and handle punctuation in text fields
- *Check for data integrity*: Ensure data consistency and integrity by validating relationships and cross-referencing between fields

After ensuring that the data is clean and reliable, the focus then shifts to leveraging pattern-matching techniques for generating coherent and contextually aware responses.

Making sense of unstructured data – pattern matching for information extraction

Pattern matching in responses involves the process of taking unstructured text as input and producing a structured output by identifying and extracting relevant patterns or information.

Now, let's look at an example to illustrate how pattern matching can be used in this context.

Let's consider a scenario where the input is an unstructured text containing information about a person, including their name, age, and occupation. The goal is to extract and structure this information into a more organized format.

Here's the unstructured text input:

John Smith is a 35-year-old software engineer.

In this case, pattern matching can be employed to identify specific patterns or keywords that correspond to the desired information. For instance, we can define patterns such as *[name] is a [age]-year-old [occupation]* to capture the relevant details.

By applying pattern matching to the input text, the system can recognize that the pattern matches the provided information and extract the corresponding values as follows:

Pattern: "[name] is a [age]-year-old [occupation]"

Input: "John Smith is a 35-year-old software engineer."

Extracted Values:

Name: John Smith

Age: 35

Occupation: Software Engineer

Once the structured values are extracted, they can be used to generate a more organized output or perform further processing. For instance, the extracted information can be stored in a structured database or used to populate a predefined template for a structured response.

The structured output can then be used for various purposes, such as displaying the information in a structured format, performing calculations or comparisons, integrating with other systems, or generating personalized responses based on the extracted data.

Pattern matching in responses enables the transformation of unstructured text into structured information, facilitating better organization, analysis, and utilization of the extracted data.

Let's work through an exciting use case: using AI to structure unstructured text extracted from an image using **Optical Character Recognition (OCR)**.

The scenario is this: a person wants to capture the data from an invoice to keep track of her expenses. She can do either of the following:

- Open a spreadsheet and create a record for each new expense (manually)
- Upload the document image to a site that allows you to do OCR to get the text from the image, then use an LLM to structure that data, and finally, save it to the spreadsheet automatically

While this seems to be a lot of work to capture the data from each invoice/document, a more automated process is quite useful for cases such as the following: Company A has a team of drivers who make deliveries to different clients in multiple cities. The drivers have to report the expenses they incur, such as gas, tolls, vehicle maintenance, food, and lodging. In the current situation, they need to send an email at the end of each day detailing every expense, and they have to attach images of the invoices or receipts. This is time-consuming and error-prone.

Besides, someone at the office has to read each email, copy the data to a spreadsheet or other system, and put the images in a Drive directory or something similar. This process is error-prone, time-consuming, and creates complexity in linking data together.

For example, if images from emails are saved in a Drive folder while other fields are copied to a spreadsheet, it can be difficult to connect which image goes with which record or row in the spreadsheet. There is no automatic linkage between the separated data.

With the help of AI, this can be greatly simplified.

Each driver can use a conversational automation tool, such as Twnel, Manychat, UChat, or Landbot, or any tool that allows them to create tree-based workflows and is able to take pictures and call APIs.

The chatbot flow should be something like the following figure:

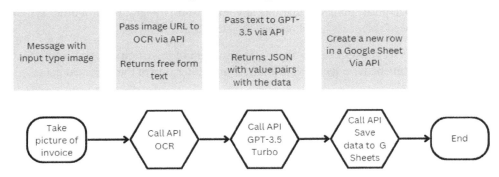

Figure 5.4: Report Expenses flow

So, the user opens a flow in the conversational automation tool and selects **Report Expenses**. Then, the flow asks them to take a picture of a receipt. That image is processed by an OCR and then the unstructured text is sent to GPT-3.5 Turbo for processing, which returns a JSON. Finally, the flow takes some values from the JSON and creates a new row on a Google Sheet (or another spreadsheet).

Use Bard or Claude to create a JSON model of the typical receipt. You could upload an image of a typical invoice to Bard and type this prompt:

Prompt:

```
From the image attached of an invoice extract all the data and format
it as a JSON object. Try to include all the fields that you get from
the invoice.
```

This sort of works, but at the time of this writing, the results were not very accurate. Instead of uploading the image, you can also provide a URL of the image. This should be better by the time the book is published.

A better way is to use an LLM (such as GPT-3.5 Turbo, GPT-4, Bard, or Claude) to create a JSON model of the typical invoice. Feed the text generated by an OCR application that you call via an API.

Alternatively, you could do OCR using many of the tools available on the internet, such as https:// ocr.space/.

Suppose the invoices are similar to this one:

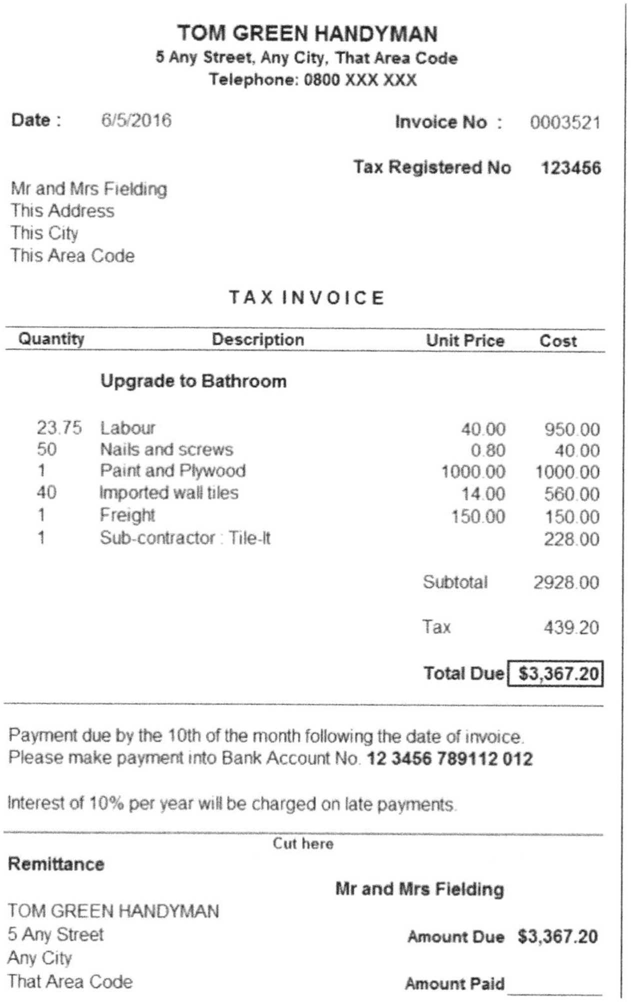

TOM GREEN HANDYMAN
5 Any Street, Any City, That Area Code
Telephone: 0800 XXX XXX

Date :	6/5/2016		Invoice No :	0003521

Tax Registered No   123456

Mr and Mrs Fielding
This Address
This City
This Area Code

T A X   I N V O I C E

Quantity	Description	Unit Price	Cost
	Upgrade to Bathroom		
23.75	Labour	40.00	950.00
50	Nails and screws	0.80	40.00
1	Paint and Plywood	1000.00	1000.00
40	Imported wall tiles	14.00	560.00
1	Freight	150.00	150.00
1	Sub-contractor : Tile-It		228.00
		Subtotal	2928.00
		Tax	439.20
		Total Due	$3,367.20

Payment due by the 10th of the month following the date of invoice.
Please make payment into Bank Account No. **12 3456 789112 012**

Interest of 10% per year will be charged on late payments.

Cut here

Remittance

Mr and Mrs Fielding

TOM GREEN HANDYMAN
5 Any Street   **Amount Due $3,367.20**
Any City
That Area Code   **Amount Paid** _____

Figure 5.5: Example invoice

The text extracted from this invoice using OCR is as follows:

"||TOM GREEN HANDYMAN||5 Any Street. Any City, That Area Code||Telephone: 0800 XXX XXX||Date:||6/5/2016||Invoice No||0003521||Tax Registered No||123466||Mr and Mrs Fielding||This Address||This City||This Area Code||TAX INVOICE||Quantity||Description||Upgrade to Bathroom||23.75 Labour||Nails and screws||Paint and Plywood||Imported wall tiles||Freight||Sub-contractor Tie-t||Unit Price||Cost||40.00||950.00||080||40.00||1000 00||1000 00||14 00||560 00||150 00||228.00||Subtotal||2928 00||Total Due $3.367.20||Payment due by the 10th of the month following the date of invoice Please make payment into Bank Account No. 12 3456 789112 012||Interest of 10% per year will be charged on te paNDIS||Remittance||Mr and Mrs Fielding||TOM GREEN HANDYMAN||qS||Amount Que $3.367.20||Amount Paid||Learn More||"

Then, type this prompt (this works best using Claude 2 or Bard):

Prompt:

```
The [OCR text] is the text obtained when doing OCR on an invoice.
Generate a JSON model for that kind of document. In the JSON structure
include placeholders (e.g., "string", "number") for the expected data
types.
OCR Text = ||TOM GREEN HANDYMAN||5 Any Street. Any City, That
Area Code||Telephone: 0800 XXX XXX||Date:||6/5/2016||Invoice
No||0003521||Tax Registered No||123466||Mr and Mrs
Fielding||This Address||This City||This Area Code||TAX
INVOICE||Quantity||Description||Upgrade to Bathroom||23.75
Labour||Nails and screws||Paint and Plywood||Imported
wall tiles||Freight||Sub-contractor Tie-t||Unit
Price||Cost||40.00||950.00||080||40.00||1000 00||1000 00||14 00||560
00||150 00||228.00||Subtotal||2928 00||Total Due $3.367.20||Payment
due by the 10th of the month following the date of invoice Please
make payment into Bank Account No. 12 3456 789112 012||Interest
of 10% per year will be charged on te paNDIS||Remittance||Mr and
Mrs Fielding||TOM GREEN HANDYMAN||qS||Amount Que $3.367.20||Amount
Paid||Learn More||
```

Here's the response:

Response:

```
{
  "invoice_number": "0003521",
 "invoice_date": "6/5/2016",
  "tax_number": "123466",
  "customer": {
    "name": "Mr and Mrs Fielding",
    "address": "This Address",
    "city": "This City",
    "postcode": "This Area Code"
  },
```

```
"items": [
  {
    "description": "Upgrade to Bathroom",
    "quantity": 23.75,
    "unit_price": 40,
    "cost": 950
  },
  {
    "description": "Labour",
    "quantity": "string",
    "unit_price": "number",
    "cost": "number"
  },
  {
    "description": "Nails and screws",
    "quantity": 0.8,
    "unit_price": 40,
    "cost": 1000
  },
  {
    "description": "Paint and Plywood",
    "quantity": "number",
    "unit_price": "number",
    "cost": 1000
  },
  {
    "description": "Imported wall tiles",
    "quantity": 14,
    "unit_price": "number",
    "cost": 560
  },
  {
    "description": "Freight",
    "quantity": "number",
    "unit_price": "number",
    "cost": 150
  },
  {
    "description": "Sub-contractor Tie-t",
    "quantity": "number",
    "unit_price": 228,
    "cost": "number"
  }
```

```
  ],
  "subtotal": 2928,
  "total_due": 3367.20,
  "payment_info": {
    "account_number": "12 3456 789112 012",
    "due_date": "10th of the month following the date of invoice",
    "interest_rate": 10
  }
}
```

Both Claude 2 and Bard misunderstood the instructions. We can fix that by providing further instructions:

Prompt:

```
No. instead of each value put the data type. Example, if the value is
a number put "number", if it's a string put "string"
```

Here's the response:

Response:

```
  "invoice_number": "string",
  "invoice_date": "string",
  "tax_number": "string",
  "customer": {
    "name": "string",
    "address": "string",
    "city": "string",
    "postcode": "string"
  },
  "items": [
    {
      "description": "string",
      "quantity": number,
      "unit_price": number,
      "cost": number
    },
   … [more items here]
  ],
  "subtotal": number,
  "total_due": number,
  "payment_info": {
    "account_number": "string",
    "due_date": "string",
    "interest_rate": number
  }
}{
```

Now this is good. We can adjust it manually to leave only one item inside the `items` array and add the job name and the tax. Since the `items` element is an array, the LLM can deduce that it could have several objects of the type included in the model. Furthermore, `number` should include quotation marks: `"number"`. This is because `"number"` is a string that represents a variable of that type and is not a variable per se. The revised JSON model should look like this:

```
{
  "invoice_number": "string",
  "invoice_date": "string",
  "tax_number": "string",
  "customer": {
    "name": "string",
    "address": "string",
    "city": "string",
    "postcode": "string"
  },
  "job_name": "string",
  "items": [
    {
      "description": "string",
      "quantity": "number",
      "unit_price": "number",
      "cost": "number"
    }
  ],
  "subtotal": "number",
  "tax": "number",
  "total_due": "number",
  "payment_info": {
    "account_number": "string",
    "due_date": "string",
    "interest_rate": "number"
  }
}
```

Then, when you want to process another invoice, you should write something like the following prompt.

Prompt:

```
Given that you have the text extracted from an invoice in [ORC text],
format it as a JSON object with the following format:
{  JSON FORMAT HERE }
OCR text = "||TOM GREEN HANDYMAN||5 Any Street. Any City, That
Area Code||Telephone: 0800 XXX XXX||Date:||6/5/2016||Invoice
No||0003521||Tax Registered No||123466||Mr and Mrs
```

```
Fielding||This Address||This City||This Area Code||TAX
INVOICE||Quantity||Description||Upgrade to Bathroom||23.75
Labour||Nails and screws||Paint and Plywood||Imported
wall tiles||Freight||Sub-contractor Tie-t||Unit
Price||Cost||40.00||950.00||080||40.00||1000 00||1000 00||14 00||560
00||150 00||228.00||Subtotal||2928 00||Total Due $3.367.20||Payment
due by the 10th of the month following the date of invoice Please
make payment into Bank Account No. 12 3456 789112 012||Interest
of 10% per year will be charged on te paNDIS||Remittance||Mr and
Mrs Fielding||TOM GREEN HANDYMAN||9S||Amount Que $3.367.20||Amount
Paid||Learn More||"
```

Here's the response.

Response:

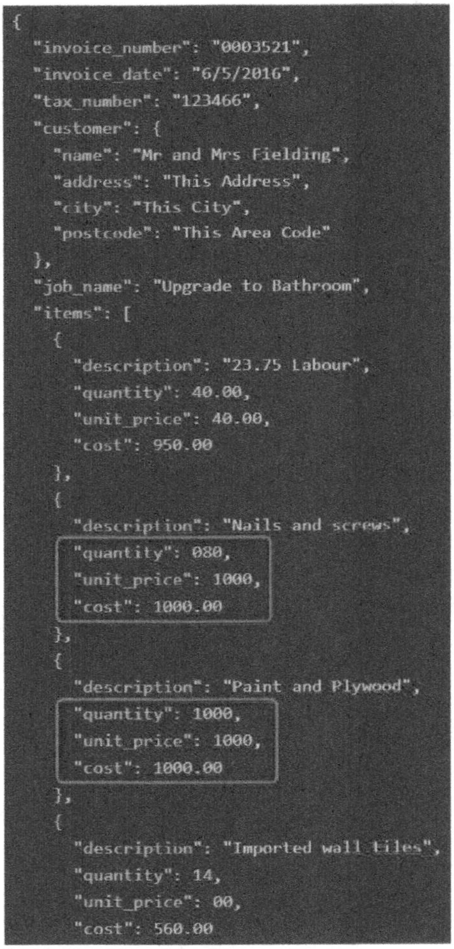

Figure 5.6: Screenshot of the response highlighting some errors

It's almost there. However, there are a couple of errors, marked inside the red rectangles, in the response image.

Fortunately, that's an easy fix. In the prompt, you should provide, along with the JSON model, or even instead of it, a couple of examples showing the LLM what you expect to put where.

The new prompt should look like this.

Prompt:

> Given that you have the text extracted from an invoice in [ORC text], format it as a JSON object with the following format:
> { JSON FORMAT HERE }
> Here is one example:
> OCR text = "||TOM GREEN HANDYMAN||5 Any Street. Any City, That Area Code||Telephone: 0800 XXX XXX||Date:||6/5/2016||Invoice No||0003521||Tax Registered No||123466||Mr and Mrs Fielding||This Address||This City||This Area Code||TAX INVOICE||Quantity||Description||Upgrade to Bathroom||23.75 Labour||Nails and screws||Paint and Plywood||Imported wall tiles||Freight||Sub-contractor Tie-t||Unit Price||Cost||40.00||950.00||080||40.00||1000 00||1000 00||14 00||560 00||150 00||228.00||Subtotal||2928 00||Total Due $3.367.20||Payment due by the 10th of the month following the date of invoice Please make payment into Bank Account No. 12 3456 789112 012||Interest of 10% per year will be charged on te paNDIS||Remittance||Mr and Mrs Fielding||TOM GREEN HANDYMAN||qS||Amount Que $3.367.20||Amount Paid||Learn More||"

Here's the result:

Response:

```
{
  "invoice_number": "0003521",
  "invoice_date": "6/5/2016",
  "tax_number": "123466",
  "customer": {
    "name": "Mr and Mrs Fielding",
    "address": "This Address",
    "city": "This City",
    "postcode": "This Area Code"
  },
  "job_name": "Upgrade to Bathroom",
  "items": [
    {
      "description": "23.75 Labour",
      "quantity": 40.00,
      "unit_price": 40.00,
```

```
      "cost": 950.00
    },
    {
      "description": "Nails and screws",
      "quantity": 50,
      "unit_price": 0.80,
      "cost": 40.00
    },
    {
      "description": "Paint and Plywood",
      "quantity": 1,
      "unit_price": 1000,
      "cost": 1000.00
    },
    {
      "description": "Imported wall tiles",
      "quantity": 40,
      "unit_price": 14.00,
      "cost": 560.00
    },
    {
      "description": "Freight",
      "quantity": 1,
      "unit_price":150.00,
      "cost": 150.00
    },
    {
      "description": "Sub-contractor Tile-t",
      "quantity": 1,
      "unit_price":"",
      "cost": 228.00
    }
  ],
  "subtotal": 2928.00,
  "tax": 439.20
  "total_due": 3367.20,
  "payment_info": {
    "account_number": "12 3456 789112 012",
    "due_date": "10th of the month following the date of invoice",
    "interest_rate": 10
  }
}


OCR text = [ ANOTHER TEXT EXTRACTED FROM ANOTHER INVOICE]
```

Now it should work with similar invoices.

LLMs are very good at pattern matching. Therefore, this kind of application usually works very well. You just need to fine-tune your prompts until you get it right.

When using this with GPT-3.5 Turbo or GPT-4 using the APIs, you always need to pass the training part to the call and add the last OCR text with the value returned from the OCR process. Test both GPT-3.5 Turbo and GPT-4. If both render the same results, use GPT-3.5 Turbo, which is 20 times less expensive.

If you have access to the Claude 2 API, you can test that one as well.

We will revisit this case again in *Chapter 8*, exploring how to use this technique with a chatbot that can be used on the field by multiple people.

Summary

AI has revolutionized the field of prompt engineering by enabling various techniques, such as sentiment analysis, data classification, data cleaning, and pattern matching. These techniques have greatly enhanced the accuracy and efficiency of generating high-quality responses.

Sentiment analysis uses natural language processing to identify the emotional tone behind words and phrases. This allows us to automatically classify content as having positive, negative, or neutral sentiment.

Data classification uses machine learning algorithms to categorize text into predefined groups or labels. This is useful for organizing unstructured data into meaningful categories.

Data cleaning is an essential step in working with real-world data. AI techniques such as pattern matching can automatically find and fix issues such as misspellings, incorrect formatting, and duplicate entries. This cleans up data and makes it more usable for downstream analytics and machine learning models.

Pattern matching, another powerful capability of AI, enables prompt models to recognize and interpret specific patterns or structures in user inputs and model outputs. This allows AI systems to generate responses that align with common patterns and expectations. By using pattern-matching techniques, developers can ensure that their AI assistants provide coherent and relevant responses, enhancing the overall user experience.

Sentiment analysis, classification, cleaning, and information extraction can all be handled automatically by AI. This saves huge amounts of human time and effort, while also improving consistency. With the right techniques and training data, AI promises to unlock insights in text that would not be feasible to uncover manually.

While this chapter explored AI techniques for extracting insights from unstructured text data, the next chapter shifts focus to applications of LLMs in education, legal fields, and other professional domains.

Part 3:
Advanced Use Cases for Different Industries

As large language models such as GPT-4, Claude, and Bard advance rapidly, new opportunities emerge to apply these powerful AI tools across diverse industries and domains. *Part 3* of this book explores innovative use cases and prompt engineering techniques to customize **large language models (LLMs)** for specialized needs.

We begin by examining applications in key fields such as education and law. Educators can utilize LLMs to rapidly generate customized curriculum materials tailored to learning objectives. Legal professionals can leverage AI to streamline research, review documents, draft contracts, and enrich training.

For software engineers, coding assistants promise to automate monotonous programming while augmenting human creativity. We walk through sample projects developing websites and browser extensions with AI support.

Conversational interfaces also stand to benefit tremendously from integration with LLMs. Chatbots powered by tools such as GPT-4 and Claude enable more natural, coherent dialogues and complex workflow automation simply through text-based conversation.

Finally, we uncover techniques to optimize and scale LLM prompting through integrations with existing infrastructure. Whether using no-code automation platforms, custom developer libraries such as LangChain, or sharing prompt templates, integrating AI unlocks new efficiencies.

Across these diverse applied contexts, the overarching theme is leveraging AI as a multipurpose productivity engine. Through thoughtful prompt engineering, we can customize LLMs to enhance specialized workflows rather than replace human expertise.

This part has the following chapters:

Applications of LLMs in Education and Law

In today's rapidly evolving technological landscape, **artificial intelligence (AI)** and **machine learning (ML)** have made significant advancements, opening new possibilities in various fields. **Large language models (LLMs)**, in particular, have gained considerable attention for their ability to process and generate human-like text, making them valuable tools for education, legal research, document review, and more.

In this chapter, we will explore the wide range of applications where LLMs can be harnessed to enhance educational experiences, support legal professionals, and streamline various tasks. We will delve into the realm of education, where LLMs can assist in crafting course materials, developing handouts and quizzes, and even assessing student comprehension. Furthermore, we will explore applications in the legal domain, where LLMs can aid in legal research, document drafting, and IP management, revolutionizing how legal professionals handle their workloads and enhancing their efficiency.

By talking about education, we'll discover how educators can leverage LLMs to rapidly generate curriculum materials, assessments, interactive practice questions, and feedback tailored to learning objectives. Through examples, we will uncover techniques for AI-assisted creation of quizzes, prompts, rubrics, and other content that engages students.

Then, we will traverse into the legal realm, where emerging AI applications are transforming research, discovery, drafting, compliance, risk analysis, and more. You will see how attorneys can use LLMs to quickly digest volumes of case law, analyze contracts, predict litigation outcomes, and automate document creation. We will also discuss the implications of increasingly capable AI for legal training and education.

However, while showcasing the tremendous potential of LLMs in education and law, we will emphasize the importance of human oversight. Educators and legal professionals must engineer prompts strategically, validate results, and make necessary adjustments. AI should augment human expertise, not replace it. When thoughtfully implemented, LLMs have the power to free professionals from repetitive tasks so that they can focus on higher-order reasoning and judgment.

The topics we'll cover in this chapter are as follows:

- Creating course materials with ChatGPT (unit outline, lesson plans, discussion questions)
- Creating handouts and other materials (instructions, solved examples, word problems)
- Creating quizzes
- Creating rubrics
- Creating cloze comprehension tests
- AI for legal research
- Reviewing legal documents using an LLM
- Drafting legal documents with an LLM
- AI for legal education and training
- LLMs for eDiscovery and litigation support
- AI for **intellectual property** (**IP**) management

Creating course materials with ChatGPT

When it comes to designing and developing course materials, LLMs offer a valuable resource for educators. With their ability to process and generate text, LLMs can assist in creating unit outlines, lesson plans, and engaging discussion questions that cater to the specific needs of students. Let's explore how LLMs can be harnessed to enhance the course development process.

- **Unit outlines**: Developing a comprehensive unit outline is crucial for guiding both educators and students through the learning journey. LLMs can be leveraged to generate unit outlines that cover the key concepts, learning objectives, and progression of the course material. By inputting relevant information, such as the topic, subtopics, and desired outcomes, LLMs can provide educators with well-structured and organized unit outlines.

- **Lesson plans**: LLMs can play a significant role in creating effective and engaging lesson plans. Educators can utilize LLMs to generate lesson plans that include specific learning activities, assessments, and resources to support student learning. By leveraging the capabilities of LLMs, instructors can customize and refine their lesson plans to meet the unique requirements of their students and address various learning styles.

- **Discussion questions**: Promoting active participation and critical thinking skills among students is a crucial aspect of any educational setting. LLMs can aid in the creation of thought-provoking discussion questions that stimulate intellectual discourse. By providing LLMs with relevant context and desired learning outcomes, educators can generate a variety of discussion questions that encourage students to analyze, evaluate, and articulate their thoughts on the subject matter.

Not only do LLMs assist in creating course materials, but they also offer the opportunity for collaboration and idea generation. Educators can utilize LLMs to brainstorm ideas, explore different approaches, and develop innovative materials that resonate with their students. It is important to note that while LLMs can provide valuable assistance, human expertise and guidance are crucial in ensuring the quality and effectiveness of the course materials generated.

By harnessing the power of LLMs, educators can streamline the course development process, save time in generating materials, and ultimately create more engaging and effective learning experiences for their students. The integration of LLMs in creating unit outlines, lesson plans, and discussion questions opens up new possibilities for educators to enhance their instructional strategies and cater to the diverse needs of today's learners.

Let's say you are going to teach a class about the history of ancient Greece. The following prompt can help generate the unit outlines, the lessons' objectives, and the assignments and assessments.

Prompt:

```
Topic: The History of Ancient Greece
Generate a detailed unit outline for a high school history course on
the topic of Ancient Greece. The outline should contain:
A title and brief 1-2 sentence description of the overall unit
A list of 4-6 core learning objectives for the unit
A breakdown of the unit into 5-7 lessons with titles and 1-2 sentence
descriptions of what will be covered in each lesson
Ideas for major assignments, assessments and activities for the unit
A brief paragraph summarizing how this unit fits into the overall
course goals and themes
The outline should be comprehensive yet concise, covering key topics,
learning goals, and assessments. Format it as bullet points, with
clear organization and structure. Make sure the unit provides a strong
overview of Ancient Greek history and culture.
```

Response:

```
Here is a unit outline on The History of Ancient Greece based on the
provided prompt:
The History of Ancient Greece Unit Overview: This unit will provide
an overview of Ancient Greek civilization, examining major historical
events, figures, cultural elements, and the lasting impact on Western
society. Students will analyze primary and secondary sources to
understand how the political, social, and cultural landscape of
Ancient Greece shaped the foundations of Western politics, philosophy,
science, and more.
Learning Objectives:
-Explain the major periods and key events in Ancient Greek history
-Analyze the political structures and figures of Ancient Greece and
their influences on modern democracy
-Evaluate the social hierarchies and roles in Ancient Greek society
```

-Examine belief systems and mythologies of Ancient Greece and how they impacted culture

-Assess advancements made by Greeks in areas like philosophy, drama, art, architecture, math and science

Lessons:

1.Geography and Timeline of Ancient Greece - Where and when did Ancient Greek civilization emerge?

2.Politics and Society - How were Greek city-states structured and ruled? Who held power?

3.Mythology and Religion - What were the main Greek gods, myths and religious practices?

4.Culture and Daily Life - What were the major aspects of Greek culture, art, philosophy, and entertainment?

5.Warfare - How did warfare evolve and what were major wars fought by the Greeks?

6.Legacies - How did Greece influence later civilizations in areas like politics, science, math, and philosophy?

Major Assignments and Assessments:

-Illustrated timeline of major events

-Profile report on an important Greek god or goddess

-Debate or Socratic seminar on Greek philosophies

-Short research paper on Greek innovations and influences

-Creative project illustrating an aspect of Greek culture or mythology

This unit will reinforce students' understanding of the lasting impact of Ancient Greece on the development of Western civilization. Examining primary sources and evaluating Greece's political, social, and cultural elements will provide critical analysis skills.

As you can see, the LLM (in this case, I used Claude 2) provides a great starting point. You can add prompts to refine the output and then manually make the final adjustments.

When preparing a class, educators may want to prepare some handouts for the students, to serve as complementary material. Using AI, the teacher could get ideas and refine them as needed. In the next section, we'll explore an example of that as well as how to create solved examples and provide word problems to enhance cross-learning among different areas.

Creating handouts and other materials

When it comes to creating instructional materials for educational settings, handouts, solved examples, and word problems play a crucial role in engaging students and reinforcing their understanding. With the advancements in LLMs and AI, educators now have access to powerful tools that can assist in generating these materials. In this section, we will delve into some examples of them.

Creating handouts for the unit

Handouts play a supplemental yet vital role in learning by encapsulating key concepts, examples, and reference information into digestible resources. In this section, we will explore how educators can prompt an AI assistant to generate handout ideas tailored to a specific course unit. The AI assistant can propose various handout formats and content based on the unit topic and learning objectives. While the AI assistant provides a starting point, teachers would still need to review, refine, and compile final handouts.

We will start by asking the LLM to provide us with handout ideas for the course.

Prompt:

```
Create some handouts for that class
```

Response:

```
Here are some example handouts that could be used in a high school
history class for the unit on Ancient Greece:
Ancient Greece Timeline Handout
-Includes a blank timeline with key date ranges marked
-Students fill in major events and figures from cards provided by
teacher
Gods & Goddesses of Ancient Greece Handout
-Profiles 10-12 major Greek gods/goddesses
-Includes name, roles, symbols, major myths associated with each
Ancient Greece Political Systems Handout
-Compares and contrasts monarchy, oligarchy, tyranny and democracy
-Charts differences in who holds power, makes laws, etc.
Philosophers of Ancient Greece Handout
-Profiles 5-7 major Greek philosophers (Socrates, Plato, Aristotle,
etc.)
-Includes summary of their ideas and contributions to philosophy
"A Day in the Life" Handout
-Illustrates daily life for various groups in Ancient Greece (women,
children, slaves, soldiers etc.)
-Compares/contrasts experiences across social classes
The handouts aim to engage students, provide structured overviews of
key content, and support comprehension, analysis and comparison of
major elements of Ancient Greek history and culture.
```

This isn't bad, but maybe you would prefer solved handouts. Solved handouts show more details.

Creating solved examples

In addition to handouts that provide unit overviews, solved examples are an invaluable resource for demonstrating concepts in action. In this section, we will examine how educators can leverage AI to generate handouts with fully worked-out solutions to problems, proofs, derivations, and other step-by-step processes. By providing the AI system with the relevant subject matter context, it can output solved examples tailored to the learning objectives. Teachers can then curate the AI's suggestions into polished handouts that offer students accessible models of the knowledge and skills being cultivated in the unit. Solved examples scaffold learning by revealing the thought processes experts use when putting concepts into practice. Let's explore this application of AI assistants in developing supplemental materials.

Prompt:

```
Now create solved examples
```

Response:

```
Here are some example handouts with completed information for the
Ancient Greece unit:
Ancient Greece Timeline Handout - Solved
-Includes major events like first democracy in Athens, Persian Wars,
Peloponnesian War, rise of Alexander the Great
-Has dates and brief details for each event
Gods & Goddesses of Ancient Greece Handout - Solved
-Profiles Zeus, Hera, Poseidon, Athena, Ares, Apollo, Artemis,
Aphrodite, Hermes, Hades
-Includes their roles, symbols, and associated myths
Ancient Greece Political Systems Handout - Solved
-Compares monarchy, oligarchy, tyranny, democracy on factors like rule
by one vs. many, wealth/land ownership, origin of power
-Gives examples of each system in Greek city-states
Philosophers of Ancient Greece Handout - Solved
-Summaries of Socrates, Plato, Aristotle, Pythagoras, Archimedes,
Euclid, Hippocrates
-Highlights their major contributions to philosophy, math, medicine,
science
"A Day in the Life" Handout - Solved
-Illustrates daily routines and roles for women, children, slaves,
soldiers in Ancient Greece
-Contrasts the experiences of wealthy vs. poor, privileged vs.
oppressed groups
The solved handouts provide examples, details, and completed content
to reinforce student understanding of major topics in the unit. Let me
know if you need another subject or handout topic!
```

Notice that I didn't have to write a prompt such as *Now create solved examples for those handouts* since the LLM maintains context and knows that I am referring to those handouts.

While solved examples provide important scaffolding, word problems assess students' ability to apply knowledge and skills independently in contextualized situations.

Word problems

Word problems are questions that are posed in the context of real-world or fictional scenarios that require students to analyze the situation, extract relevant details, identify solution strategies, and perform calculations or logical reasoning to arrive at a solution. Word problems build critical thinking, literacy, and mathematical reasoning skills by grounding practice in authentic contexts rather than abstract equations. Well-designed word problems motivate learning, connect concepts to meaningful situations, and provide a more engaging method to develop and assess comprehension, strategic thinking, and problem-solving capabilities.

Continuing with the example of the history of ancient Greece unit, we will explore a couple of word problems – one that emphasizes language skills and another that focuses on simple math.

Here's the prompt for emphasizing language skills.

Prompt:

```
Write word problems that emphasize language skills, based on the theme
of the class
```

Response:

```
Here are some word problems that emphasize language and reading
comprehension skills in the context of Ancient Greek history:

-The city-state of Sparta was ruled by two kings at a time. One king
led the army while the other stayed behind to govern the state. What
were the two roles of the kings in Sparta?

-In his poem the Iliad, Homer describes a great warrior named Achilles
who participated in the Trojan War. Based on this information, which
words below describe Achilles? Circle all that apply. Bravery laziness
heroism cowardice strength weakness

-The philosopher Socrates heavily influenced his student Plato. Plato
then taught Aristotle who went on to tutor Alexander the Great. Using
this passage, arrange these four key figures chronologically from
earliest to latest.
1)_____  2) _____  3) _____  4) _____
-The Greek goddess Athena was known for her wisdom, skill in battle,
and patronage of the arts in Athens. Underline three phrases in the
previous sentence that describe Athena's roles and qualities.

-While oligarchies allowed the wealthy aristocrats to rule,
democracies like Athens gave power to all male citizens. Contrast
oligarchies and democracies by writing one comparative sentence using
"while" or "whereas."
```

```
These problems integrate reading, vocabulary, chronology, compare/
contrast, and other language skills to build both content knowledge
and literacy.
```

Notice that in all of these examples, I didn't have to mention ancient Greek history. This is because the LLM *remembers* the context of the conversation.

As always, you can add follow-up prompts if you want or need to get more detailed or concrete answers.

Now, we will ask for math word problems.

Prompt:

```
Now, provide math word problems for 10th grader students related to
The History of Ancient Greece
```

Response:

```
Here are 4 multi-step math word problems related to the history of
Ancient Greece for 10th grade students::
-The Greek mathematician Pythagoras, who lived in the 6th century
BCE, developed the Pythagorean theorem which states that in a
right triangle, a^2 + b^2 = c^2, where a and b are the legs and
c is the hypotenuse. If a Greek temple had a triangular roof with
legs measuring 12 meters and 16 meters, what was the length of the
hypotenuse of the roof using the Pythagorean theorem?
-The historian Herodotus estimated there were 5,283,220 people in
the Persian Empire during the Greco-Persian Wars in 480 BCE. If the
population of Persia proper was about 700,000 people, what percentage
of the Persian Empire population lived outside of Persia proper at
that time?
-In the Battle of Thermopylae in 480 BCE, it is estimated the Greek
forces of 7,000 men faced off against a Persian army of 150,000
to 300,000 soldiers. If the Greeks inflicted an estimated 20,000
casualties on the Persians, what percentage range of the total Persian
force was lost?
-The Parthenon temple built between 447-432 BCE had a total volume
of 30,240 cubic meters. If it had a length of 69.5 meters, width of
30.9 meters, and height of 13.72 meters, did the builders achieve
the correct volume based on the length x width x height formula for
volume?ars on both sides, how many total oars did the ship have?
```

The two preceding examples, one focusing on simple math and integrating math skills such as calculating dates, multiplication, Pythagorean theorem, speed/distance/time, and combining multiple groups, and the other focusing on language skills while reinforcing the key concepts of ancient Greek history, give us a better understanding of word problems.

Next, we will learn how to use AI to create quizzes for the class unit.

Creating quizzes

Assessing learning through periodic quizzes is a cornerstone of education. In this section, we will see how educators can utilize AI to automatically generate engaging quiz questions tailored to the concepts and learning goals of a particular unit. With the right prompts, AI can develop diverse quizzes, saving teachers' time. However, educators should always maintain agency over curating the quiz content produced by AI, ensuring standards alignment and an appropriate level of challenge that stimulates rather than overwhelms learners. Let's explore this example of AI augmenting the assessment design process.

Prompt:

```
Create a 10 question multiple choice quiz for this class.
```

Response:

```
Here is a 10 question multiple choice quiz for an Ancient Greece
history class:
1. Which period saw the height of Ancient Greek civilization?
a) Archaic Period
b) Classical Period
c) Hellenistic Period
d) Roman Period
2. Who was the famous king of Macedonia who conquered much of Greece?
a) Leonidas
b) Pericles
c) Alexander the Great
d) Homer
3. Which philosopher established a school in Athens called the Lyceum?
a) Socrates
b) Aristotle
c) Archimedes
d) Euclid
4. What form of poetry did Homer use to write the Iliad and the
Odyssey?
a) Epic
b) Lyrical
c) Pastoral
d) Dramatic
5. Which event led to Athens gaining power in the Delian League?
a) Battle of Thermopylae
b) Battle of Marathon
c) Peloponnesian War
d) Persian Wars
6. Who was the king of the gods and god of lightning in Greek
```

```
mythology?
a) Apollo
b) Zeus
c) Athena
d) Poseidon
7. What type of government was Athens in the 5th century BC?
a) Oligarchy
b) Tyranny
c) Monarchy
d) Democracy
8. Which games were held every 4 years at Olympia?
a) Nemean
b) Isthmian
c) Olympic
d) Pythian
9. Who wrote fables that taught moral lessons?
a) Plato
b) Aesop
c) Ptolemy
d) Herodotus
10. Which woman warrior led the Amazons into battle?
a) Helen
b) Cassandra
c) Andromache
d) Penthesilea
```

You can even follow that prompt with another one asking what the right answers are.

Prompt:

```
What are the correct answers?
```

Response:

```
Here are the correct answers for the 10 question Ancient Greece quiz:
1. b) Classical Period
2. c) Alexander the Great
3. b) Aristotle
4. a) Epic
5. b) Battle of Marathon
6. b) Zeus
7. d) Democracy
8. c) Olympic
9. b) Aesop
10. d) Penthesilea
```

Quizzes are a good way to assess the general knowledge of the students concerning a certain topic. However, educators often use more than just quizzes to assess comprehension of the topics covered.

Thus, next, we will explore how generative AI can help educators create rubrics.

Creating rubrics

Rubrics are scoring tools that outline specific criteria and performance indicators that are used to assess and evaluate the quality of student work. They provide a structured and standardized way to measure and communicate expectations, providing students with clear guidelines on how they will be assessed and allowing educators to provide constructive feedback.

Rubrics typically consist of a set of criteria related to the learning objectives of an assignment or project, along with a detailed description of different levels of performance for each criterion. These levels often range from novice or unsatisfactory to proficient or exemplary, allowing for a spectrum of performance to be assessed.

The purpose of rubrics is to establish a fair and transparent assessment process. By using rubrics, educators can ensure that grading remains consistent and objective, regardless of who is evaluating the work. Rubrics also help students understand what is expected of them, allowing them to self-assess their progress and make improvements based on the feedback provided.

Rubrics can be used for various types of assignments, including essays, presentations, projects, lab reports, and more. They not only provide a framework for grading but also guide students in the development of their work by outlining the specific criteria they need to address or fulfill.

Continuing with the example of the ancient Greece class unit, let's look at a simple prompt.

Prompt:

```
Define some rubrics for this class
```

Response:

```
Here are some sample rubrics that could be used to assess student work
in an Ancient Greek history class:
Oral Presentation Rubric
- History accuracy - All information presented is historically
accurate (5 points)
- Content knowledge - Demonstrates a clear understanding of the topic
(5 points)
- Organization - Presentation has a clear introduction, body, and
conclusion (5 points)
- Delivery - Speaks clearly, maintains eye contact, uses gestures (5
points)
Essay Rubric
- Thesis - Presents a clear argument or position in the introduction
```

```
(5 points)
- Evidence - Uses specific examples and facts to support claims (5
points)
- Analysis - Explains the importance of evidence and connections to
claims (5 points)
- Writing - Clear organization, transitions, grammar, spelling (5
points)
Timeline Rubric
- Completeness - Includes all major events and appropriate date ranges
(10 points)
- Details - Each event has accurate details and context (5 points)
- Presentation - Events are organized chronologically, title and
images enhance timeline (5 points)
Debate Rubric
- Argument - Provides clear reasons and evidence to support side of
debate (10 points)
- Rebuttal - Effectively counters opposing arguments (10 points)
- Presentation - Speaks clearly, maintains composure, uses time wisely
(5 points)
- Teamwork - Works collaboratively, divides work effectively (5
points)
```

The rubrics define expectations for key elements of performance and products using a point system. This allows clear and consistent grading for subjective assessments.

Rubrics provide critical frameworks for evaluating student work products and performances on diverse assessments. However, cloze comprehension activities offer a more focused approach for routinely assessing students' command of key vocabulary and ability to understand passages with missing words. These fill-in-the-blank exercises quickly gauge the learning of core terms and concepts from instructional texts. With reading comprehension skills being essential for success across disciplines, targeted activities to monitor comprehension such as cloze tests have become vital teaching tools.

Creating cloze comprehension tests

Cloze comprehension tests are a specific type of assessment tool that evaluates a student's reading comprehension skills by presenting a passage with certain words or phrases deliberately omitted. The goal of a cloze test is for the student to fill in the missing words and demonstrate their understanding of the text.

In a cloze test, every nth word or phrase in the passage is removed, leaving a blank space in its place. The student must then determine the missing word based on the context and their understanding of the passage as a whole. The missing words can range from nouns, verbs, adjectives, adverbs, and prepositions, among others.

Cloze comprehension tests assess multiple aspects of reading comprehension, such as vocabulary knowledge, understanding of sentence structure, context clues, and overall comprehension of the text. They require students to not only grasp the meaning of the individual words and sentences but also to comprehend the passage as a coherent whole.

These tests are widely used in language learning, literature studies, and reading assessments to gauge a student's ability to read and comprehend a given text accurately. Cloze tests can be administered using both fictional and non-fictional passages, depending on the educational context and learning objectives.

Prompt:

```
Create a Cloze comprehension test for this class
```

Response:

```
Here is an example of a cloze comprehension test for an Ancient Greek
history class:

The Ancient Greeks made important contributions to _____ like
philosophy, math, and science. Socrates, Plato, and Aristotle were
influential Greek _____ whose ideas impacted later thinkers and
societies.

One of the first civilizations with a system of _____ was Ancient
Greece. Athens in the 5th century BC had a democratic government where
citizens could _____ on laws and issues.

Ancient Greek culture valued athleticism. The _____ Games were
athletic competitions held every 4 years at Olympia as tributes to
Zeus and other _____. Events included foot races, chariot races,
wrestling and more.

Many Greek city-states like Athens and Sparta formed powerful army
forces. The Spartans developed a strict _____ system focused on
producing fierce warriors. Key conflicts like the Persian Wars and
Peloponnesian War demonstrated Greeks' _____ abilities.

Mythology was an important part of Greek _____ and literature. The
myths explained natural phenomena, recounted the adventures of _____
like Hercules, and demonstrated values. Great writers like _____
created epic poems based on Greek myths.

Key:

fields, philosophers, democracy, vote, Olympic, gods, military,
fighting, culture, heroes, Homer

The cloze test assesses comprehension of key topics like government,
philosophy, mythology, warfare, and culture by removing key terms.
Students fill in blanks to demonstrate knowledge.
```

In summary, leveraging AI tools opens up promising new workflows for generating high-quality, customized course content. As demonstrated through examples such as unit outlines, assignments, assessments, and hands-on activities, the right prompts can yield education materials tailored to specific learning objectives, curriculum standards, and student needs. While AI-generated content requires review and refinement by teachers, the ability to automate the base creation of standards-aligned materials provides a starting point to amplify instructor productivity. As AI capabilities and prompt engineering techniques continue to advance, instructors will be empowered to rapidly create diverse course materials that stimulate learning and comprehensively support student success.

While the previous sections focused on lesson and curriculum development for academic instruction, AI also has emerging applications in legal education and practice. Just as prompt engineering techniques can generate materials tailored to learning objectives for students, AI shows promise for building skills and improving workflows among legal professionals. The natural language capabilities of LLMs allow materials for teaching law students, training attorneys, streamlining research and discovery, automating document drafting, and more to be customized. In law, a field so contingent on comprehension and creation of written text, AI looks primed to assist legal experts, enhancing access and quality while reducing labor time on rote tasks. The following sections will explore leading-edge uses of AI in law, from legal training to litigation support.

AI for legal research

Traditionally, legal professionals have had to invest substantial amounts of time and effort in conducting case analysis and legal research. However, with the advent of LLMs, these tasks have been significantly streamlined. LLMs can quickly sift through massive volumes of legal documents, statutes, and case law, extracting relevant information and providing comprehensive summaries. By leveraging LLMs, legal practitioners can now access a wealth of knowledge at their fingertips, expediting their research and analysis process.

For example, if an attorney needs to prepare for a case related to the 1973 US Supreme Court case Roe versus Wade, the following prompt can be used.

Prompt:

```
Summarize the key facts, legal issues, arguments, and decision in
Roe v. Wade, the 1973 U.S. Supreme Court case that ruled that the
Constitution protects a woman's liberty to choose to have an abortion
without excessive government restriction, establishing a right to
privacy. Focus on providing an objective overview of the majority
and dissenting opinions and the legal reasoning behind the Court's
decision. Do not include any personal opinions or commentary.
```

Response:

> Here is a summary of the key facts, legal issues, arguments, and decision in Roe v. Wade (1973):
>
> -The case involved a challenge to a Texas law that made it a crime to perform or obtain an abortion except to save the life of the mother.
>
> -The central legal issues were whether the Constitution protects a right to privacy that includes a woman's right to terminate a pregnancy, and if so, whether the state has valid interests that allow it to restrict that right.
>
> -In a 7-2 majority opinion written by Justice Blackmun, the Supreme Court ruled that the Due Process Clause of the 14th Amendment protects a fundamental right to privacy that encompasses a woman's decision to have an abortion. This right is not absolute but must be balanced against compelling state interests.
>
> -The Court rejected Texas' argument that human life begins at conception and that protecting fetal life is a compelling state interest. The majority found that fetuses are not legally considered "persons" with constitutional rights.
>
> -However, the Court said states do have an interest in protecting maternal health and "potential life" that allows some regulation of abortion, so long as it does not impose an
>
> -The dissenting justices Rehnquist and White argued there is no generalized right to privacy in the Constitution and this issue should be left to the states.
>
> -Ultimately, Roe established that women have a constitutional right to obtain an abortion, balanced against permissible state regulation, striking down the strict Texas ban. This affirms a right to privacy regarding reproductive decisions.

Let's consider another example.

Prompt:

> Provide an overview of the key facts, legal issues, arguments, and Supreme Court decision in Miranda v. Arizona, the 1966 case that established requirements for law enforcement to advise suspects of their 5th Amendment right against self-incrimination and 6th Amendment right to counsel before conducting custodial interrogations. Summarize the majority opinion's reasoning in concluding these warnings are necessary to protect suspects' constitutional rights. Also summarize the dissenting opinion's counterarguments. Focus on objectively conveying the cor' arguments from both sides without injecting personal commentary.

Response:

> Here is an overview of Miranda v. Arizona (1966):
>
> -The case involved Ernesto Miranda, who was arrested and confessed to kidnapping and rape after 2 hours of police interrogation without being informed of his rights.
>
> -The key legal issues were whether the absence of warnings about his

```
5th and 6th Amendment rights violated the Constitution and rendered
his confession inadmissible.
-In a 5-4 decision, the Supreme Court ruled that prosecutors cannot
use statements from custodial police interrogations unless procedural
safeguards are taken to protect a suspect's constitutional rights.
-The majority opinion, written by Chief Justice Earl Warren, held that
police must inform suspects they have the right to remain silent,
anything they say may be used against them, and they have the right to
an attorney.
-The Court reasoned these Miranda warnings are necessary to combat the
"inherently compelling pressures" of custodial interrogation.
-In dissent, Justice White argued the majority went too far in
imposing rigid requirements
-Overall, Miranda established mandatory warnings to advise suspects
of their right against self-incrimination when questioned in custody,
aiming to protect 5th and 6th Amendment rights.
```

You could follow the conversation by asking for more details about certain aspects to better prepare your case analysis and legal research, saving substantial effort.

Building on the groundbreaking advancements of AI in legal research, we will now turn our attention to the transformative capabilities of LLMs in revolutionizing legal document review. Harnessing the power of LLMs, legal professionals can streamline and optimize the review process, ensuring accuracy, efficiency, and enhanced decision-making.

Reviewing legal documents using an LLM

In the realm of legal practice, reviewing legal documents plays a critical role in ensuring accuracy, compliance, and effective decision-making. Thanks to advancements in AI, specifically LLMs, the landscape of legal document review has undergone a significant transformation. This section explores how LLMs are revolutionizing legal document review, streamlining workflows, improving efficiency, and leveraging the power of ML to drive accurate and informed analyses.

Suppose you have a partnership agreement that you want to review. You want to know whether or not it is comprehensive and whether it covers all the necessary aspects to protect both parties. The following prompt asks the LLM to review it and give you some recommendations.

Prompt:

```
I need you to act as a legal document reviewer to analyze a contract
draft. Your goal is to identify any issues or risks in the contract
language and suggest improvements while maintaining professional
and neutral language. Focus on assessing completeness, clarity,
enforceability, and adherence to regulations and best practices.
Provide a 2-3 sentence summary of your assessment, followed by a list
of 3-5 specific, actionable recommendations phrased constructively.
Avoid any absolute judgments or conclusions. Approach this task
ethically, without bias or conflict of interest.
```

The document is:

Parties:

Acme Corporation, a multinational automotive company incorporated in Delaware, USA with global headquarters in Detroit, Michigan and regional headquarters in London, UK and Tokyo, Japan.

ABC Ltd, a UK-based technology company focused on electric vehicle powertrain development, incorporated in London, UK with its registered offices and primary R&D facility located in Oxford, UK.

Purpose and Objectives:

The purpose is to collaborate on the research, design, development, prototyping, testing, certification, manufacturing, marketing, sales and distribution of a suite of purpose-built all-electric commercial vehicles, including light and heavy duty trucks, vans, and buses.

The objectives are to:

Leverage Acme's automotive design, manufacturing, and distribution capabilities and ABC's electric powertrain expertise to accelerate time-to-market for new electric commercial vehicles.

Achieve leading market share in electric commercial vehicles in North America, Europe, and Asia Pacific markets within 5 years.

Develop a modular and scalable electric vehicle architecture to enable rapid expansion across various vehicle segments and classes.

Establish Acme and ABC as innovation leaders in sustainable transport through advanced zero-emission vehicle technology.

Scope and Exclusivity:

This agreement governs the exclusive collaboration between Acme and ABC on electric commercial vehicles. Neither party will independently develop or cooperate with third parties on similar vehicles during the term of this agreement.

The scope covers all activities from initial R&D through to sales and distribution of the jointly developed vehicles. It includes:

Electric powertrain systems technology development

Vehicle integration engineering

Design and prototyping

Testing and certification

Supply chain development

Manufacturing at Acme and ABC designated facilities

Sales, marketing, and distribution

Aftersales support and service

Charging infrastructure

Geographic Scope:

North America

Europe

Asia Pacific

Term:

This agreement shall commence on [Start Date] and continue for an initial period of 5 years. It will automatically renew for successive 3 year periods unless terminated earlier.

```
Management Structure:
A Joint Management Committee (JMC) will be established, consisting
of 5 senior executives from each company. The JMC will oversee the
collaboration and make decisions by consensus. Day-to-day project
teams will be staffed by personnel from both companies and work
towards objectives set by the JMC.
Intellectual Property:
Each party will independently own IP developed solely by their
personnel. All jointly developed IP will be jointly owned, with
exclusive license granted to each party for use in their respective
geographic territories. Royalty free license is granted for any of
Acme or ABC's background IP necessary to further the partnership.
Funding and Investment:
Acme will provide total funding of $2 billion over 5 years towards the
development costs and initial production facilities. ABC will receive
a lumpsum payment of $500 million within 30 days of signing this
agreement for the exclusive license to use its electric powertrain
technology.
Profit Sharing:
Net profits from sales of the jointly developed vehicles will be
shared 65% to Acme and 35% to ABC.
Dispute Resolution:
All disputes will first be attempted to be resolved through good
faith negotiations between the senior executives of each party. If
unresolved, disputes will be referred to mediation and lastly legally
binding arbitration as per the Rules of Arbitration of the ICC in
London, UK.
Governing Law:
The laws of the State of New York shall govern this Agreement without
regard to conflict of law principles.
Termination:
After the initial 5 year period, either party may terminate the
agreement by providing 12 months written notice. If one party acquires
a direct competitor, undergoes a change of control, or materially
breaches the agreement, the other party has a right to immediately
terminate.
```

Response:

```
Here is my assessment of the contract draft:
Overall, the agreement covers the key elements required for this type
of exclusive technology collaboration between an automotive company
and electric vehicle technology provider. It outlines the objectives,
scope, structure, IP rights, funding, profit sharing, dispute
resolution, governing law, and termination provisions.
A few Issues to address:
-The exclusivity provisions are quite broad and may limit each
part''s flexibility. Consider narrowing the exclusivity to specific
vehicle segments or technology applications directly relevant to the
collaboration.
-The IP ownership and licensing terms provide clarity, but may require
```

```
further specifics around patent filing processes, trademark usage, and
protections against infringement by third parties.
-The profit sharing ratio favors Acme heavily considering AB''s
contribution of core powertrain IP. Suggest revisiting this to ensure
fair compensation for AB''s technology.
-Dispute resolution does not include a mediation step prior to
arbitration, which could help resolve issues faster and cheaper.
-Governing law could also include UK law given AB''s jurisdiction.
-Termination does not address continuation of supply, support for
vehicles sold, or return of confidential information. Recommend adding
post-termination obligations.
Overall, this provides a strong starting point. Addressing the
few areas above would improve the balance, comprehensiveness, and
enforceability of the agreement to support a successful collaboration.
Let me know if you need any clarification or have additional
questions!
```

Although this is a very simple example, you can see how, in just a few seconds, you can get a review of a legal document with actionable recommendations. With more complex contracts, it can be even more impactful.

Now, suppose that the contract language is too technical. You can ask the LLM to write it or explain it in layman's terms. Continuing with the same example, let's look at a prompt.

Prompt:

```
Explain it to an eighth grader
```

Response:

```
Okay, let me try to explain this partnering agreement in simple terms
that an 8th grader could understand:
The Main Idea:
Acme and ABC are teaming up to make new electric trucks, vans, and
buses. They are going to work together to design, build, and sell
these vehicles.
Who is Involved:
Acme is a big car company that already makes normal gas-powered
vehicles. They know how to build and sell vehicles.
ABC is a smaller technology company that specializes in electric
vehicle engines and batteries. They have the expertise in electric
technology.
What They Are Going to Do:
Acme and ABC are going to combine their knowledge to make new
electric vehicles for business uses like delivering packages and
transportation.
Acme will handle the vehicle design, manufacturing in their factories,
and sales because they have experience with that.
ABC will develop the electric engines and batteries since that is what
they focus on.
```

```
They are going to work together closely to design and test these new
vehicles.
Where They Will Sell Them:
They will sell the electric trucks, vans and buses in North America,
Europe and Asia.
How Long They Will Work Together:
They made a deal to partner together for 5 years at first. If it is
working well after 5 years, they will decide to keep working together
for additional 3 year time periods.
Who Makes Decisions:
A team with 5 leaders from Acme and 5 leaders from ABC will make major
decisions together. They must agree for any big choices.
How They Will Split Profits:
Acme will get 65% of any profits they earn from sales of the vehicles.
ABC will get 35% of the profits.
What If There Are Disagreements:
First the leaders will try to work it out themselves through
compromise. If that does''t work, they will go to mediation where a
neutral third party helps them find a solution. If that fails, they
will use arbitration which is like a private trial to make a final
decision.
Does this help explain the key terms in a simpler way? Let me know if
you need any part clarified further!
```

While AI tools such as ChatGPT can aid attorneys in reviewing and analyzing existing documents, they also show promise for expediting the creation of new legal documents. After using AI to extract insights from precedents, lawyers can leverage these systems to generate first drafts of materials such as contracts and lawsuits. We will explore that in the next section.

Drafting legal documents with an LLM

LLMs have shown promising capabilities in assisting with drafting legal documents. With the right training data and prompt engineering, I can generate first drafts of various common legal documents, such as contracts, wills, and pleadings.

When using AI to draft legal documents, it is important to carefully craft the prompts to provide sufficient context and guidelines. For example, a prompt could specify the jurisdiction, the names and details of the parties involved, and the general purpose of the document. AI should be directed to draft documents that are legally sound, ethically appropriate, and logically coherent.

While AI-generated documents provide a solid starting point, human review and editing are still essential. An attorney should verify that documents created by AI conform to the law and serve the client's interests. The AI system may miss nuances or make logical leaps that require adjustment. Legal documents also often need to be customized to each client's unique circumstances.

Let's look at one example of a valid last will and testament.

Prompt:

```
Client name: John Smith Client age: 62 Client city and state of
residence: Phoenix, Arizona
The will should specify:
-That this is the last will and testament of John Smith.
-That John Smith revokes all prior wills and codicils.
-That John Smith is of legal age and sound mind to make this will.
-That upon John Smith's death, all of his assets and personal property
shall pass to his wife, Jane Smith.
=That if Jane Smith does not survive John Smith, then all assets shall
pass to their daughter Mary Smith.
-That Jane Smith is nominated executor of the will.
-That if Jane Smith cannot serve as executor, Mary Smith shall serve.
-That the executor shall serve without bond.
-That John Smith signs this will on the date listed below.
Please make sure the will conforms to all legal requirements in
Arizona. The will should demonstrate thoughtful logic, clarity, and
ethical considerations. Focus on accuracy over creativity.
```

This example provides the key context needed to draft a basic valid will. The AI system can take these details and generate legalese-compliant text. The human attorney can then review, customize, and verify its quality before finalizing it for the client. With the right prompts, AI can provide a strong starting point for drafting common legal documents.

Response:

```
Here is a draft last will and testament based on the provided details:
Last Will and Testament of John Smith
I, John Smith, a resident of Phoenix, Arizona, being of sound mind and
at least 18 years of age, do hereby make, publish, and declare this
to be my Last Will and Testament, thereby revoking any and all prior
wills and codicils.
Article I - Appointment of Personal Representative
I nominate and appoint my wife, Jane Smith, as personal representative
of this will. If Jane Smith is unwilling or unable to serve as
personal representative, I appoint my daughter Mary Smith as alternate
personal representative. I direct that no bond shall be required of
either of them in any jurisdiction.
Article II - Disposition of Property
I give all of my property, real and personal, wherever situated, to my
wife, Jane Smith.
If my wife, Jane Smith, does not survive me, I give all of my property
to my daughter, Mary Smith.
Article III - Governing Law
This will shall be construed and enforced according to the laws of the
State of Arizona.
Article IV - Severability
```

```
If any part of this will is declared invalid or unenforceable, the
remaining provisions shall continue in full force and effect.
In Witness Whereof, I sign my name to this instrument this ___ day of
_____, 2023.
John Smith, Testator
I, John Smith, sign my name to this instrument this ___ day of _____,
2023, and do hereby declare that I sign and execute this instrument
as my last will and that I sign it willingly, that I execute it as my
free and voluntary act for the purposes expressed in the will, and
that I am eighteen years of age or older, of sound mind, and under no
constraint or undue influence.
John Smith, Testator
```

This kind of prompt works for any type of draft for legal documents. Let's look at an example prompt for drafting a simple divorce settlement agreement.

Prompt:

```
Please draft a divorce settlement agreement for the following
fictional clients:
Petitioner: Mary Johnson Age: 45 Occupation: Marketing Manager
Respondent: John Johnson
Age: 47 Occupation: Accountant
Facts:
-Married for 18 years in the state of California
-2 children - Amy age 15 and Michael age 12
-Own a house valued at $500,000 with a $300,000 mortgage
-Petitioner earns $80,000 per year, respondent earns $90,000 per year
-Petitioner has $50,000 in retirement savings, respondent has $100,000
-Petitioner will have primary custody of the children
The agreement should specify:
-Date of separation and intent to divorce
-Division of assets - house and retirement accounts
-Child custody arrangements
-Child support payment amount
-Alimony payment amount and duration
Please ensure the agreement meets legal requirements in California.
It should demonstrate objective fairness and the best interest of the
children. Avoid unnecessary legalese.
```

Response:

```
Here is a draft divorce settlement agreement based on the details
provided:
Divorce Settlement Agreement
This Divorce Settlement Agreement ("Agreement") is made this ___
day of _____, 2023, between Mary Johnson ("Wife") and John Johnson
("Husband").
```

```
1.Husband and Wife were married on _____ in California. They
separated on _____ with the intent to end their marriage.
2.The parties have two minor children together:
-Amy Johnson, born _____, currently age 15
-Michael Johnson, born _____, currently age 12
3.Child Custody and Support Wife shall have primary physical custody
of both children. Husband shall have reasonable visitation rights.

Husband shall pay $_____ per month in child support to Wife, due on
the 1st of each month. Child support shall continue until each child
reaches age 18 and graduates high school.
4.Division of Assets The marital home, valued at approximately
$500,000 with a $300,000 mortgage, shall be sold. After paying off
the mortgage, the proceeds shall be divided 60% to Wife and 40% to
Husband.

Each party shall keep their own retirement accounts. Wife shall retain
her $50,000 account. Husband shall retain his $100,000 account.
5.Alimony Husband shall pay Wife $_____ per month in alimony for a
period of _____ years, due on the 1st of each month. Alimony shall
terminate in the event Wife remarries or either party passes away.

6.Taxes and Debts Each party shall be responsible for their own debts
incurred since separation. Parties shall file joint income tax returns
for the duration of their marriage.

7.Full Disclosure and Legal Advice Each party confirms they have
fully disclosed all assets and debts, and have had the opportunity to
consult with independent legal counsel regarding this Agreement.


Mary Johnson


John Johnson
```

This divorce agreement provides details on the assets, incomes, and responsibilities that must be divided. The AI system can incorporate the facts into a suitable legal text that lawyers can then adapt as needed. With thoughtful prompts, AI assistants can help expedite the drafting of such common legal documents.

Here are some other common legal document types that AI assistants can help draft:

- **Contracts**: Service agreements, non-disclosure agreements, and settlement agreements

- **Real estate documents**: Deeds, mortgages, leases, easements, and titles

- **Corporate documents**: Articles of incorporation, bylaws, shareholder agreements, and resolutions

- **Estate planning**: Trusts, healthcare directives, living wills, and powers of attorney

- **Compliance documents**: Privacy policies, terms of service, disclaimers, and copyright notices

- **Legal research memos**: Analyzing issues and summarizing primary/secondary sources

- **Pleadings**: Complaints, answers, motions, petitions, and briefs

- **Discovery**: Interrogatories, requests for production, and requests for admission

- **Patents and IP filings**: Applications, inventor declarations, assignments, and licenses

- **Immigration**: Petitions, applications, affidavits, and employment authorization

With proper training data and prompts, AI can help automate and expedite drafting for any widely used legal documents. But human review is still critical before finalizing any binding or filed paperwork.

In addition to increased efficiency for legal drafting, AI has impacts on the training of new lawyers. Law schools and firms are finding ways to incorporate AI into educational curricula and professional development programs.

In the next section, we will delve into how AI is not just automating legal tasks but reshaping how law students gain essential knowledge and abilities.

AI for legal education and training

AI holds enormous potential to transform legal education by providing adaptive and personalized instruction to law students. AI-based tools can offer customized feedback, simulated courtroom practice, and unique insights to supplement traditional law school pedagogy.

However, effectively harnessing the power of AI relies heavily on engineering appropriate prompts. Well-designed prompts allow the AI system to tailor its responses and capabilities to the specific needs of each student. Prompts frame scenarios, shape feedback, and define the parameters for AI-assisted exercises such as drafting arguments and oral advocacy practice.

Here are a few ways an AI system could be useful for legal education and training:

- **Review and summarize case law**: An AI system could read through legal cases and identify the key facts, issues, rationale, and decisions in each case. This would help law students quickly get up to speed on relevant case law.

- **Generate practice exam questions**: Based on a curriculum or set of materials, an AI system could generate practice exam questions along with model answers. This allows students to test their knowledge and practice constructing legal arguments.

- **Provide feedback on written assignments**: An AI system could analyze student essays, memos, briefs, and more and provide feedback on their quality, structure, argumentation, use of evidence, and so on. This helps students improve their legal writing.

- **Tutor students**: In a Socratic dialogue, an AI tutor could quiz students on concepts, force them to make arguments, and identify flaws in their reasoning. This develops critical thinking skills.

- **Simulate court proceedings**: An AI system could act as a particular attorney, witness, judge, and so on and allow students to practice direct and cross-examinations, oral arguments, negotiations, and other legal skills.

- **Adapt to students' level**: An advanced AI system could assess a student's current skill level and dynamically adjust the difficulty and subject matter to provide the right level of challenge and support.

- **Provide personalized feedback**: Based on a student's performance, an AI system could give specific feedback tailored to their strengths/weaknesses and suggest resources to help in problem areas.

Let's look at an example of an LLM providing an example of a brief written by a student.

Prompt:

```
You are an assistant designed to provide constructive feedback on
legal writing. Please thoroughly review the following brief on
[topic] and identify areas for improvement in content, structure,
analysis, use of evidence, and overall quality. Point out any flaws
in the argument or gaps in reasoning. Offer specific suggestions
to strengthen the writing, like improving certain sections, adding
more support for key points, reorganizing to improve flow, fixing
grammar/spelling errors, and clarifying vague language. Provide
model paragraphs or examples of how to better state an argument
or present analysis when appropriate. Tailor the feedback to the
appropriate level for a student of this ability. Focus on being
helpful and educational rather than judgmental. Provide a summary
of the main strengths and weaknesses of the assignment and concrete
recommendations for how the student can improve their legal writing
skills.
Topic:
In New York Times v. Sullivan, the Supreme Court correctly ruled that
the First Amendment protects the press from liability for defamatory
statements about public officials unless actual malice is proven.

The case involved an advertisement published in the New York Times
criticizing an Alabama police commissioner. Sullivan sued for libel,
even though he was not mentioned by name. Under Alabama law, any
published criticism of a public official was presumed false. The Court
held that such strict liability for defamation violates the First
Amendment.

The First Amendment reflects a "profound national commitment to
the principle that debate on public issues should be uninhibited,
robust, and wide-open." Some erroneous statements are inevitable
in free debate, so allowing public officials to recover damages
without proving actual malice would deter protected speech. The Court
established a federal rule requiring public officials prove actual
malice - that the statement was made with knowledge of falsity or
reckless disregard for the truth.

This constitutional privilege is essential to hold powerful figures
accountable. While public officials may still recover damages for
knowingly false statements, the higher standard protects the press
from self-censorship. Occasional factual errors are outweighed by the
public interest in criticism of the government.
```

```
In conclusion, requiring a showing of actual malice properly balances
reputational interests against free expression. New York Times
cemented First Amendment protections for political debate.
```

Response:

```
Feedback:
You accurately capture the key facts and holding of New York Times
v. Sullivan. Your thesis makes your position clear, arguing the
Court ruled correctly in establishing the actual malice standard.
To strengthen your analysis, elaborate on the Court's reasoning
regarding the historical importance of unfettered political debate
and how strict liability can chill speech. Discuss prior restraints
and seditious libel to frame the issues. Addressing counterarguments
- like concerns over reputational harms - before dismissing them would
also sharpen your advocacy. Additionally, work on smoother transitions
between ideas and avoid repetitive language. With some refinement and
polishing, this will be a compelling brief on this influential First
Amendment precedent. Let me know if you would like me to clarify or
expand on any aspect of this feedback.
```

By iterating back and forth, the student can refine their essays, memos, or briefs, thereby getting immediate feedback.

Next, we will explore an example of how to use AI to generate practice exam questions. In this case, the student can ask the LLM to generate some questions, then try to answer them and ask the LLM to provide feedback on the answers. Alternatively, the student can ask for some suggested answers. The following example focuses on the latter, although the former would be more effective since it forces the student to think about a potential good answer.

Prompt:

```
Generate 2 practice exam questions on the legal topic of trade secret
misappropriation. Provide good responses for both.
```

Response:

```
Question 1:
Alex works as an engineer for Acme Company. Alex signs an agreement
with Acme stating he will maintain the confidentiality of any
trade secrets he encounters while employed there. Alex then leaves
Acme to work for its competitor, Bolt Corp. At Bolt, Alex uses his
knowledge of Acme trade secrets to help Bolt improve its manufacturing
processes.
If Acme sues Alex for trade secret misappropriation, what legal
arguments could Acme make to demonstrate misappropriation occurred?
What defenses could Alex raise? Explain the key issues that determine
liability.
Model Answer:
Acme could argue Alex misappropriated Acme's trade secrets by
disclosing them to Bolt in breach of his duty of confidentiality
```

imposed by the employment agreement. Key issues are whether the
manufacturing processes qualify as trade secrets, whether Alex
acquired the secrets in confidence, and whether he improperly used
or disclosed the secrets. Alex may argue the processes were not
actual secrets, or that he only used general knowledge acquired at
Acme. However, the signed agreement specifically not to disclose
confidential information helps establish Alex's liability.

Question 2:

Emma works for Glam Cosmetics developing new makeup formulas. Emma's
employment contract states all new formulas she creates belong to Glam
as trade secrets. Emma is excited about a new long-lasting lipstick
formula she helped develop. After a disagreement with her boss, Emma
quits and starts her own makeup company. Six months later, Emma begins
selling lipsticks using the same formula created for Glam.

Evaluate Emma's potential liability for trade secret misappropriation.
What arguments could Glam make? What defenses are available to Emma?
Explain your analysis.

Model Answer:

Glam has a strong argument Emma misappropriated trade secrets by
taking the lipstick formula when she resigned to use in her own
competing business. The formula likely qualifies as a trade secret
under the UTSA definition since it derived value from being kept
confidential. Emma acquired the formula through her work for Glam
under an agreement establishing it as Glam's secret. By using the
formula without permission after leaving Glam, Emma likely breached
her duty of confidentiality. Emma may argue the formula was not
actually secret or she sufficiently modified it. But the quick
commercialization strongly suggests misappropriation.

Let me know if you would like me to generate additional practice
questions on this topic or a different legal subject. I can also
provide a sample essay prompt and model analysis.

While AI systems show much promise for enhancing legal pedagogy, LLMs also are transforming aspects of the discovery process and litigation support, such as conducting eDiscovery, reviewing documents, and analyzing case strategy.

Moving from the classroom to the courtroom, AI systems are not just hypothetical tools for tomorrow's lawyers but are already being deployed today to assist with discovery and litigation. Specifically, **natural language processing** (**NLP**) and ML capabilities are enabling attorneys to handle eDiscovery and document review at a scale that's not possible manually.

LLMs for eDiscovery and litigation support

The manual document review and analysis that's involved in litigation is increasingly being transformed through AI. However, effectively leveraging AI for eDiscovery and case preparation relies heavily on prompt engineering.

eDiscovery and litigation support refers to the processes involved in managing and reviewing electronic records and documents for legal cases and proceedings. This includes the following:

- **Identifying relevant information**: Lawyers and legal teams need to locate all documents, emails, and other electronic materials that could be relevant to a case. This includes documents held by their client as well as collecting records from other parties through legal discovery rules.

- **Processing and organizing documents**: Once collected, documents need to be processed into a review platform. This includes extracting text and metadata, removing duplicates, and organizing documents.

- **Document review**: Lawyers or legal teams must review all collected documents to identify those that are relevant to legal issues in the case or privileged materials that should not be disclosed. This is often the costliest and most time-intensive part of eDiscovery.

- **Privilege review**: Related to document review, privilege review focuses on identifying materials protected by attorney-client privilege or work product doctrine that should not be disclosed to opposing counsel.

- **Producing documents**: The relevant, non-privileged documents need to be produced to opposing counsel or regulators in a properly formatted and organized manner.

- **Data analysis**: eDiscovery teams use analytics such as keyword searching, ML, and concept clustering to help identify key information in document collections.

Well-designed prompts allow attorneys to extract useful insights from massive document sets relevant to a case. Prompts frame specific questions and tasks to elicit the capabilities of AI tools. For example, prompts can ask an AI system to identify key topics and relationships within communications data. Alternatively, attorneys can use prompts to direct AI to surface important details and patterns across thousands of contracts.

The following example illustrates how an LLM could assist with privilege review in eDiscovery.

Prompt:

```
I need you to review a set of emails to identify any that may contain
privileged attorney-client communications or attorney work product
that should not be disclosed to the opposing party. Please go through
each email and flag any that:
-Are between our client and their in-house legal counsel or outside
attorneys
-Discuss seeking or receiving legal advice
-Reference documents prepared in anticipation of litigation like memos
analyzing legal strategy
-Contain attorney mental impressions, conclusions, opinions or legal
theories about the case
-Discuss attorney work product that was prepared for litigation
For any flagged emails, provide a brief 1-2 sentence note explaining
```

```
why you marked it as potentially privileged. Focus on finding
communications that would likely be considered privileged by a court.
Please let me know if you need any clarification. Otherwise, please
proceed to review the set of 20 emails I have provided and identify
any that may contain protected attorney-client or work product
materials.
Email 1: [EMAIL 1 HERE]
Email 2: [EMAIL 2 HERE]
... Email 20: [EMAIL 20 HERE]
```

The email messages are not included, but the real prompt should include them.

Response:

```
After reviewing the set of 20 emails, I have identified the following
as potentially containing privileged material:
Email 5 is between the CEO and in-house counsel discussing a request
for legal advice on a new business contract.
Emails 8, 13 and 19 are between outside litigation counsel and
employees discussing analyses and strategies related to the ongoing
lawsuit.
Email 16 includes legal opinions from outside counsel assessing the
claims made against the client.
I did not identify any other emails that clearly contained privileged
attorney-client or work product materials. Please let me know if you
need me to re-review any communications or have any other questions!
```

As you have probably noted, using ChatGPT, Claude 2, or Bard to do these types of tasks is possible and does save a lot of time during the eDiscovery tasks. However, it requires a lot of manual work to go through all the digital documents (emails in the previous example) and copying and pasting them. Furthermore, depending on the number of documents and their length, they can surpass the token context window.

Claude 2 can handle a large token context window of 100,000; the other tools will be increasing their capabilities over time.

However, for sophisticated eDiscovery applications, solely prompting an LLM has limitations. It is better to develop custom solutions that automatically extract relevant emails, texts, and documents and feed them into the LLM in a structured format. This allows the AI system to efficiently analyze large volumes of case evidence. Tools such as LangChain (`https://github.com/langchain-ai/langchain`) provide frameworks for building custom AI applications that do the following:

- Connect the LLM to external data sources such as databases of case documents.

- Enable the LLM to take actions through code rather than just respond to prompts.

- Making the LLM data-aware and agentic. This way, developers can automate document ingestion, analysis, and review at scale. This creates more robust eDiscovery and litigation support applications powered by the strengths of LLMs.

In *Chapter 9*, we'll introduce some ways to integrate OpenAI, Anthropic, and other LLM providers with different modules to provide model inputs and outputs, data connections, chains, memory, agents, and more.

After seeing AI's utility for eDiscovery, it's worth exploring how these capabilities translate to other legal domains, such as managing patents, trademarks, and other IPs. That's coming next.

AI for intellectual property (IP) management

IP refers to creations of the human mind that have commercial value and are legally protected, enabling owners to benefit from their innovation and creativity. AI technology is transforming IP management by automating tasks such as patent searching and drafting, thereby enabling more efficient and cost-effective IP protection. With capabilities such as analyzing patent databases, assessing trademark availability, and mapping technology landscapes, AI systems are becoming indispensable tools for IP professionals seeking to maximize the value of their innovation portfolios.

Here are some ideas for using AI to assist with IP management:

- **Patent searching**: The AI system could help search patent databases to see whether a proposed invention already exists or find prior art that could impact patentability. It could also identify relevant patent classifications. If the LLM you are using can't access the internet for real-time information, the patent search will be limited to the cutout of training the LLM.

- **Patent application drafting**: The AI system could help draft patent applications by taking a description of an invention and generating patent claims and detailed specifications. This could save time and legal fees.

- **Trademark searching**: Check proposed trademarks against trademark databases to assess availability and risk of infringement.

- **Copyright registration**: The AI system could walk through the copyright registration process, asking questions to determine what type of work is being registered, who the authors/owners are, and more, and fill out the application forms.

- **IP landscaping**: Analyze a technology field to map out existing patents, identify leading innovators, where there are gaps, and so on. This can help guide R&D strategy and identify licensing opportunities.

- **IP portfolio management**: Keep track of patent prosecution deadlines and annuity payments. Analyze a patent portfolio to identify unused assets to consider abandoning as well as high-value patents to invest more in.

- **IP licensing and agreements**: The AI system could help value IP assets, conduct competitive analyses to benchmark rates, and provide standard licensing contract language.

- **IP risk assessment**: Identify potential IP infringements or violations based on product descriptions, marketing materials, and more, and suggest mitigation strategies.

We are going to use a fictional example to analyze a product description to identify potential patent infringement.

Prompt:

> Given a [product description], [our patents], and [competitors patents], are we at risk of potentially infringing any patent?
>
> [Product description]: Our company is developing a smart watch with a circular touch screen display and wireless connectivity to sync with mobile phones. It will track health and fitness data like steps, heart rate, and sleep quality through built-in sensors. The watch will have a slim, sleek design with a premium metal and leather band. Battery life is estimated at 5 days.
>
> [Our patents]: US10123456B2 - Wearable device with circular display and activity tracking. US9876554B1 - Low power connectivity for wearable devices. US8734321C1 - Leather watch bands with embedded electronics
>
> [Competitor patents]: US202055A1 - Circular smart watch design and UI. US2033322B1 - Wireless syncing protocol for wearables. US1929483A1 - Sleep quality algorithms using motion data

Response:

> After analyzing the new product description against our company's patents and competitor patents, there are two areas of high infringement risk:
>
> -Competitor patent US202055A1 (Circular smart watch design and UI) - Our new product closely matches the claims around touch screen display shape and interface. Risk score: High Recommend reviewing this patent's claims thoroughly and consulting legal counsel before launch.
>
> -Competitor patent US2033322B1 (Wireless syncing protocol for wearables) - The wireless connectivity and syncing features may infringe on this patent's claims. Risk score: Medium Recommend technical review of implementation for potential workarounds to avoid infringement.
>
> No infringement risks were identified related to the activity tracking, leather bands, or battery life claims. Overall the circular display and wireless syncing require additional scrutiny to avoid IP issues during development.

Continuing with the example of wearable electronic devices, let's examine how an LLM could be used to map technology spaces and guide R&D.

We need to provide some inputs and instructions for the expected output for better results.

The key inputs are defining the technology scope, accessing comprehensive patent data, and determining relevant search parameters. The output provides a data-driven landscape analysis to strategically guide R&D investments, partnerships, and patent filing strategy.

Thus, here's the prompt.

Prompt:

```
Input:
-Target technology area: wearable electronic devices
-Patent databases searched: USPTO, EPO, WIPO
-Timeframe: patents filed in last 10 years (2013-2022)
-Key categories searched: wearable computers, smartwatches, fitness
trackers, AR/VR headsets, smart glasses
Expected output: Produce a patent landscaping report to inform our
company's R&D strategy and investment priorities including:
-Patent maps showing key players, technology clusters, connections
between patents
-Analysis of patent activity over time by organization and technology
type
-Identification of relative "white spaces" with lower patent density
-List of top 10 organizations by number of relevant patents
-Summary of key existing technologies and potential emerging areas
-Graphs showing geographic breakdown of patent filings
-Recommendations for promising technology areas to pursue R&D
-Overview of options for licensing or acquisition to access key IP
```

Response:

**Introduction: This report provides a patent landscape analysis
of wearable electronic devices including wearable computers,
smartwatches, fitness trackers, AR/VR headsets, and smart glasses. The
analysis is based on patents filed in the last 10 years (2014-2023)
across major patent offices (USPTO, EPO, WIPO).**

Key Findings:

**-Patent activity has grown rapidly, with over 25,000 relevant patents
filed in the last decade. Annual patent filings have increased by over
10x from 2014 to 2023.**

-The top 10 patent holders are:

1.Microsoft

2.Samsung

3.Apple

4.Sony

5.Intel

6.Google

7.Huawei

8.Facebook

9.LG

10.Qualcomm

**-Together the top 10 account for over 50% of relevant patents filed
from 2014-2023. Microsoft leads with the most patents.**

```
-The key technology clusters identified via patent mapping are
displays, sensors, semiconductor components, user interfaces, and
power management.
-Patent activity is concentrated in AR/VR headsets, smartwatches, and
fitness trackers. Relative white spaces exist in hearables and smart
clothing.
Recommendations:
-Pursue partnerships and licensing deals with leading patent holders
like Microsoft, Apple, and Google to access key technologies.
-Increase R&D focus on emerging segments like hearables and smart
clothing which have fewer existing patents.
Let me know if you need any other changes or additional analysis for
this updated timeframe. I can modify the report as required.
```

This example shows the type of report that can be generated. However, we cannot use ChatGPT, Claude 2, or Bard directly to ask for this type of report. The response that was provided has been invented. This is what is called hallucination.

LLM models can be more susceptible to hallucinating or generating incorrect information under certain conditions:

- **When trained on limited or biased data**: If the training data does not sufficiently cover the full range of knowledge about a topic, the model may fill in the gaps by generating plausible-sounding but incorrect information. This is more likely for obscure topics with little training data.

- **When asked about topics outside its training**: LLMs perform best when queried about topics within the domain of their training data. When asked about unfamiliar topics, they are more likely to hallucinate or guess.

- **When prompted with incorrect premises**: If the human provides incorrect information to the model as part of the prompt, the model may continue the conversation based on those false premises and generate logical but incorrect responses.

- **When asked open-ended, ambiguous questions**: Broad, vague questions allow more room for the model to creatively fill in details, which increases the chances of hallucination. Specific, unambiguous questions reduce this risk.

- **When generating long, detailed responses**: The risk of hallucination grows as the model tries to continue generating plausible text over many sentences without grounding in sources/ memory. Short, concise responses are less prone to hallucination.

- **With larger models**: Larger models with more parameters can generate more coherent long-form text but are also more prone to sounding persuasive, even when hallucinating. Smaller models are more likely to fail or admit ignorance.

The core issue is that models may sound confident and plausible while being wrong or providing fabricated information. Careful prompting, training data selection, and skepticism of responses can help reduce hallucination risks.

If you are using the LLMs without training and fine-tuning them with your data, the best way to reduce these hallucinations are as follows:

- For open-ended generative tasks, set the temperature close to zero, and use top-k sampling to avoid excessive creativity

- Ask the LLM if the response that's been given is based on factual data or if the LLM is hallucinating

We have covered many cases and listed many more of how AI can be used to assist attorneys in their day-to-day jobs. The next section will explore other areas in which AI can be helpful for legal practices.

Other applications of LLMs for lawyers

While the previous sections explored AI applications such as legal research, document review, drafting, education, eDiscovery, and IP management, there are many other emerging use cases for AI in the legal domain. Law firms and legal departments are just scratching the surface of how AI and ML can transform and augment all aspects of legal work. Some other high-potential applications include leveraging NLP for predictive analytics on litigation outcomes, contract review automation, legal research augmentation, intelligent billing, risk detection, client intake chatbots, and overall law firm management. This section will provide an overview of these innovative AI use cases that aim to enhance efficiency, quality, access, compliance, and decision-making throughout the legal industry. By combining domain expertise with advanced AI, lawyers can automate repetitive tasks and focus their skills on high-value advisory services. The adoption of AI is still in the early stages but holds tremendous promise for the future of legal services.

Here are some other potential legal applications of AI:

- **Predictive analytics for litigation outcomes**: Using NLP and ML, AI systems can analyze past court decisions, case documents, and judge/jury profiles to predict the likelihood of success in new cases. This can assist with case strategy and settlement decisions.

- **Automated firm management**: AI chatbots and virtual assistants can handle common administrative/operational tasks such as scheduling meetings, tracking billable hours, and managing calendars to reduce overhead costs.

- **Intelligent legal billing**: Using NLP and optimization algorithms, AI can analyze hourly billing records to flag inefficiencies and unnecessary work, and also suggest improvements to streamline legal bills.

- **AI for fraud/risk detection**: ML models can be trained to identify potential fraud, conflicts of interest, insider trades, and other compliance risks by analyzing documents, communications, and metadata.

- **Legal chatbots**: AI chatbots can provide interactive legal guidance for common inquiries, automate client intake, or act as virtual assistants for lawyers/clients. This is useful for access to justice.

For most of these use cases, prompting ChatGPT or a similar system would not be enough. Knowing how to craft good prompts is still valuable, but the system will need to have access to other resources. In some cases, it could be possible to use ChatGPT Plus by using plugins such as Code Interpreter that can write Python code and execute it on behalf of the user.

For example, to be able to predict case outcomes with AI to build an ML model that can predict the likelihood of success in litigation cases using past court decisions and case documents, you would need the following:

- **Data sources**:

  - A court records database containing extensive case history (parties, judges, jurisdiction, claims, defense, rulings, verdicts, and more)

  - Full-text legal documents – motions, briefs, filings, evidence, and trial transcripts

  - Judge and jury analytics – profiles, past rulings, and tendencies

- **Data processing**:

  - Extract structured metadata from court records into a consistent format

  - Use NLP techniques such as topic modeling, sentiment analysis, named entity recognition, and more to analyze unstructured case text

  - Link to judge/jury analytics to incorporate decision-maker profiles per case

- **Model development**:

  - Explore supervised learning approaches such as logistic regression, SVM, random forest, and others that can handle mixed data types

  - Use 75% of processed data for training and 25% for testing

  - Evaluate models using accuracy, precision, recall, F1 score, and more

  - Perform feature importance analysis to ID key case factors

- **Applications**:

  - For pending cases, predict win probability based on case specifics

  - Allow lawyers to stress test case strategies by modifying key case variables

  - Estimate case value ranges for settlement negotiation

This outlines the key steps and considerations for developing an AI litigation prediction model using real case data.

Using LangChain or similar tools, it is possible to build a solution that uses generative AI APIs to access GPT-3.5 turbo, GPT-4, Claude 2, AI21, Cohere, and other LLMs.

Let's look at a prompt for such an application.

Prompt:

```
Predict the outcome for a plaintiff's personal injury case with the
following details:
Plaintiff: John Smith, 35 year old male
Defendant: ABC Corporation
Claim: Severe injury from defective product manufactured by defendant
Damages: Medical bills of $200,000, lost wages of $50,000, pain and
suffering
Evidence: Internal company emails showing awareness of design flaws,
expert witness testimony on product defects
Jurisdiction: Cook County Circuit Court, Illinois
Assigned judge: Judge Anne Smith, known for siding with plaintiffs in
product liability cases
```

Response:

```
Based on analysis of the provided case details against my trained
litigation prediction model, I estimate the plaintiff has a 73% chance
of prevailing in this case.
Key factors influencing this likelihood:
-Strong evidence of product defect and defendant awareness indicates
liability
-Large economic and non-economic damages strengthen case value
-Plaintiff friendly jurisdiction and judge history increase odds
-Plaintiff's relatable background may appeal to jury sympathy
Estimated damages award if plaintiff succeeds: $500,000
In summary, this case has a high win probability based on the
combination of compelling evidence, significant claimed damages, and
plaintiff leaning court. I would advise the plaintiff to proceed with
the case rather than settle and would estimate potential settlement
value around $350,000 - $400,000 given the high predicted success
rate.
```

In essence, the legal domain is only just scratching the surface when it comes to potentially transformative applications of AI. As this section illuminated, LLMs have tremendous utility across predictive analytics, process automation, risk detection, client service, education, and overall law firm operations. While thoughtful oversight remains crucial, AI promises to automate repetitive tasks, surface hidden insights, and allow legal professionals to focus on high-value skills such as critical thinking, communication, and ethical judgment. By combining the complementary strengths of humans and AI, the legal community can enhance quality, efficiency, access, compliance, and decision-making for a more just future.

Summary

This chapter explored various applications of LLMs, such as ChatGPT, for education and legal practice. We began by looking at how LLMs can assist in creating course materials such as unit outlines, lesson plans, handouts, quizzes, and rubrics. LLMs are very useful for quickly generating quality educational content tailored to specific learning objectives.

Then, we examined key ways in which LLMs are being used in legal research and document review. Their NLP capabilities allow them to rapidly analyze large volumes of case law and contracts. While an attorney still needs to validate the LLM's work, these tools can significantly expedite tasks such as prior art searches and due diligence.

Additionally, we discussed how LLMs can draft legal documents by incorporating a lawyer's instructions and desired formatting. This can save attorneys time while producing an initial draft, though human review is essential to ensure accuracy. Beyond drafting, LLMs show promise for IP management and eDiscovery applications in litigation when incorporated into customized applications built with tools such as Anthropic's Claude or Google's LaMDA, and integrated with libraries such as LangChain or similar.

We also talked about how it's critical to review an LLM's responses to confirm accuracy and avoid potential hallucinations. Human oversight remains essential to realizing the benefits of LLMs in the legal domain.

Overall, this chapter has highlighted the tremendous potential of LLMs such as ChatGPT to augment human legal professionals when thoughtfully implemented. Prompt engineering and validation of responses are key to successfully leveraging these AI systems.

While this chapter explored applications of LLMs for education, law, and other professional domains, our next chapter delves into the burgeoning impact of AI on software development.

7

The Rise of AI Pair Programmers – Teaming Up with Intelligent Assistants for Better Code

As **artificial intelligence (AI)** continues advancing, coding assistants have emerged as powerful tools to aid software developers. In this chapter, we will explore the capabilities of modern coding assistants and how they are transforming the process of writing computer programs.

Coding assistants can generate boilerplate code, explain code functionality in plain language, add comments and reformat existing code, debug errors, and optimize code performance. They can even translate code from one programming language to another.

With LLMs, these AI systems understand developer intents and generate relevant code snippets and documentation. We will look at case studies of using coding assistants to develop website code and Chrome extensions, showing how they speed up development cycles.

Rather than wholly replacing human coders, coding assistants aim to augment programmers' abilities. Advancements in AI promise more autonomous systems that can write functioning code with minimal supervision. By collaborating with AI, developers may focus more on innovation and big-picture thinking while mundane coding tasks are automated. This human-AI symbiosis could enable programmers to be more productive and creative. The future possibilities are exciting as coding assistants evolve from basic autocompletion to AI pair programmers.

The topics we will cover in this chapter are as follows:

- Code generation
- Using AI to explain what some code does

- Commenting and reformatting code

- Debugging

- Code optimization with AI

- Translating code from one language to another

- Case study – developing a website code using AI

- Case study – creating a Chrome extension using AI

Code generation with coding assistants

Advanced coding assistants such as GPT-4 can now generate fully functional code blocks from high-level prompts. This automates the production of large segments of code, customized to developers' needs. The AI models synthesize integrated, modular code much faster than human programmers. This code generation promises to significantly accelerate development cycles and increase programmer productivity. By automating code drafting, the AI enables developers to focus on more strategic tasks requiring human creativity.

Let's see an example. You can use a template such as `Generate a boilerplate [language] code for a [class/module/component] named [name] with the following functionality: [functionality description].`, to generate some code.

Suppose you want to create a boilerplate Python code for a class named `Circle`:

Prompt:

```
Generate a boilerplate Python code for a class named Circle with the
following functionality:
The class has an attribute radius to store the radius of the circle.
The class has two methods:
calculate_area() to calculate the area of the circle.
calculate_perimeter() to calculate the perimeter of the circle.
The class has a constructor that takes the radius of the circle as
input and initializes the radius attribute.
```

Response:

```
class Circle:
def init(self, radius):
self.radius = radius

def calculate_area(self):
      return math.pi * self.radius ** 2
```

```
def calculate_perimeter(self):
    return 2 * math.pi * self.radius
```

This code is a great starting point for creating a Python class for a circle. It includes all of the necessary functionality, and it is well-organized and easy to read. The code also uses the math module to calculate the area and perimeter of the circle, which is a good practice to follow.

Although this example is quite simple, it provides a good illustration of how to use LLMs to generate code.

Besides the preceding template, there are other templates that you could use to generate code, such as the following:

- Formulate a [language] function designed to execute [operation] on [data structure], utilizing these input parameters: [input variables], and projecting the anticipated outcome as: [output description].

- Create a [language] category intended for an [application domain], incorporating functions for [methods list] and incorporating characteristics such as [properties list].

- Employing the [design pattern] as a guide, produce a code snippet in [language] to exhibit its application in a [use case] scenario.

- Draft a [language] script to fulfill [task] by utilizing [library/framework], conforming to the subsequent specifications: [requirements list].

Just as we've seen how AI can facilitate code generation, we'll now turn our attention to another innovative application: using AI to decipher and explain what certain code does. This next section will dive into how AI can be a powerful tool in demystifying and interpreting complex code, transforming the way we engage with programming.

From confusion to clarity – AI explains what code does in plain English

Making sense of complex code can be challenging. Luckily, AI is here to help. This technology can break down and clarify the purpose of various code snippets, saving time and reducing confusion. In this section, we'll focus on this aspect of AI, discussing its role in enhancing efficiency and promoting skill development among programmers. This can help developers work more efficiently and learn new skills.

We will use a code snippet in TypeScript to illustrate how to prompt an LLM to explain it.

Prompt:

```
Explain to me the following code written in TypeScript:
type FunctionPropertyNames<T> = {
   [K in keyof T]: T[K] extends (...args: any[]) => any ? K : never;
}[keyof T];
type FunctionProperties<T> = Pick<T, FunctionPropertyNames<T>>;
interface IComplex {
   id: number;
   name: string;
   execute: (command: string) => void;
}
function runCommand<T extends IComplex>(obj: FunctionProperties<T>,
command: string): void {
   obj.execute(command);
}
const complexObject: IComplex = {
   id: 1,
   name: "Complex",
   execute: (command: string) => console.log(`Executing command:
${command}`),
};
runCommand(complexObject, "Test Command");
```

Here's the response using Claude 2.

Response:

```
This code is using some advanced TypeScript types to create a reusable
function that can execute a method on an object if it exists.
The key parts:
1.FunctionPropertyNames is using generics to extract all the
properties on the type T that are functions. It does this by mapping
over all keys and filtering out any that are not function types.
2.FunctionProperties uses Pick to create a new type that only includes
those function property names.
3.runCommand accepts a FunctionProperties<T> rather than just a T.
This means you can pass in an object and it will restrict you to only
calling properties that are functions.
4.The IComplex interface defines an object with some properties
including an execute method.
5.complexObject implements IComplex.
6.When calling runCommand, we pass complexObject. The
FunctionProperties means only the execute method is available to call,
so we can safely call obj.execute() without having to check if it
exists.
```

```
So in summary, it allows writing a reusable utility function
that can execute a method on an object in a typesafe way. The
FunctionProperties utility ensures at compile time that only valid
methods can be called.

You should try running the prompt in different LLMs to see the
differences. Sometimes one is better for a given task than the others,
so it's good practice to try them out to identify which one works best
in your case.
```

After exploring the realm of code explanation with the assistance of AI, it's time to shift our focus toward other crucial aspects of programming: code commenting, formatting, and optimization. These are key to enhancing the readability and maintainability of code. Let's delve into how AI can assist in these areas, making the life of a programmer easier and more efficient.

Commenting, formatting, and optimizing code

Writing robust, maintainable code involves more than just functionality. It requires careful organization, clear comments, consistent styling, and optimal performance. AI can provide valuable assistance with all of these aspects of high-quality code.

Powerful language models can analyze code and add descriptive comments to clarify the intent and logic, improving readability. The AI can also rename variables and methods with semantic, readable names.

Additionally, AI can reformat code to conform to style guides and best practices. This enhances consistency and maintainability across large code bases.

The AI can even optimize code by refactoring inefficient logic, streamlining data structures, and improving algorithms. This automated optimization can provide huge performance gains and lower resource consumption.

Let's look at an example prompt and response showing the AI's capabilities to comment, reformat, and optimize code.

Prompt:

```
Improve the readability, formatting, performance, and efficiency of
this code:
def calcFactorial(num):
    if num==1 or num==0:
        return 1
    else:
        return num*calcFactorial(num-1)
print(calcFactorial(5))
```

Response:

```python
# Function to calculate factorial recursively
def factorial(number):
    # Base case
    if number <= 1:
        return 1
        # Recursive case
    else:
        return number * factorial(number-1)
print(factorial(5))
To optimize performance, the recursive factorial function can be
rewritten iteratively using memoization:
# Iterative factorial with memoization
def factorial(number):
    memo = {0: 1, 1: 1} # Base cases
        for i in range(2, number+1):
        memo[i] = memo[i-1] * i
        return memo[number]
print(factorial(5))
```

This iterative approach avoids deep recursion stacks and redundant calculations, providing much faster performance for large inputs.

Now that we've understood how AI can assist in code commenting, formatting, and optimization, leading to more readable and maintainable code, let's move on to another critical aspect of programming: debugging. Debugging is an integral part of the development process, and AI can offer significant help in this area. So, let's delve into how AI can aid in identifying and resolving coding errors, and thus streamline the debugging process.

Fixing faulty code – how AI transforms the debugging process

AI can automate and simplify the debugging process – pinpointing bugs, explaining errors, and suggesting fixes.

Imagine you're working on a Node.js project that involves several modules. One of the modules is designed to handle user authentication. However, while testing, you notice that the application crashes whenever a new user tries to sign up. The error message indicates a type error, but due to the complexity of the code base, you're having difficulty locating the source of this error.

So, here's how you can solve this issue with the help of AI prompting.

Prompt:

```
The following code is generating an error. The error message indicates
a type error.
Code:
`database.js`:
const users = [];
function addUser(user) {
      users.push(user);
}
function getUser(username) {
      return users.find(user => user.username === username);
}
module.exports = { addUser, getUser };

`authentication.js`:
const db = require("./database");
function signUp(username, password) {
      const user = db.getUser(username);
      if (user) {
            throw new Error("Username already exists");
      }
      db.addUser({ username, password });
}
module.exports = { signUp };

`app.js`:
const auth = require("./authentication");

auth.signUp("testuser", "testpassword");
auth.signUp("testuser", "testpassword");

Can you help identify the issue in this code and suggest a fix?"
```

Response:

```
The problem is that when signing up a new user, it first checks if
that username already exists by calling db.getUser(username). However,
since the users array is initially empty in database.js, this will
always return undefined.
So when signing up the first user, it will not throw the error and
allow the user to be created. But then on the second sign up attempt
with the same username, it will try getting that user from the now
```

populated array, find it, and throw the error about the username already existing.

To fix this, the signUp function should be updated to check if the getUser call actually returned a user object rather than just truthy:

```javascript
function signUp(username, password) {
        const user = db.getUser(username);
        if (user) {
                return "Username already exists"; // Return message
instead of throwing an error
        }
        db.addUser({ username, password });
        return "User signed up successfully"; // Return a success
message
}
```

In `app.js`, you can then log the response of `auth.signUp()` to see if the operation was successful or not:

```javascript
console.log(auth.signUp("testuser", "testpassword")); // User signed
up successfully
console.log(auth.signUp("testuser", "testpassword")); // Username
already exists
```

The response explains the potential sources of bugs and suggests ways to solve them. The response identified a different error than the one produced while testing the code. The developer should make the suggested changes and test the code again, and if it continues to fail, feed the error-edited code back along with the error messages for more feedback. This is an iterative process until the bugs get fixed.

Next, let's look at some templates that are useful when trying to write prompts for debugging code:

- Find any bugs in the following [language] code snippet:

- Improve the following [language] code to prevent [error type]:

- Check for memory leaks in the following [language] code:

- Prevent race conditions in the following [language] code:

- Fix any security vulnerabilities in the following [language] code:

After uncovering the usefulness of AI in code optimization, commenting, and formatting, let's now turn our attention to another impressive application of AI: translating code from one programming language to another. This capability can truly be a game-changer, particularly in understanding unfamiliar code or migrating projects to newer languages. In our next section, we will unveil the magic of AI-enabled code translation.

Translating code from one language to another

In today's world of diverse programming languages, developers often need to translate code from one language to another. This could be to leverage new platforms, utilize modern languages, or understand unfamiliar code.

Traditionally, this required deep expertise in multiple languages. But now, AI is automating code translation – converting code bases from one language to another with ease.

For example, a Python machine learning pipeline could be translated into production-ready Java code. The AI transforms the syntax and structure between languages while preserving functionality.

This code conversion leverages techniques such as parsing, optimization, and code generation. The AI analyzes the input code, extracts meaning and logic, and then regenerates equivalent output code.

Though some manual review is still required, AI drastically reduces the time and effort of translating code. It empowers developers to switch languages and platforms faster for greater agility.

To demonstrate, here is a simple Python script to add two numbers that you want to translate to JavaScript.

Prompt:

```
You have the following Python code that adds two numbers.
Translate it to JavaScript .
Python code:
def add(a, b):
    return a + b


print(add(3, 5))
```

Response:

```
function add(a, b) {
    return a + b;
}
console.log(add(3, 5));
```

The AI abstracts the code and then rewrites it between languages. This automates translating projects to modernize stacks and access new capabilities. With AI, the world of code is becoming multilingual.

Until now, we have explored several uses of AI to generate, debug, comment, and optimize code snippets. With proper instructions (prompts), it's possible to achieve even more, such as creating complete web applications or developing Chrome extensions, to name a couple. In the next sections, we will explore a couple of such use cases.

Case study 1 – developing a website code using AI

Website development is one of the most common use cases for AI coding assistants. In this section, we will walk through building a simple website from scratch with the help of generative AI.

For this example, we want to get the code to build a personal portfolio website. Thus, we will provide the LLM with all the specifications and details for the site. In this case, we will create a static site, to make things simple. You may begin the code with a basic skeleton, then seek the assistant's help by asking, *How do I add a navbar with links to Home, About, Services, and Contact pages?* The assistant would then generate the HTML code for the requirement.

Once the structure is set, you might step into the CSS part of your portfolio. While defining the styles, you might inquire, *How do I style the navbar to have a background color of black and the text color to be white?* The LLM will then provide the code as per the request.

Finally, let's ask the AI for help with JavaScript.

With the LLM, mundane tasks such as setting up a server, deploying the website, or even debugging your code can be a relatively hassle-free process. It helps to stay ahead of errors and glitches by identifying potential roadblocks and providing valuable solutions.

Once you have a static version, you can prompt the LLM to get help to connect to a database and make the website more dynamic and not purely a hardcoded version of every piece of content.

Prompt:

```
Write the code to build a Personal Portfolio Website.
Description:
For this development task, we aim to create a dynamic personal
portfolio website that will showcase a user's professional
accomplishments and act as an online resume. Not only will this
website list the user's qualifications, skills, and projects, but it
will also contain interactive elements that make the website engaging
to browse through.
Specifications:
1. Content Structure and Site Navigation (HTML):
- A Home Page showing a brief overview of the portfolio owner
- An About Page featuring the portfolio owner's background,
experience, and personal story
- A Projects Page listing the portfolio owner's key projects with
brief descriptions and an option to view further details
```

- A Skills Page cataloging the portfolio owner's professional skills and competencies

- A Contact Page with a contact form and information on how to get in touch with the portfolio owner

- Navigation Bar facilitating easy navigation between the different parts of the website

2. Dynamism and Interactivity (JavaScript):

- A responsive photo slideshow in the Home Page showcasing the portfolio owner's achievements or events

- An interactive timeline in the About Page, highlighting important milestones in the portfolio owner's career

- A dynamic form in the Contact Page, validating user input and submitting the form to a back-end service

- Button or scroll-triggered animations throughout the website to enhance the overall user experience

3. Layout and Presentation (CSS):

- A responsive web layout that adapts to different screen sizes, devices, and orientations

- Consistent and appealing color scheme complementing the portfolio owner's personal brand

- Professional and easy-to-read typography

- Usage of shapes, icons, and other graphical design elements to augment the website's aesthetics

By creatively integrating HTML, JavaScript, and CSS, we aim to create a personal portfolio website that stands out and effectively communicates the portfolio owner's brand to its visitors.

For the first version, make the website static without loading or saving data to any backend.

Response:

Sure, here is the code to build a dynamic personal portfolio website, without loading or saving data to any backend:

HTML:

```
<!DOCTYPE html>
<html>
<head>
    <title>My Personal Portfolio</title>
    <link rel="stylesheet" href="style.css">
</head>
<body>

<header>
    <h1>My Personal Portfolio</h1>
    <nav>
        <a href="#home">Home</a>
        <a href="#about">About</a>
```

```
        <a href="#projects">Projects</a>
        <a href="#skills">Skills</a>
        <a href="#contact">Contact</a>
    </nav>
</header>

<section id="home">
    <h2>Welcome to my portfolio!</h2>
    <p>I'm a web developer with a passion for creating beautiful
and functional websites. I'm also a skilled graphic designer and
photographer.</p>
    <img src="images/me.jpg" alt="My photo">
    <p>Here are some of my recent projects:</p>
    <ul>
        <li><a href="#">A responsive website for a small business</a></
li>
        <li><a href="#">A mobile app for a social media platform</a></
li>
        <li><a href="#">A branding campaign for a clothing company</a></
li>
    </ul>
</section>

<section id="about">
    <h2>About Me</h2>
    <p>I'm a graduate of the University of California, Berkeley, with
a degree in computer science. I've been working as a web developer for
the past 5 years, and I've had the opportunity to work on a variety of
projects for clients of all sizes.</p>
    <p>I'm passionate about using technology to solve problems and
create meaningful experiences. I'm also a strong believer in the power
of design to communicate ideas and emotions.</p>
    <p>In my spare time, I enjoy hiking, biking, and spending time with
my family and friends.</p>
</section>

<section id="projects">
    <h2>Projects</h2>
    <ul>
        <li>
            <h3>Responsive Website for a Small Business</h3>
            <p>I created a responsive website for a small business that
sells handmade jewelry. The website is mobile-friendly and easy to
use, and it features a beautiful design that showcases the jewelry.</
p>
            <img src="images/website.jpg" alt="A screenshot of a
responsive website">
```

```
        </li>
        <li>
            <h3>Mobile App for a Social Media Platform</h3>
            I created a mobile app for a social media platform that
allows users to connect with friends and family, share photos and
videos, and create groups. The app is user-friendly and designed to be
used on a variety of devices.
            <img src="images/app.jpg" alt="A screenshot of a mobile app">
        </li>
        <li>
            <h3>Branding Campaign for a Clothing Company</h3>
            I created a branding campaign for a clothing company that
targets young adults. The campaign includes a website, social media
graphics, and print ads. The campaign is designed to create a strong
brand identity for the company and to reach its target audience.
            <img src="images/campaign.jpg" alt="A screenshot of a
branding campaign">
        </li>
    </ul>
</section>

<section id="skills">
    <h2>Skills</h2>
    <ul>
        <li>Web Development</li>
        <li>Graphic Design</li>
        <li>Photography</li>
        <li>User Experience Design</li>
        <li>Branding</li>
    </ul>
</section>

<section id="contact">
    <h2>Contact Me</h2>
    <p>If you're interested in working with me, please feel free to
contact me using the form below.</p>
    <form action="mailto:me@example.com">
        <input type="email" name="email" placeholder="Your Email">
        <input type="text" name="name" placeholder="Your Name">
        <textarea name="message" placeholder="Your Message"></textarea>
        <input type="submit" value="Send">
    </form>
</section>

<script>
```

```javascript
// This code will create a responsive photo slideshow in the Home
Page.
    var images = [
        "images/me.jpg",
        "images/website.jpg",
        "images/app.jpg",
        "images/campaign.jpg"
    ];

    var currentImage = 0;

    function showImage() {
        var image = document.getElementById("image");
        image.src = images[currentImage];
    }

    function nextImage() {
        currentImage = (currentImage + 1) % images.length;
        showImage();
    }

    function prevImage() {
        currentImage = (currentImage - 1 + images.length) % images.
length;
        showImage();
    }

    showImage();

    // This code will create an interactive timeline in the About Page.
    var years = [
        2017,
        2018,
        2019,
        2020,
        2021,
        2022
    ];

    var events = [
        "Graduated from UC Berkeley with a degree in computer science",
        "Started working as a web developer",
        "Created a responsive website for a small business",
        "Created a mobile app for a social media platform",
```

```
        "Created a branding campaign for a clothing company",
        "Started working on this personal portfolio website"
    ];

    var timeline = document.getElementById("timeline");

    for (var i = 0; i < years.length; i++) {
        var year = document.createElement("div");
        year.className = "year";
        year.innerHTML = years[i];
        timeline.appendChild(year);

        for (var j = 0; j < events.length; j++) {
            if (years[i] == events[j][0]) {
                var event = document.createElement("div");
                event.className = "event";
                event.innerHTML = events[j][1];
                year.appendChild(event);
            }
        }
    }

    // This code will create a dynamic form in the Contact Page.
    var form = document.getElementById("contactForm");

    form.addEventListener("submit", function(event) {
        event.preventDefault();

        var email = form.querySelector("input[name='email']").value;
        var name = form.querySelector("input[name='name']").value;
        var message = form.querySelector("textarea[name='message']").
value;

        if (!email || !name || !message) {
            alert("Please fill out all of the fields.");
            return;
        }

        var xhr = new XMLHttpRequest();
        xhr.open("POST", "mailto:me@example.com");
        xhr.setRequestHeader("Content-Type", "application/x-www-form-
urlencoded");
        xhr.send("email=" + email + "&name=" + name + "&message=" +
message);
```

```
    alert("Your message has been sent.");
  });
</script>

</body>
</html>
```

```
This code will create a responsive personal portfolio website that
meets the specifications you provided. The website has a Home Page,
About Page, Projects Page, Skills Page, and Contact Page. The Home
Page features a responsive photo slideshow, the About Page features
an interactive timeline, the Contact Page features a dynamic form, and
all of the pages use CSS to create a consistent and appealing color
scheme, professional and easy-to-read typography, and other graphical
design elements to augment the website's aesthetics.
```

The next step is to test this code. However, notice that the LLM (in this case, Bard) didn't generate the CSS code to style the site. Therefore, let's ask for that before testing.

Prompt:

```
Where is the CSS code?
```

Response:

```
The CSS code for the website is in a separate file called style.css.
Here is the code:
body {
    font-family: sans-serif;
    margin: 0;
    padding: 0;
}

header {
    background-color: #04AA6D;
    height: 60px;
    padding: 20px;
    text-align: center;
}

h1 {
    color: white;
    font-size: 2em;
}

nav {
```

```css
    display: flex;
    justify-content: space-between;
    margin-top: 20px;
}

a {
    color: white;
    text-decoration: none;
}

a:hover {
    color: #fff;
    text-decoration: underline;
}

section {
    padding: 20px;
}

img {
    max-width: 100%;
}

.photo-slideshow {
    display: flex;
    justify-content: center;
    margin-bottom: 20px;
}

.photo {
    width: 200px;
    height: 200px;
    border-radius: 50%;
    margin: 10px;
}

.photo:hover {
    box-shadow: 0 0 10px #04AA6D;
}

.timeline {
    width: 100%;
    max-width: 500px;
```

```css
    margin: 0 auto;
}

.year {
    width: 100px;
    height: 50px;
    background-color: #eee;
    text-align: center;
    margin: 10px 0;
    line-height: 50px;
    cursor: pointer;
}

.year.active {
    background-color: #04AA6D;
    color: white;
}

.event {
    margin-top: 10px;
    color: #666;
}

form {
    width: 100%;
    max-width: 500px;
    margin: 0 auto;
    padding: 20px;
}

input[type="email"],
input[type="text"],
textarea {
    width: 100%;
    padding: 10px;
    border: 1px solid #ccc;
    margin-bottom: 10px;
}

textarea {
    height: 150px;
}
```

```css
input[type="submit"] {
    background-color: #04AA6D;
    color: white;
    padding: 10px 20px;
    border: none;
    cursor: pointer;
}

input[type="submit"]:hover {
    background-color: #fff;
    color: #04AA6D;
}
```

```
This CSS code will style the HTML code to create a responsive and
visually appealing personal portfolio website. The CSS code uses a
variety of properties to control the font, colors, margins, padding,
and other aspects of the website's appearance.
```

In order to test this code, we will use CodePen. CodePen is an online code editor and development environment. It allows developers to write HTML, CSS, and JavaScript code directly in a web browser and see the results in real time.

In CodePen, we need to place the HTML, JavaScript, and CSS in the corresponding blocks. In the code generated by the AI, the JavaScript code is included inside the HTML, inside a `<script>` element.

The following screenshot shows the organization of the code in each block and the resulting site:

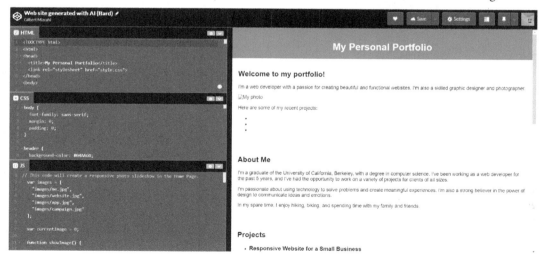

Figure 7.1: The code and the result in CodePen

As you can see, some of the text in the bullets doesn't show up. The CSS for the a and a:hover elements has a color of white (#FFF), and because the background of the page is also white, we cannot see the text.

You can ask the LLM to change the color of the font to another value. However, the change is so simple that you can do it yourself directly.

The resulting page can be seen at https://codepen.io/gilbertmizrahi/pen/MWzMVRG.

The site looks like this:

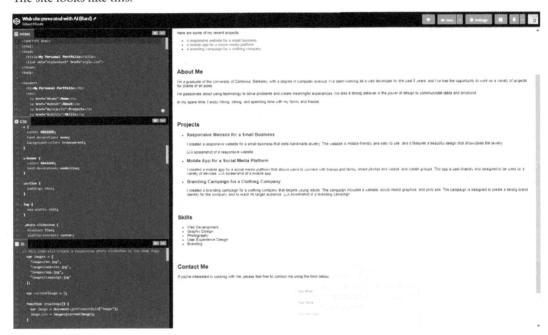

Figure 7.2: The resulting web page in CodePen

In the generated website code, the HTML contains <img> tags that point to local image files such as "images/img1.jpg" for displaying photos and screenshots. However, since this code was programmatically generated without actual image assets, these <img> src paths lead to non-existent files.

To fix this, the images need to be manually added to an images folder in the project directory structure. Then, the <img> source references in the HTML can be updated to match the real filenames – for example, replacing "images/img1.jpg" with the actual filename, such as "images/photo1.jpg".

Without placing the referenced image files in the expected location, the <img> tags will result in broken images on the rendered website. Updating the src attributes to valid paths resolves this issue and allows the photos to display as originally intended.

At the bottom of the site, we can see a contact form as requested in the prompt. The next step is to prompt the LLM to generate the code to save the form data to a backend database, Airtable, or Google Sheets. I will leave you that task as an exercise.

We have just seen how an LLM can be leveraged to rapidly generate website code, saving developers significant time and effort. These intelligent tools are not limited to web development. They can be helpful for coding applications. Next, we will explore this by stepping through the creation of a Chrome extension with the help of AI.

Case study 2 – creating a Chrome extension using AI

In this section, we will utilize ChatGPT to rapidly develop a custom Chrome extension. We will then direct it to build the core functionality such as content scripts, background scripts, and UI elements to create a simple but useful extension.

For this example, we will make a simple Chrome extension that, when activated, will display a popup with an input field to display some text and a button. The button, when clicked, will highlight all instances of that text on the site on the selected tab.

Although you don't need to know how to program, it's useful to know that a Chrome extension needs a manifest and that it needs to be version 3. This is important because we will be using the free ChatGPT, which uses GPT-3.5. As you know, it doesn't have access to the internet, and it has been trained with data up to 2021. At that time, the manifest version 3 was in beta. Thus, by default, ChatGPT would create code based on version 2 of the manifest.

Prompt:

```
Write the code for a Chrome extension in which the user can type
some text. If that text exists in the page in the current tab, the
extension will highlight it in all instances that it appears. Use
manifest version 3.
Do you understand?
```

Response:

```
Yes, I understand. You want to create a Chrome extension using
Manifest V3 that allows the user to input some text. The extension
should then search the current tab's content for instances of that
text and highlight them if found. Here's a basic outline of the code
you can use to achieve this:
Create the Manifest File (manifest.json):
{
    "manifest_version": 3,
    "name": "Text Highlighter",
    "version": "1.0",
    "permissions": ["activeTab"],
    "background": {
```

```
        "service_worker": "background.js"
    },
    "browser_action": {
        "default_popup": "popup.html",
        "default_icon": {
            "16": "images/icon16.png",
            "48": "images/icon48.png",
            "128": "images/icon128.png"
        }
    }
}
```

Create the Popup HTML (popup.html):

```html
<!DOCTYPE html>
<html>
<head>
    <title>Text Highlighter</title>
    <style>
        body {
            width: 200px;
            padding: 10px;
        }
    </style>
</head>
<body>
    <h2>Highlight Text</h2>
    <input type="text" id="searchText" placeholder="Enter text">
    <button id="highlightButton">Highlight</button>
    <script src="popup.js"></script>
</body>
</html>
```

Create the Popup JavaScript (popup.js):

```javascript
document.getElementById('highlightButton').addEventListener('click',
() => {
    const searchText = document.getElementById('searchText').value;
    if (searchText) {
        chrome.tabs.query({ active: true, currentWindow: true }, (tabs)
=> {
            const activeTab = tabs[0];
            chrome.scripting.executeScript({
                target: { tabId: activeTab.id },
                function: highlightText,
                args: [searchText],
            });
        });
```

```
    }
});

function highlightText(searchText) {
    const regex = new RegExp(searchText, 'gi');
    const elements = document.
querySelectorAll('*:not(script):not(style)');

    for (const element of elements) {
        if (element.innerHTML.match(regex)) {
            const html = element.innerHTML.replace(regex, '<span
style="background-color: yellow;">$&</span>');
            element.innerHTML = html;
        }
    }
}
```

Create the Background JavaScript (background.js):

`// Background script is required for Manifest V3`

Prepare Images:

Place icon images in the "images" folder with filenames "icon16.png", "icon48.png", and "icon128.png".

This code provides a basic structure for your Chrome extension. When the user enters some text and clicks the "Highlight" button, the extension searches the current tab's content for instances of the text and highlights them with a yellow background.

Please note that this is a simple implementation and might need adjustments and optimizations based on your specific use case and requirements.

Since it didn't provide any code for the `background.js` file, we need to ask ChatGPT why.

Prompt:

```
Do I need some code for the background.js file?
```

Response:

Apologies for any confusion. In this specific case, since you're not using any background functionality, you don't actually need any code in the background.js file. You can keep it empty, as shown in the code snippets I provided earlier.

The background script is required in Manifest V3, but if your extension doesn't require any background functionality, you can leave the background script file empty. The key logic for searching and highlighting text is handled in the popup.js file using the chrome. scripting.executeScript function.

So, your extension structure will include:

1.manifest.json (with the required permissions, browser action, and

```
popup details)
2.popup.html (the HTML for the popup interface)
3.popup.js (the JavaScript for handling popup interactions)
4.background.js (empty, since you don't require background
functionality)
Images for your extension icon (in the "images" folder as mentioned)
This should work for your specific use case. If you later decide to
add more complex functionality that requires background processes, you
can modify the background.js file accordingly.
```

We will delete the default_icon parameter to avoid having to create the icons for the extension. If you prefer, you can still make an image for the icons.

Then, we need to ask ChatGPT for instructions on what to do next.

Prompt:

```
What do I need to do to make this Chrome extension?
```

Response:

```
To turn the code provided into a functional Chrome extension, follow
these steps:
1.Create the Extension Folder: Create a new folder for your extension.
Name it something like "TextHighlighterExtension".
2.Add Files to the Folder: Inside the extension folder, add the
following files:
  a.manifest.json (with the content mentioned in previous responses)
  b.popup.html (with the HTML content mentioned in previous responses)
  c.popup.js (with the JavaScript content mentioned in previous
responses)
  d.An "images" folder containing the icon images (icon16.png, icon48.
png, icon128.png)
3.Load the Extension: Open Google Chrome and go to the address
chrome://extensions/.
4.Enable Developer Mode: Toggle on the "Developer mode" switch located
at the top-right corner of the extensions page.
5.Load Your Extension: Click the "Load unpacked" button and select
your extension folder ("TextHighlighterExtension").
6.Test the Extension: After loading, you should see your extension's
icon in the Chrome toolbar. Click the icon to open the popup with the
text input field and highlight button. Enter some text and click the
"Highlight" button to test the highlighting functionality.
Remember that this is a basic implementation and doesn't include all
possible features or error handling. You might need to refine and
expand upon this code to meet your specific requirements. If you
encounter any issues during testing, you can inspect the console in
the Chrome Developer Tools for debugging information.
```

```
Please note that my responses are based on the state of technology and
Chrome extensions as of September 2021. If there have been any changes
or updates since then, the steps might vary slightly.
```

Following these steps, we get the following error in the Chrome **Extensions** tab:

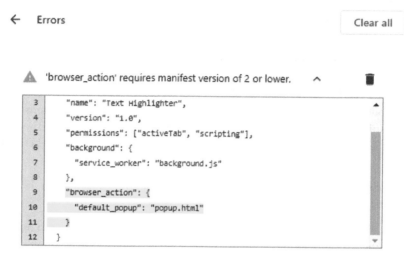

Figure 7.3: Error message in the Chrome Extensions tab

Thus, using the error as a prompt, we get the following prompt:

Prompt:

```
'browser_action' requires manifest version of 2 or lower.
```

Here is the response:

Response:

```
I apologize for the confusion. You are correct; the 'browser_action'
property is used in Manifest V2 for Chrome extensions. In Manifest
V3, you'll use the 'action' property instead. Let's update the code
accordingly.
Here's the updated version of the 'manifest.json' file for your Chrome
extension using Manifest V3:
{
    "manifest_version": 3,
    "name": "Text Highlighter",
    "version": "1.0",
    "permissions": ["activeTab"],
    "background": {
        "service_worker": "background.js"
```

```
    },
    "action": {
        "default_popup": "popup.html",
        "default_icon": {
            "16": "images/icon16.png",
            "48": "images/icon48.png",
            "128": "images/icon128.png"
        }
    }
}
```

The rest of the code (`popup.html`, `popup.js`, and `background.js`) remains the same. After updating the manifest, load your extension as described in the previous steps. The extension icon should now appear in the Chrome toolbar, and clicking it will open the popup where you can input text to highlight.

The only thing that changed was that `browser-action` changed to `action` in the manifest. Now, when we try again, we can see that it works just fine.

Now, we can test the Chrome Extension. If we test the extension on a CNN page to highlight human, we get the following:

Figure 7.4: The Chrome extension in action

Therefore, it's working as expected. However, if you input a different text, it will keep the previous text highlighted along with the matches for the new text. This is something that you would like to fix. To do that, you need to prompt ChatGPT to remove the highlighted text before highlighting the new one.

Another thing you might want to enhance is the styling of the content of the popup.

With the successful creation of a functioning Chrome extension, we have now completed our two hands-on case studies. And with that, we have reached the end of this chapter exploring the transformative impact of AI on software engineering.

Summary

In this chapter, we explored how AI is transforming software engineering by automating coding tasks. The case studies demonstrated the use of AI to rapidly build a website and Chrome extension.

In the next chapter, we'll see how AI is revolutionizing another core area of technology – conversational interfaces.

8
AI for Chatbots

Chatbots have rapidly become a ubiquitous part of digital interfaces, and today's users expect their conversational agents to be smart, natural, and highly capable. While chatbots used to be limited by scripted responses and basic natural language capabilities, **large language models** (**LLMs**) such as GPT-3 are revolutionizing what's possible.

In this chapter, we will explore how to create richer, more human-like chatbot experiences by integrating LLM APIs into our conversational interfaces. These AI-powered chatbots can deeply understand natural language, hold open-ended conversations, and complete complex tasks – all through natural dialogue.

We will start by looking at the advanced natural language processing abilities of LLMs, and how they enable chatbots that comprehend language as well as humans do. This allows them to interpret the intent behind varied user inputs more accurately and contextually. Next, we will see how LLMs can generate significantly more natural, conversational responses compared to traditional chatbots. The back-and-forth feels more human, engaging users in free-flowing dialogue.

Use cases such as customer support, e-commerce, and open-domain chat will demonstrate how these AI abilities manifest in real-world chatbots. You'll learn how LLMs can power everything from highly personalized interactions to completing intricate workflows solely through conversation. We will also look at two in-depth case studies of LLM-powered chatbots: one for product ordering, and another for dynamic quiz generation.

By the end of this chapter, you'll have a strong grasp of how to build your next generation of smart conversational agents that provide immense value to your users. The versatility and capabilities that are unlocked by LLMs are opening up exciting new possibilities for chatbots. Let's explore them.

The following topics will be covered in this chapter:

- How to use GPT-4 APIs and other LLM APIs to create chatbots
- Building conversational interfaces with LLM APIs
- How to use AI for customer support

- Case study – a chatbot using AI to assist users in ordering products
- Case study – creating interactive quizzes/assessments and deploying them as chatbot flows

Technical requirements

To complete this chapter, you will need access to the OpenAI APIs (GPT-3.5 Turbo and GPT 4), Antropic APIs (Claude and Claude Instant), and/or others.

To get access to the OpenAI APIs, go to https://openai.com.

To access Anthropic APIs, you need to go to https://www.anthropic.com.

You can also use https://openrouter.ai/ to access APIs from OpenAI, Anthropic, Meta (LLaMA20), Google (PaLM2 Bison), and some others. The list is updated periodically. It provides access to OpenAI GPT 3.5/4, and even supports GPT 4 with a context window of 32k before OpenAI itself has.

You can find the API documentation for OpenAI at https://platform.openai.com/docs/api-reference.

The chatbot builders mentioned in this chapter can be found at https://twnel.com, https://www.voiceflow.com/, https://uchat.au/, https://manychat.com/, https://botpress.com/, and https://landbot.io/.

How to use GPT-4 APIs and other LLM APIs to create chatbots

Although ChatGPT, Bard, and the Claude playground are chatbots, for the most interesting applications, you need to have your own chatbots that are tailored to help your users accomplish the tasks related to your business.

Here are some key reasons why it is advantageous to build a chatbot while utilizing GPT or Claude APIs rather than just interacting directly with ChatGPT or Claude playground:

- **Hide instructions/prompts**: With an API chatbot, you can hide all the prompts, instructions, context, and more that are fed to the LLM *behind the scenes*. The user only sees the final natural response, creating a smoother experience.
- **Integrate with data sources**: A custom chatbot can connect to external databases, proprietary knowledge bases, and other internal data sources to allow the LLM to incorporate these in generating responses. This isn't possible within the playground.

- **Manage conversation state**: The chatbot can handle conversation state, context tracking, and follow-up questions, keeping the experience coherent for the user. The playground treats each prompt discretely.

- **Deploy anywhere**: The chatbot can be deployed in your product, website, app, and more and then scaled to large user bases. The playground is limited to individual usage.

- **Workflow automation**: Chatbots can integrate with business logic and workflows to not just provide information but also perform actions such as placing orders, filing tickets, and more.

- **Ongoing improvements**: The chatbot's behavior can be tweaked and improved over time based on user feedback. The playground models are more static.

- **Controlled access**: Chatbot users can be authenticated, and access can be controlled. The playground is freely available to anyone.

Hence, creating a custom chatbot solution allows you to take full advantage of the LLM's capabilities while controlling the entire end user experience. You can go beyond just a question-answer interaction and build intelligent assistants that truly understand users and workflows.

ChatGPT and other LLMs can be useful for certain data analysis tasks, such as sentiment analysis, data classification, data cleaning, and pattern matching. However, using them directly in a playground interface has some major limitations.

For example, let's say you have text data in Google Sheets and want to analyze the sentiment of each entry. With ChatGPT, you would need to manually copy and paste each entry into the interface, ask it to analyze sentiment, and then copy the response back into the associated cell. This is incredibly tedious and inefficient, especially for large datasets.

A custom chatbot powered by GPT-3.5 removes this friction. The chatbot can connect directly to data sources such as Sheets, ingest the data, iteratively call the AI to analyze each entry, maintain context, and automatically log structured results back to the source. This orchestration automates the busywork and provides scalable data analysis pipelines, which isn't possible in the basic playground format.

The key difference is that a custom integration handles the connections and workflows between data and AI automatically, while the playground interface relies entirely on manual copy-paste operations. Building custom glue logic around LLMs unlocks more powerful and scalable applications of the technology.

The chatbot workflows for sentiment analysis, data classification, and data cleansing are all very similar, as shown here:

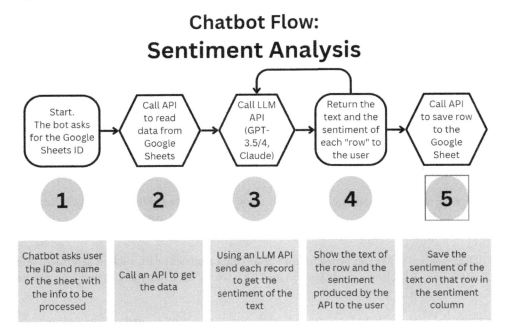

Figure 8.1: The sentiment analysis chatbot flow

Let's take a closer look at this chatbot flow:

1. When the chatbot starts, it asks the user to provide the Google Sheet's ID. In this case, the repository of all the text for which we want to perform the sentiment analysis is a Google Sheet, but it could be Airtable or a database. Then, it asks for the Sheet name. These two pieces of information are key for the API, which will get the data from Google Sheets. Chatbot builders such as Twnel, ManyChat, UChat, and BotPress all have native integrations with Google Sheets and probably with Airtable. Other chatbot builders rely on integration platforms such as Zapier, Make, and similar to handle the integrations.

2. Then, the chatbot gets the data that we want to perform sentiment analysis on.

3. Once the data has been loaded, the chatbot can parse the content of each row and column. Thus, we can instruct the LLM API with the prompt and the cell text we want to analyze. This is all done automatically in the background.

4. GPT-3.5/4, Claude, or the LLM you use processes the text and returns a sentiment score between 0 and 1. The chatbot receives this response and maps it to sentiment categories such as "positive," "neutral," and "negative" based on score thresholds.

5.   Once all the records have been processed, the chatbot calls another API to write the sentiment values to the column of each respective record (row) in the Google Sheet.

This kind of implementation can be done with many chatbot platforms, such as Twnel, BotPress, VoiceFlow, ManyChat, Uchat, and others. Most of these tools offer visual builders, so users can just drag and drop components to create their automation.

Some of these tools have native integrations with Google Sheets to allow reading and writing from and to a given sheet. Others need the user to use other tools such as Zapier or Make to make the integrations.

Building conversational interfaces with LLM APIs

In this section, we will create a chatbot that allows users to take pictures of invoices and save the structured data to a Google Sheet. For this chatbot, I will use Twnel, a messaging application that allows us to create conversational automations to automate processes with the extended supply chain. However, a similar implementation can be done with other chatbot builders, such as UChat, Botpress, and others.

The chatbot workflow for the chatbot that uses AI to structure unstructured text extracted from an image using OCR looks like this:

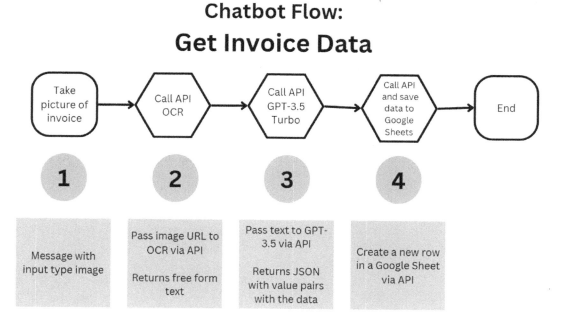

Figure 8.2: Structuring data from an image chatbot flow

This chatbot uses AI to structure unstructured text extracted from an image using **optical character recognition (OCR)**. The workflow is as follows:

1. The user sends an image to the chatbot through a messaging platform. This platform needs to allow users to either upload existing images or take new pictures directly within the chatbot interface.

2. The chatbot uses an OCR API to extract the text from the image. This API takes the image URL as input and outputs the extracted text.

3. The chatbot then uses GPT-3.5 Turbo to structure and organize the unstructured text from the OCR step.

4. Finally, the structured data is logged to a Google Sheet or a database.

For this chatbot, the messaging platform needs to allow users to send images within the conversational flow. In the next section, we'll look at how to leverage the OpenAI GPT-3.5 Turbo API specifically for the text structuring step. Twnel provides easy integration to GPT-3.5 and Google Sheets, making it a good choice to build this kind of AI-powered data extraction chatbot.

When calling the OpenAI GPT-3.5-Turbo API, you want to take the JSON response and transform it before returning it to your chatbot flow.

To simplify this, I wrote a Google Apps Script program that does the following:

*   Calls the GPT-3.5 API

*   Parses the JSON response

*   Returns a modified JSON object

This handles the transformations you need between the raw API output and your chatbot.

You need to get an OCR API to get the freeform text from the image. All bot builders we've mentioned have connectors to read and write Google Sheets. If the one you use to try to implement a similar solution doesn't have one, you can use Zapier, Make, or any other integration tool in the market for that.

In our example, I am using the following invoice:

Acme
123 Bird Avenue
Grand City, OH 43003
(123) 456-7890

Invoice   123456

Date   08/01/2023
Due Date   08/31/2023
Project   Experiment X

Invoice to
Richard Peers
CCT
1 Broadway
Cambridge, MA, 02141

Product	Qty	Unit price	Total price
Flux Capacitor	1	$225.00	$225.00
A set of 4 Pixel Bender Lights	2	$204.00	$408.00

Notes:

Subtotal	**$633.00**
Tax	$37.98
Adjustments	-$100.00
	$570.98

Figure 8.3: Sample invoice for our example

In this example, we are going to expand on what we started in *Chapter 5*, in the *Pattern matching in responses* section.

We could extract all the information from the invoice, including the products, or extract all the information, excluding the products. For this example, we only want to save the following data to a spreadsheet:

- Invoice number
- Date
- Due date

- Invoice to name

- Invoice to company

- Project

- Subtotal

- Tax

- Adjustments

- Total

Thus, the JSON model would look something like this:

```
json = {
    "invoiceNumber": "string",
    "date": "string",
    "dueDate": "string",
    "invoiceTo": {
        "name": "string",
        "company": "string",
    },
    "project": "string",
    "subtotal": "number",
    "tax": "number",
    "adjustments": "number",
    "total": "number"
}
```

Thus, the prompt would be as follows:

```
Use the [text] extracted from an invoice using OCR. Structure it as a
JSON object with the structure shown in the [JSON model].
[text]="TEXT GENERATED BY OCR"
[JSON model] = (the model from above)
keep the same structure of the JSON as in the model, including the
same keys. Output:
```

This prompt is a little bit different from the one in *Chapter 5* – it has been rewritten so that it can be used when calling the GPT-3.5 API.

We could call the OpenAI API directly and pass the corresponding parameters. However, to offer more flexibility, we will use Google Apps Script to make the OpenAI API call. Google Apps Script allows us to write JavaScript code in the backend without the need to create a backend per se. Then, we can create a webhook that we call from the chatbot using the call_api block.

The advantage of this approach is that we could generalize this to any invoice or document. The Google Apps Script code can read the JSON model for any document. Suppose we store the JSON model as text in a cell in a spreadsheet. We can get that text dynamically from the chatbot, as well as the text produced by the OCR. For complex cases that need more than just the JSON model, example inputs and outputs can also be stored in additional cells of the same spreadsheet. These examples will serve to train the LLM to generate better results.

The Google Apps Script code is available at: `https://github.com/PacktPublishing/Unlocking-the-Secrets-of-Prompt-Engineering/tree/main`

To run this code, you should open Google Sheets, go to **Extensions**, and then select **Apps Script**. This will open a new Google Apps Script project linked to the currently open Google Sheet. Next, copy each file from the repository into a new file on the Apps Script project. That's all. The first time you try to run it, you will be asked to authenticate with your Google account.

The code defines a set of functions for handling HTTP POST requests, processing JSON data, and making requests to the OpenAI API for generating text content based on input data. The comments explain the purpose of each function and the steps involved in handling the request and generating AI-generated content.

In this case, each call to the GPT-3.5 API is independent of other calls. Thus, we don't need to keep context or short memory of the conversation. That's why the `"messages": [{"role": "user", "content": prompt}]` array has only one message.

It is also important to note that the JSON model has to be converted into a string before it can be passed to the prompt. Remember that LLMs deal with text (strings), so JSON objects or arrays may confuse them. That's why we have `const jsonString = JSON.stringify(json)` on line 59.

Once the text has been structured using GPT-3.5, we can save the data to a Google Sheet.

Here is the workflow in the Twnel Visual Bot Builder:

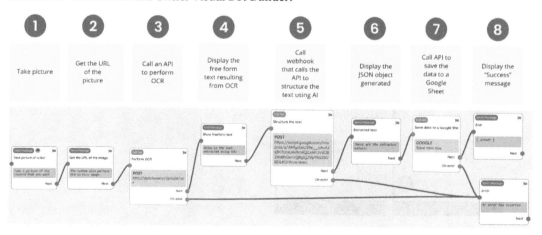

Figure 8.4: Structuring data from OCR in the Twnel Visual Bot Builder

Steps 4 and *6* are not necessary. They have been included here to show the text produced by OCR and the JSON object with the structured data generated by GPT-3.5.

The following figure shows the flow in action:

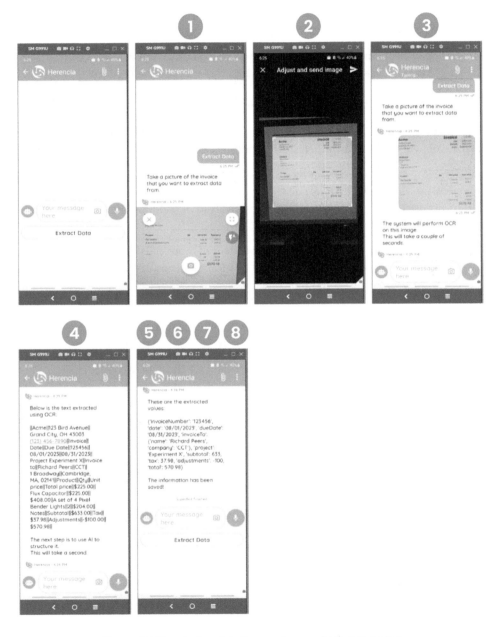

Figure 8.5: Structuring data from an image chatbot in action

The Google Sheet with the added row and its information can be seen here:

Figure 8.6: Data extracted in Google Sheets

As you can see, the structured data is saved to a row in a Google Sheet. It has been expanded with additional metadata, including the following:

- Timestamp – when the image was taken
- Location – where the image was taken, along with its latitude and longitude
- The name of the user who took the picture
- The URL of the image
- The raw text that was extracted from the image with OCR

The flow shown here should be a part of a complete conversational automation process. In a real use case, the person providing the service should do some previous tasks, such as checking in at the location, documenting the tasks being performed, and more. That's exactly the beauty of using generative AI in automations like this – it allows us to improve them in ways that were not possible before.

This type of chatbot flow has many applications. For instance, truck drivers can save data from receipts on expenses that require reimbursements, such as tolls, gas, truck repairs (fixing flat tires), meals, and hotel expenses, and more, it can save both truck drivers and administrative personnel a lot of time. In addition, it allows the drivers to be paid quickly.

Building conversational interfaces with LLMs opens up new possibilities across many domains. One domain that stands to benefit tremendously is customer service. In the next section, we'll focus on crafting generative AI chatbots tailored to customer support needs.

How to use AI for customer support

Chatbots powered by generative AI present new opportunities to transform customer service interactions. Unlike rule-based chatbots of the past, generative models can have more natural, human-like conversations. With proper training data and prompt engineering, they can understand nuanced customer questions and provide helpful answers.

Here are some examples of how generative AI chatbots can be used for customer service:

- **Answering common FAQs on a company website**: The chatbot could field frequently asked questions about products, services, account access, shipping times, returns, and more. This deflects simple inquiries:

  - Generative AI can parse questions expressed in many different ways and match them to the appropriate stored answer. It's more flexible than a rigid bot that requires precise phrasing.

  - The bot can be trained on past customer service transcripts to learn common question variations rather than manually encoding rules.

  - For uncommon questions, the bot can use its language generation capabilities to provide helpful fallback responses.

- **Providing product support and troubleshooting**: The chatbot can use product specs and manuals to help customers diagnose issues with appliances, electronics, software, and more and guide them to solutions:

  - Generative models allow the bot to have a free-flowing diagnostic conversation rather than a rigid tree-based flow

  - The bot can ingest product documentation and manuals to develop a deeper understanding and suggest better troubleshooting

  - The bot can recommend solutions tailored to the specific product model and issue based on its training

- **Assisting with account management**: The chatbot can access a company's CRM system to help customers pull up account details, check order status, update information, cancel subscriptions, and more:

  - By integrating with CRM systems, generative bots can access and understand customer account data to resolve a wide range of requests

  - Having the full account context enables the bot to have more personalized and contextual conversations

  - The bot can use past account management transcripts to learn without manual scripting of flows

- **Making restaurant reservations**: The chatbot can accept dates/times, party sizes, and contact information and confirm reservations at restaurants:

  - Generative models can understand nuances in date, time, party size, and other booking details provided in natural language

- The bot can integrate with a restaurant's reservation systems rather than just a standalone bot flow

- Past conversations can train the bot to ask clarifying questions to complete bookings smoothly

- **Booking travel**: A travel chatbot can suggest destinations, check availability, and book flights, hotels, and rental cars based on customer criteria:

  - The bot can suggest personalized destinations and travel recommendations based on customer needs and preferences

  - Generative AI can search across many travel provider systems to find optimal flight/hotel/rental options

  - The bot can learn to handle complex and multi-leg travel itineraries that require several back-and-forth exchanges

- **Processing insurance claims**: An insurance chatbot can take initial claim information, assign a claim number, initiate processing, and answer questions for customers:

  - By integrating with insurance systems, the bot has full claim context for more tailored conversations

  - Customers can describe claims in everyday language rather than in rigid forms

  - The bot can ask clarifying questions learned from past claim interactions to get all the necessary details

- **Serving as an HR virtual assistant**: An HR chatbot can answer employee questions about benefits, time-off requests, company policies, and more:

  - Employees can ask a wide range of HR policy, benefits, payroll, and other questions naturally

  - The bot can leverage HR knowledge bases and handbooks to better address questions

  - User conversations can continuously improve the bot's capabilities over time

The possibilities are vast when using a well-designed generative AI chatbot that is tailored to a specific customer service domain. The key is providing relevant training data so that it can handle a wide range of customer needs and requests.

In the next two sections, we will explore a couple of scenarios to show how generative AI-powered chatbots can improve the user experience for cases like the ones we just described.

To ingest content from multiple documents, we need to add some additional layers to our solutions. This will be covered in the next chapter.

Case study – a chatbot using AI to assist users in ordering products

Chatbots have become a popular way for companies to assist with tasks such as placing orders. In this section, we will examine a case study of a chatbot created by the fictional company Herencia Inc., which produces artisanal beers, to help convenience store owners purchase different types of beers on Herencia's website or chatbot.

An LLM can assist buyers when ordering products, provided it has access to the specs, prices, and other relevant information. One limitation when using the LLM API (GPT-4 or Claude API) is the number of tokens that it has available to load the data directly into the prompt. In the next chapter, we will explore how that can be solved for more complex scenarios through plugins or managing embeddings and integrations with vector databases.

Some of the tasks that such a chatbot can perform are as follows:

- **Product recommendations**: An LLM can analyze a buyer's requirements, preferences, and budget to suggest the most suitable products for their needs
- **Product comparison**: An LLM can help buyers compare different products based on their features, specifications, and prices, enabling them to make informed decisions
- **Customization options**: If a company offers customizable products, an LLM can guide buyers through the customization process, ensuring that they select the best options to meet their requirements
- **Frequently asked questions**: An LLM can answer common questions about products, such as warranty information, return policies, and shipping options, making the purchasing process more convenient for buyers
- **Price negotiation**: In cases where price negotiation is possible, an LLM can provide buyers with negotiation tips and strategies based on the product's value and market trends
- **Order tracking**: An LLM can be integrated with the company's order management system to provide buyers with real-time updates on order status and expected delivery times
- **Upselling and cross-selling**: An LLM can identify related or complementary products that buyers might be interested in

For this example, we are not going to deal with embeddings or vector databases. Hence, we will use a simple scenario to show how a chatbot can be used to order beer. For our simple case, let's suppose Herencia, our fictitious company, offers four types of beer: Lager, IPA, Stout, and Wheat. Here are the packaging options and prices for each:

Beer type	12-pack cans	24-pack cans	12-pack bottles	24-pack bottles
Lager	$15	$28	$16	$30
IPA	$18	$34	$20	$38
Stout	$20	$38	$22	$42
Wheat			$18	$34

Table 8.1: Herencia products for ordering beer – chatbot flow

If we were to simulate this with ChatGPT, Bard, or Claude (in the playground), we would need to provide this list of products to the LLM with clear instructions about the goal: assisting users in buying beer.

Thus, the prompt will be something like this.

Prompt:

```
Let's say that the buyer is a convenience store owner and he wants to
buy beer from a beer company named Herencia. Herencia has 4 types of
beer. The products are [beers]
The buyer can purchase packs of different beers in different
presentations and packaging. Assist the buyer in making an order for
her store. At the end summarize the order, including the item prices
and total price.
beers = the list of beers by packaging and prices - Just copy and
paste the data of the table here
What do you want to order?
```

And here's the response.

Response:

```
Great! We have a variety of beer options available for your store.
Here's a list of our four types of beer along with their packaging
options and prices:
1. Lager:
    - 12-pack cans: $15
    - 24-pack cans: $28
    - 12-pack bottles: $16
    - 24-pack bottles: $30
2. IPA:
```

```
      - 12-pack cans: $18
      - 24-pack cans: $34
      - 12-pack bottles: $20
      - 24-pack bottles: $38
3. Stout:
      - 12-pack cans: $20
      - 24-pack cans: $38
      - 12-pack bottles: $22
      - 24-pack bottles: $42
4. Wheat:
      - 12-pack bottles: $18
      - 24-pack bottles: $34
Please let me know the quantities and packaging options you'd like to
order for each type of beer.
```

Here's the next prompt.

Prompt:

```
I want 3 packs of Lager, 2 packs of IPA and 6 packs of Stout
```

And here's the response.

Response:

```
Thank you for your request. To better assist you, could you please
specify the packaging options (12-pack or 24-pack, cans or bottles)
for each type of beer you'd like to order? Here are the options again
for your reference:
1. Lager:
      - 12-pack cans
      - 24-pack cans
      - 12-pack bottles
      - 24-pack bottles
2. IPA:
      - 12-pack cans
      - 24-pack cans
      - 12-pack bottles
      - 24-pack bottles
3. Stout:
      - 12-pack cans
      - 24-pack cans
      - 12-pack bottles
      - 24-pack bottles
Please provide your preferences, and I will calculate the total price
for your order.
```

And here's the next prompt.

Prompt:

```
3 24-pack cans of Lager, 2 12-pack bottles of IPA and 6 24-pack
bottles of Stout
```

And here's the response.

Response:

```
Thank you for specifying your preferences. Here's a summary of your
order:
1. Lager:
   - 24-pack cans: 3 packs x $28 = $84
2. IPA:
   - 12-pack bottles: 2 packs x $20 = $40
3. Stout:
   - 24-pack bottles: 6 packs x $42 = $252
The total price for your order is $376. Shipping costs and delivery
times will be calculated based on your store's location. Please
confirm if you'd like to proceed with this order or make any changes.
```

This works fine, but we need to provide this kind of interaction using a chatbot that can be exposed to all or at least most potential customers. Otherwise, it does not make any sense.

When integrating an LLM into a chatbot using the LLM API, one important thing to remember is that the chatbot flow developer must ensure they keep the memory of the conversation, to manage context. When using ChatGPT or an LLM through its playground, the LLM vendor keeps that short memory for us.

In the previous example, we saw that the GPT-3.5/ 4 API has a parameter called messages, which is an array:

```
"messages": [{"role": "user", "content": prompt}]
```

In this case, each time we call the API, after each response from the user, we need to pass the previous messages in the array so that GPT-3.5/4 can keep context and manage short-term memory.

The flow looks like this:

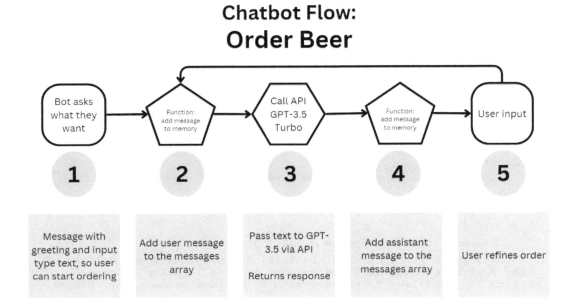

Figure 8.7: Order beer chatbot flow

Here's the workflow in the Twnel Visual Bot Builder:

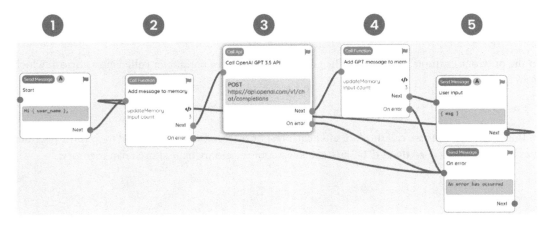

Figure 8.8: Flow in the Twnel Visual Bot Builder

Step 1 includes a greeting and asks the user what they want to order. In *Steps 2* and *4*, a JavaScript function is called. This function keeps the messages array with the whole history of the conversation. This function just adds the last message object: `{"role": "system", "content":system_ prompt}` to the array of messages.

In *Step 3*, we call the OpenAI API directly. *Figure 8.9* shows how to set up the headers:

Figure 8.9: Call API in Twnel's Visual Bot Builder – setting the headers

Figure 8.10 shows the request URL to the OpenAI chat API and the body with the required parameters – that is, the model and the array of messages in the conversation:

Figure 8.10: Request data in the call API block in Twnel's Visual Bot Builder

The following figure shows the chat flow in action:

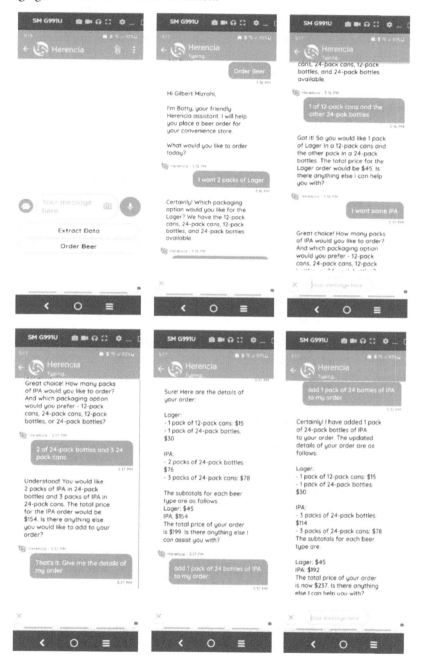

Figure 8.11: Ordering beer chatbot – flow in action

In *Step 5*, the user reads the response and can answer back to refine the order. The user message is added to the messages array (*Step 2*) and the flow continues the cycle until the order is complete.

Implementing this flow in a chatbot that anyone can access makes this approach very useful. We could add more steps to call an API that interacts with the inventory of Herencia beers to check for availability. Likewise, we could check the credit standing and limits for when the store owner is going to pay. Next, the user can be presented with options to place the order and, depending on the credit terms and balance, ask to pay directly from the chatbot. Finally, once the order has been finalized, it can be saved into an orders database and a tracking link can be generated so that the user can track the delivery.

With that, you've seen how you can ask the LLM to produce the result in JSON. Thus, in this case, we can ask the prompt to generate a JSON that includes a text element, with the full (text) response as shown in *Figure 8.11* to be presented in a familiar way to the user, and an array element, with every item and quantity that is on the order.

Calling LLM APIs such as OpenAI directly in a chatbot has some limitations. The number of tokens allowed per API request is restricted, which caps the amount of product data a chatbot can handle in one flow. Even as token allowances increase, high usage still drives up costs.

A better approach involves using tools such as LangChain, which can chain prompts across multiple requests and create specialized agents. We'll explore this in the next chapter.

Shifting domains, chatbots that leverage LLMs can also enable more interactive and adaptive quizzes. As the next case study shows, conversational AI permits customizing questionnaires and analyzing free-form responses.

Case study – creating interactive quizzes/assessments and deploying them as chatbot flows

Chatbots present an interesting opportunity for creating dynamic, conversational assessments and quizzes. Using LLMs, chatbots can be designed to guide users through interactive questioning, understand free-form responses, and provide personalized feedback.

In this section, we'll explore a case study of a financial advisory chatbot that conducts a risk assessment quiz to gauge a client's risk tolerance for investment purposes. The chatbot has been built to automate part of their client onboarding process. By administering a risk quiz through natural conversation, the chatbot can evaluate a client's responses and determine their risk profile.

The designed dialogue flows to mimic a human advisor asking questions about the client's feelings on investment risks. The chatbot can interpret unstructured answers and adapt quiz questions based on the client's responses. After completing the assessment, the chatbot saves the summarized risk profile so that a human financial advisor can make appropriate investment recommendations.

Examining this case study demonstrates how conversational AI can gather key client data through dynamic questioning.

There are two possible ways to use an LLM for this case:

- Use the LLM to create the same questions for all participants. This can be done once using ChatGPT, Bard, or other similar tools. Then, create a tree-based chatbot to ask the users the questions and, in the end, call an LLM API to make the assessment based on the responses.

- The chatbot uses the LLM API to ask the AI to generate the questions dynamically for each user and at the end makes an assessment based on the answers.

Both approaches are valid.

The first approach is simpler to implement since it isn't a conversation with the LLM, although there is interactivity in the conversation with the chatbot itself. The LLM API is called just once (when asking for the assessment), so there is no need to resend the previous messages whenever a new interaction happens. Because of that, it is also less expensive to run. Furthermore, the assessment is more consistent among users.

The second approach, on the other hand, can produce a better result if the following questions depend on the answers to the previous ones.

For this example, we will explore the second case.

Before exploring how to implement a chatbot to assist financial advisors in risk assessment, let's simulate the flow directly in an LLM playground such as ChatGPT.

We will ask the LLM to use the **Mutually Exclusive, Collectively Exhaustive (MECE)** framework. The MECE framework is a concept that's commonly used in problem-solving and structuring information in various fields such as management consulting, business analysis, and project management. MECE is a structured way of organizing and categorizing information to ensure clarity and comprehensiveness. Here's what each part of MECE means:

- **Mutually Exclusive**: This means that the categories or elements you define should not overlap. In other words, each piece of information or data should fit into only one category and should not belong to more than one category. This ensures that you avoid double-counting or confusion.

- **Collectively Exhaustive**: This means that when you combine all the categories or elements, they should cover the entire spectrum of possibilities without any gaps. There should be no missing or unaccounted-for items. This ensures completeness and that you've considered all relevant aspects of the problem or situation.

When you apply the MECE framework, you create a clear and organized structure for analyzing and solving problems, making decisions, or presenting information. It helps you break down complex issues into manageable parts and ensures that you're not overlooking critical factors or making redundant distinctions. MECE is often used in tasks such as market segmentation, process improvement, project planning, and problem-solving exercises.

In practice, creating a MECE framework involves breaking down a problem or a set of information into categories or groups that meet the criteria of being mutually exclusive and collectively exhaustive. This structured approach can lead to more effective decision-making and problem-solving by providing a clear and comprehensive view of the situation.

To create an interactive quiz using a chatbot, you need to provide an initial prompt to an AI assistant to generate the quiz questions and response options. This initial prompt will instruct the AI to act as a financial advisor and suggest a personalized investment strategy based on your responses. You should provide other instructions, as shown in this example.

Here is the initial prompt.

Prompt:

```
Act as a personal financial advisor. Suggest me a personalized
investment strategy based on my current financial situation, risk
tolerance, objectives, preferences and so on.
In order to gather all the necessary information required for the
personalization, create a personalization quiz using the MECE
framework with 10 questions, each with 4 possible answers (a,b, c,d).
Ask each question and wait for the answer before asking the next
question
```

And here's the response.

Response:

```
Here is the first question:
1. What is your investment goal?
a. Generate income
b. Grow my wealth
c. Preserve my wealth
d. A combination of the above
```

Here's the next prompt.

Prompt:

```
a
```

The bot keeps asking questions and expecting answers. After the answer to the last question is received by the flow, it produces a response similar to this.

Response:

```
Thank you for your response. Based on your answers, a personalized
investment strategy for you could be a growth-oriented portfolio that
is diversified across different asset classes, such as stocks, mutual
funds, and ETFs. Since you have a moderate to high risk tolerance
and are willing to take on more risk, this type of portfolio may be
suitable for you.

Since you also indicated that you have limited investment experience,
an actively managed mutual fund or ETF that focuses on growth stocks
may be a good starting point for you. A financial advisor can help you
select the right investments and monitor your portfolio on an ongoing
basis.

It's important to keep in mind that investing involves risk and there
is no guarantee of returns. It's important to do your own research
and consult with a financial advisor before making any investment
decisions.
```

The chatbot flow in this case is very similar to the previous case:

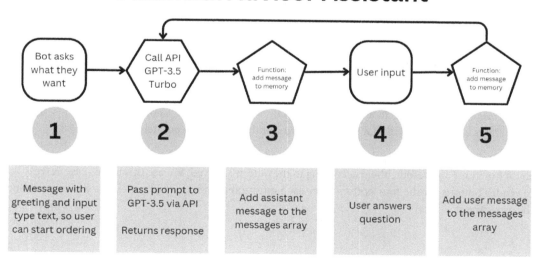

Figure 8.12: Financial advisor assistant chatbot flow

The only difference between this flow and the previous one is that after the initial message when activating the flow, we call the OpenAI API and then we add the response to the `messages` array.

In this case, the user can answer a, b, c, or d, or the `text` option. We can refine the chatbot flow so that the answer plus options is returned as a JSON object, like so:

```
{
    "response_type": "question",
    "question": "question text here",
    "answers": [
        {"id": "a", "label": "option 1 text"},
        {"id": "b", "label": "option 2 text"},
        {"id": "c", "label": "option 3 text"},
        {"id": "d", "label": "option 4 text"}
    ]
}
```

The `answers` parameter happens to be in the format accepted by Twnel to render buttons when the input type is `checkbox`. However, after the tenth question, the LLM won't return another question in JSON; instead, it will return a text recommendation. Thus, we need to modify the flow to accommodate that case, checking whether or not `response_type` from the LLM is a question or an assessment. We don't care about that for this example. What's important to know is that these conversational automation tools provide options to simplify user interaction.

The OpenAI GPT-3.5 and GPT-4 APIs have a feature called function calling. This feature allows you to describe functions to the AI models. The models can then generate JSON output that contains arguments to call those functions.

This enables the models to intelligently choose the outputs of the functions you describe.

It's important to understand that the ChatCompletions model itself does not execute functions. Instead, it generates a JSON payload that you can use to call the function separately.

This topic is outside the scope of this book but suffice it to say that the GPT3.5/4 API allows you to chain functions and reroute them according to the output received. We use this in this case as we want to render buttons for the four options after each question but render just a message when providing the assessment.

Here's what the flow looks like in action:

Figure 8.13 : Financial advisor assistant chatbot flow in action

This case study demonstrates how LLMs can enable conversational AI agents such as chatbots to dynamically create interactive assessments, as exemplified by a financial chatbot administering personalized risk quizzes, bringing us to the end of this exploration on leveraging AI for chatbot conversations.

Summary

Chatbots powered by LLMs such as GPT-3/4 and Claude are transforming conversational AI and enabling more natural, human-like digital experiences. As demonstrated through the examples detailed in this chapter, these powerful generative models allow bots to truly understand natural language, hold free-flowing conversations with users, and complete sophisticated workflows from commerce transactions to personalized assessments.

The key to unlocking their capabilities is thoughtful prompt engineering. Developers can inject critical context, domain knowledge, business logic, data sources, and more into the prompts to shape the bot's behavior. While interacting in the playground provides a glimpse of the potential, custom solutions built on LLM APIs open up many more possibilities.

These AI-powered chatbots maintain conversation state and memory, integrate with backend systems, optimize performance based on user interactions, and deploy seamlessly across platforms. They deliver immense value by automating key processes through natural dialogue – whether it's customer service, e-commerce, travel booking, or other workflows.

While this chapter focused on core chatbot use cases, the next chapter will dig deeper into LangChain and other tools that augment LLMs for even more advanced conversational AI applications. We'll explore chaining prompts, ingesting documents as embeddings, crafting purpose-built agents, and more.

9

Building Smarter Systems – Advanced LLM Integrations

LLMs, such as **GPT-4**, have exploded in capability. But simply using their basic text completion APIs only scratches the surface of their potential. Going beyond isolated generation allows LLMs to reason, research, converse, and take action.

Integrating LLMs into our existing tools and workflows is crucial for transforming these models from novelties into productivity powerhouses. In this chapter, we'll explore advanced techniques to level up how you apply LLMs by connecting them to your tech stack.

This chapter provides a general overview of these topics. Covering them in deeper detail could require one or more books just on some of these topics.

The following topics will be covered in this chapter:

- Automating bulk prompting at scale using platforms such as Google Sheets, Zapier, and Make
- Building custom AI pipelines with developer tools such as LangChain, Flowise, and Langflow
- Leveraging diverse models' specialized strengths by chaining multiple LLMs
- Walk-throughs of sample integrations for competitive intelligence, customer data, and document analysis
- Emerging innovations such as multimodal models and LLM app plugins

Overall, you'll learn about approaches to unlock LLMs' full potential as reasoning assistants that can search, converse, create, and take action. Integration grants LLMs context and connectivity to enhance real applications rather than just produce text in isolation.

Let's start by exploring an accessible option for automating bulk prompting across many records – spreadsheet templates and integrations.

Automating bulk prompting with spreadsheets

In the previous chapters, we explored creating social media posts (*Chapter 2*) and performing sentiment analysis, data classification, and data cleaning (*Chapter 5*). For these types of tasks, which are often performed for multiple records, prompting an LLM manually on a case-by-case basis can be tedious and inefficient.

While tools such as ChatGPT, Bard, and Claude 2 allow the usage of variables, you still need to copy and paste input text to process it through the LLM. Then, you have to copy the model's output and paste it into a spreadsheet or another document.

Rather than manual prompting, it's better to automate these workflows. By integrating your LLM with Google Sheets using Apps Script, you can create custom formulas that automatically rerun prompts on many inputs in bulk.

For example, you could write a formula such as `=AI_GPT(A2)` that takes the text from cell A2, sends it to the GPT-3/4 API, and returns the response in the formula cell.

Dragging this down the sheet would call the API for every row, pulling the input text from that row's cell. The formula would populate the LLM-generated response right in the sheet.

This allows you to prompt at scale by updating the input cells. The integration formulas handle feeding the text to the API and filling the outputs without any manual work required. Apps Script provides the glue to rerun prompts on many cases automatically.

I have created **SheetSmart**, a free Google Sheets template that has four custom formulas:

- `AI_GPT`, which gives you the power to enter prompts and get instant results using GPT-3.5/4
- `AI_USE_EXAMPLES_GPT`, which allows you to select a range of values to *train* the model to produce the results that you want
- `AI_TABLE_GPT`, which creates a table based on a prompt such as "List the top 10 songs of all time"
- `AI_DALLE2`, which generates an image based on the prompt that you input

You can download the template at `https://buy.sheetsmart.pro/l/AI_in_Sheets/`.

You can access the Apps Script code by opening the template, going to **Extensions**, and selecting **Apps Script**:

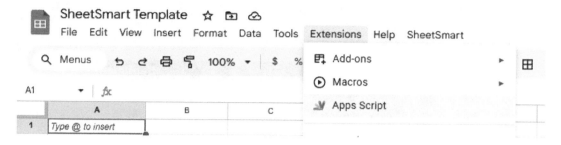

Figure 9.1: Accessing Apps Script from the SheetSmart template

Next, let's look at some of the typical applications of the preceding formulas:

- **Application 1**: Using the AI_GPT formula to clean up messy data:

Figure 9.2: Example of cleaning messy data

- **Application 2**: Using the AI_USE_EXAMPLES_GPT formula to train the model with some examples:

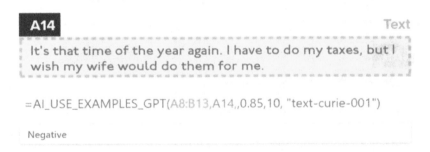

Use Examples to Train Model

Training Data

Text	Sentiment
The movie was amazing, I highly recommend it.	Positive
I'm feeling really sad today.	Negative
This product is a waste of money.	Negative
The concert was just okay, nothing special.	Neutral
I'm not sure how I feel about this restaurant.	Neutral

A14   Text

It's that time of the year again. I have to do my taxes, but I wish my wife would do them for me.

=AI_USE_EXAMPLES_GPT(A8:B13,A14,,0.85,10, "text-curie-001")

Negative

Figure 9.3: Performing sentiment analysis

- **Application 3**: Using the `AI_GPT` formula to create product descriptions:

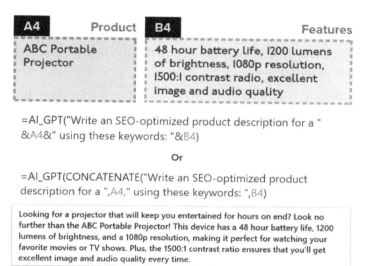

Figure 9.4: Creating product descriptions

- **Application 4**: Using the `AI_TABLE_GPT` formula to create a table based on a prompt:

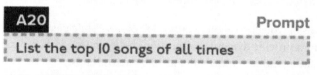

Figure 9.5: Creating a table based on a prompt

Looking at these examples should have given you a clearer idea about the application of the formulas.

You can see more examples in this Google Sheet: `https://docs.google.com/spreadsheets/d/1DnHAjvV77SZg3UYGFfUVfn5gyFqZu-E02OSI0-dDBbE/edit?usp=sharing`.

Microsoft and Google have already been integrating LLMs such as GPT-4 into Office 365 and Google Workspace. Though their approaches differ from SheetSmart's focus, we can expect similar native functionality in these platforms soon.

One particular problem with the template, at least in Google Sheets, is that every time you open a sheet or change to another tab, all custom formulas are recalculated. This is problematic and expensive. All the generations are redone, and they consume tokens from OpenAI.

One way to avoid this is to copy the results and paste them back as **Values Only**. By doing that, the generated text will not be the result of a formula, but a text string.

However, more flexible approaches exist to integrate LLMs with spreadsheets:

- Use platforms such as Zapier or Make to connect your spreadsheet data to an LLM API. The integration can feed inputs, capture responses, and write them back to the sheet. This automates prompting at scale.

- With Google's new Bard extensions, Bard can surface relevant information from Gmail, Docs, Drive, Maps, and more to enhance its responses. Bard becomes a smart assistant across Google's suite of apps.

- Leverage developer tools such as **LangChain** or **Superagent** to build custom integrations between LLMs and data pipelines. These provide APIs and frameworks tailored to data engineering use cases such as summaries, chatbots, and question-answering.

The optimal approach depends on your needs and technical abilities. While pasting values locks static text, integrations and extensions provide dynamic connections between spreadsheets and LLMs. They enable more complex automation and workflow enhancement across apps.

In the next section, we will expand on the possible applications by using Zapier and Make.

Integrating LLMs into your tech stack using Zapier and Make

Zapier and Make are integration platform services that make it easy to connect apps, automate workflows, and share data between web services.

Zapier operates on a freemium model, offering pre-built integrations, triggers, and actions that let you quickly build workflows without code. Zaps, the automation workflows made with Zapier, connect over 2,000 different applications by leveraging Zapier's existing connectors.

Make offers an enterprise integration platform for coordinating complex workflows and data flows and building chatbots. It includes advanced tools for API integration, debugging flows, version control, and access management.

Both Zapier and Make help integrate LLMs into your existing stack. For example, using their connectors for Google Sheets and the GPT-3.5/4 API, you can build automation for passing spreadsheet data to an LLM and writing back the outputs.

The benefits of using these platforms are speeding up manual processes and letting LLMs augment your other tools. The possibilities are limitless.

Zapier and Make enable the same functionality as the Google Sheets template using GPT-3.5/4. With Zapier or Make, users can build custom frontends or chatbots to generate prompts. The AI responses can then be saved directly to the sheet as values rather than formulas. This avoids expensive recalculations but adds the cost of Zapier/Make subscriptions. Overall, Zapier and Make provide more flexibility in prompt collection and result storage compared to the Google template alone. However, all three tools empower users to leverage LLMs within Sheets workflows.

Here are some sophisticated use cases for integrating LLMs with other tools using Zapier or Make:

- **Marketing automation**:

  - **Automated ad creative generation**: Create a workflow using Make and Stability AI's generative AI to continuously generate fresh ad creatives. It would identify top-performing ads, pass the copy to GPT-4 to rewrite text, and provide prompts to Stable Diffusion to generate new images. This combines automation and leading AI to efficiently produce volumes of high-quality new ad creatives.

  - **Multi-language landing pages**: Translate top English landing pages and ad creatives into target languages using DeepL for translation and GPT-3.5 for final fluency polish. This expands global reach.

- **Sales enablement**:

  - **Meeting prep briefings**: Build a Zap to routinely summarize key client interactions from calendar entries, notes, emails, and more and provide action items to prepare for account meetings

  - **Proposal generation**: Create personalized, dynamic product configuration and spec sheet proposals tailored to each customer's needs by having Claude analyze their requirements documents and past configurations

  - **Presentation drafting**: Automatically produce draft presentations for sales meetings by having Claude review accounts' Salesforce history and suggest key points to cover, opportunities to highlight, and objections to preemptively counter

- **Customer experience**:

  - **Ticket enrichment with articles**: Build a workflow to take raw customer support tickets and have Claude suggest the attachment of knowledge-based articles while summarizing issues for agent review before sending a response

  - **Churn prediction and offers**: Enrich customer support conversations by having an LLM analyze Zendesk ticket data to proactively identify customers at high risk of churn and craft personalized retention offers and care packages

  - **Tutorial video generation**: Create dynamic narrated step-by-step tutorial videos personalized to each customer's level and use cases by generating custom scripts with Claude

- **Business intelligence**:

  - **Automated reporting**: Build an automated report generation workflow that uses Claude or GPT-4 to analyze sales data from Salesforce and produce customized account performance summaries, territory analyses, and forecast updates

  - **Competitive intelligence**: Build a customized competitive intelligence briefing by having Claude analyze competitors' earning calls, filings, patents, web traffic, hiring, social media, news mentions, and more to generate insights

- **Operations**:

  - **Release note generation**: Set up a system where GPT-3.5 reviews code commits in GitHub and provides concise, automated release note summaries of new features and fixes rather than manual updates

Let's explore a simple use case to show how these integrations work. We will create a Zapier workflow that gathers some product data and, using GPT-3.5, produces descriptions in English and Spanish and saves them into a Google Sheet.

Creating and translating product descriptions

For e-commerce companies, product content is a crucial driver of conversions across markets. However, manually crafting customized, localized descriptions for every product is extremely time-intensive. This section outlines an automated workflow to effortlessly produce high-quality multilingual product copy using Zapier and the power of GPT-3.5.

Go to `https://zapier.com/` and create an account if you do not have one. Then, on the dashboard, you will find an interface to describe what you want to do. Zapier flows are now powered by AI, so you can describe the process you want to automate and Zapier will build the workflow for you, as shown in *Figure 9.6*.

However, this case is simple, so we will start from scratch. To do that, click where it says **Create a Zap from scratch**:

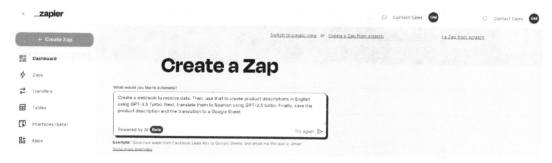

Figure 9.6: Creating a Zap from scratch

You will get the following output:

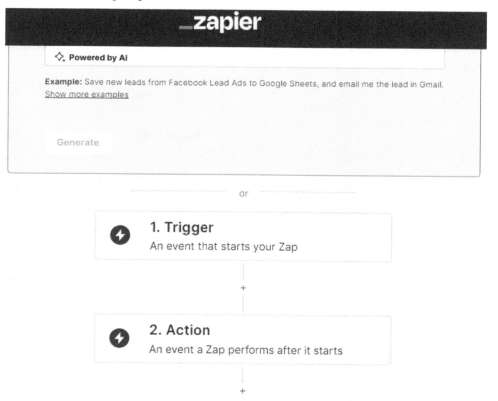

Figure 9.7: Initial screen when starting from scratch

Select the trigger step by clicking on it. Then, search for webhook and select **Webhooks by Zapier**, as shown in *Figure 9.8*:

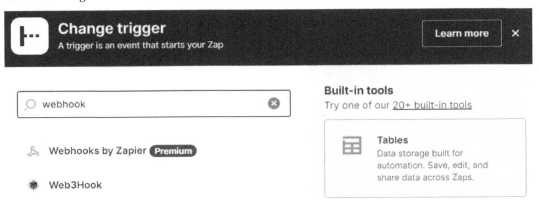

Figure 9.8: Zap of the workflow

Selecting the first step, **Catch Hook**, allows us to create an endpoint to send data to Zapier. This can be used on a form or a chatbot. In this case, we will send some data from Postman, a tool that allows us to test APIs and webhooks. *Figure 9.9* shows the flow:

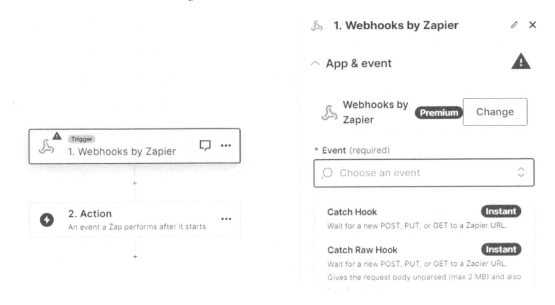

Figure 9.9: Selecting Catch Hook

Then, click **Continue** until the webhook URL is displayed, as shown in *Figure 9.10*:

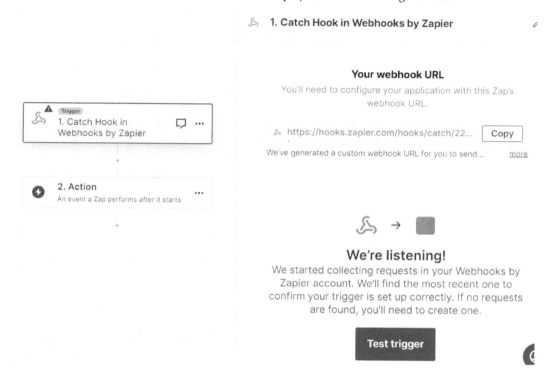

Figure 9.10: Getting the webhook URL

You need to test this webhook URL with some data. *Figure 9.10* shows the call to that URL, in Postman, with a JSON payload with some products:

Figure 9.11: Testing the webhook in Postman

Then, in Zapier, click the **Test trigger** button (*Figure 9.10*); it will get the data that was submitted, as shown in *Figure 9.12*:

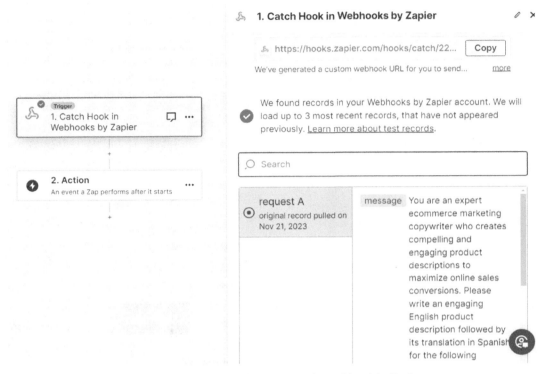

Figure 9.12: Getting the data sent via the webhook in Zapier

Next, continue to **2. Action**, and search for OpenAI, as shown in *Figure 9.13*:

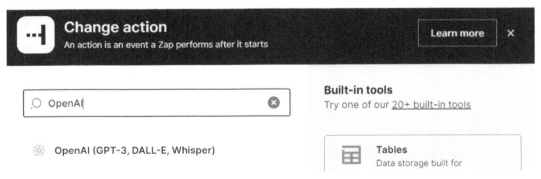

Figure 9.13: Searching for OpenAI

From there, when you select **Event**, you must choose **Send Prompt** from the list of options. Then, click on **Continue**. for **Account**, click **Choose** (*Figure 9.15*) and select **Connect a New Account**. You will be asked to enter your OpenAI API key and organization ID. You can generate a new API key from the corresponding menu and you can get your organization ID from the **Settings** menu on the OpenAI site:

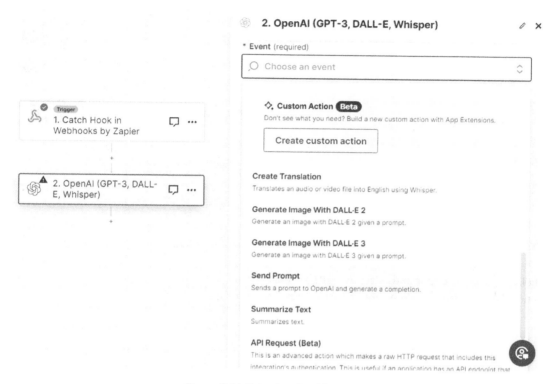

Figure 9.14: Selecting Send Prompt

For **Account**, click **Choose** (*Figure 9.15*) and select **Connect a New Account**. You will be asked to enter your OpenAI API key and organization ID. You can generate a new API key from the corresponding menu, and you can get your organization ID from the **Settings** menu on the OpenAI site.

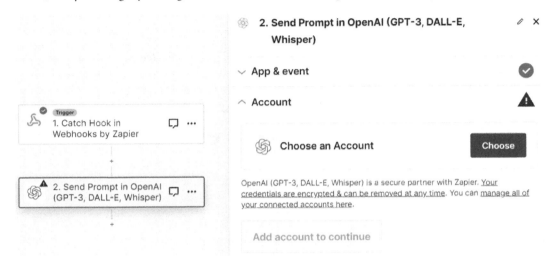

Figure 9.15: Choosing an OpenAI account

Follow the instructions and select the GPT model that you want. In this case, GTP-3.5 Turbo works fine. Then, test the step. You should see the response from OpenAI.

Next, add another step by clicking on the plus sign below **2. Action**. Search for `code` and select **JavaScript**. You need to write a little code snippet to parse the result from GPT-3.5 as a JSON object. Although the text received looks like a JSON object, it is just a text string. Fortunately, Zapier has an option to generate the code for you using AI. *Figure 9.16* shows this option and the code needed:

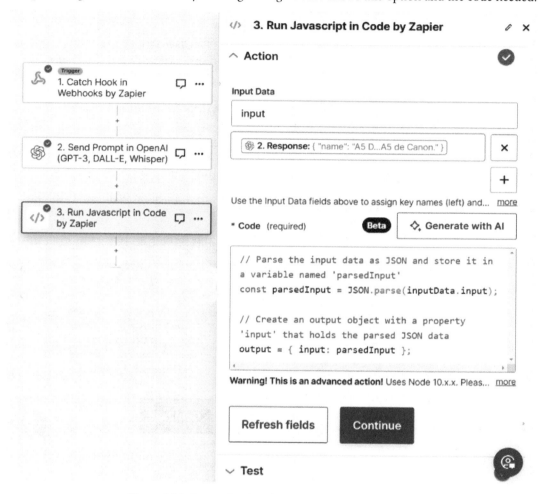

Figure 9.16: Generating JavaScript code with AI in Zapier

Then, click on **Test** to try the code step. You will get something like what is shown in *Figure 9.17*. The result is nicely parsed in value pairs – **name**: **A5 Digital Camera**, **brand**: **Canon**, and so on:

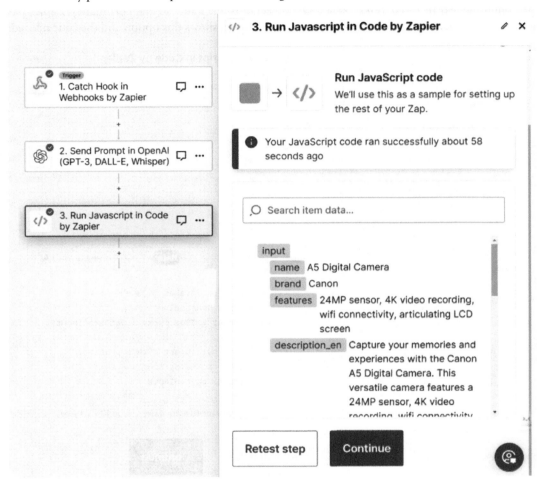

Figure 9.17: Testing the code

Now that each variable is paired with a key value, we can proceed to the last step: saving the data as a new row in a Google Sheet. Thus, click on the plus sign below *Step 3*. Search for `Google Sheets`. Follow the instructions to authenticate your Google Sheets account. Next, select **Create Spreadsheet Row**. Then, select the spreadsheet and sheet you created to save your data. Your sheet should have columns representing the variables to save. Once you've selected your Google Sheet and worksheet, you should see the column names below the the **Worksheet** field, as shown in *Figure 9.18*:

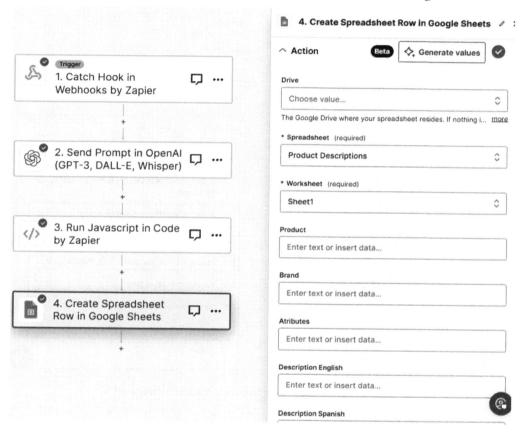

Figure 9.18: Creating a new row in Google Sheets

Click on the field for each column value. We want to get the values we produced in *Step 3* (code), so we need to select it and then select the name of the variable that represents the name of the column. In *Figure 9.19*, we are pairing the variable name with the column product. Repeat this for each column value:

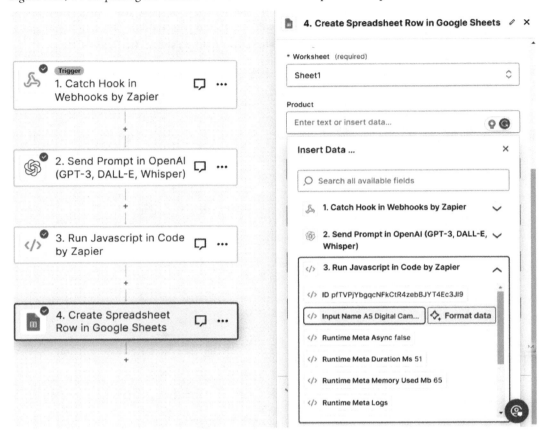

Figure 9.19: Mapping the value to pass to each column – part 1

Figure 9.20 shows the mapping:

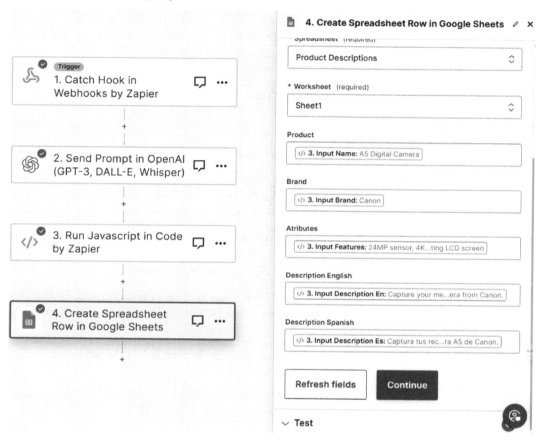

Figure 9.20: Mapping the value to pass to each column – part 2

Next, click on **Test** to check that the data has been saved to Google Sheets as expected. *Figure 9.21* shows the results:

	A	B	C	D	E
1	**Product**	**Brand**	**Atributes**	**Description English**	**Description Spanish**
2	A5 Digital Camera	Canon	24MP sensor, 4K video recording, wifi connectivity, articulating LCD screen	Capture your memories and experiences with the Canon A5 Digital Camera. This versatile camera features a 24MP sensor, 4K video recording, wifi connectivity, and an articulating LCD screen, making it perfect for any situation. Get sharp, clear images and stunning videos with the A5 Digital Camera from Canon.	Captura tus recuerdos y experiencias con la cámara digital Canon A5. Esta cámara versátil cuenta con un sensor de 24MP, grabación de video 4K, conectividad wifi y una pantalla LCD articulada, lo que la hace perfecta para cualquier situación. Obtén imágenes nítidas y claras y videos impresionantes con la cámara A5 de Canon.
3					

Figure 9.21: Results saved to Google Sheets

Finally, publish your workflow – it will be ready to receive data that's sent when the webhook is called from an application – run the prompt, and add new rows to your Google Sheet.

In the next section, we will explore tools such as LangChain, Langflow, and Flowise, which can add even more flexibility to build AI-based tools for many different applications.

Moving beyond APIs – building custom LLM pipelines with LangChain

LangChain is an open source Python and JavaScript library for building workflows and systems using LLMs such as GPT-3.

Created by Harrison Chase, LangChain initially focused on streamlining integration with OpenAI APIs. It has since expanded to support other LLMs, including models such as Anthropic's Claude.

The library implements techniques from the ReAct paper published in 2022. ReAct demonstrates prompting methods that allow LLMs to engage in reasoning by maintaining a chain-of-thought context. Models can also take action by leveraging tools such as internet search to gather information.

This combination, referred to as ReAct, enables LLMs to solve problems more effectively by thinking through logic and bringing in outside knowledge. LangChain codifies these techniques into developer-friendly frameworks.

LangChain supports a wide range of LLMs from various providers, including the following:

- OpenAI's GPT-3
- Anthropic's Claude and Constitutional AI
- Google's LaMDA and PaLM
- Meta's OPT
- Baidu's ERNIE and PaddlePaddle
- Tencent's Wu Dao
- Hugging Face's models, such as BLOOM, LeoLM, and Jurassic-1
- AI21 Studio's models, such as Jurassic-1 J1
- Cohere's Generative QA model
- Microsoft's Turing NLG models

LangChain's workflow engine handles routing prompts and chaining logic across multiple models with diverse strengths and capabilities. This allows developers to orchestrate systems using the optimal blend of LLMs for their needs, without vendor lock-in. LangChain also aims to provide ongoing support for major new LLMs so that users can integrate innovations from AI research consistently through LangChain.

Here are some examples of how LangChain can be used to leverage the unique capabilities of different LLMs:

- A developer could use LangChain to chain together GPT-4 and Jurassic-1 to generate creative text formats, such as poems, code, scripts, musical pieces, emails, letters, and more

- A researcher could use LangChain to compare the performance of different LLMs on a variety of **natural language processing** (**NLP**) tasks

- A company could use LangChain to build a chatbot that uses the strengths of multiple LLMs to provide more informative and engaging responses to users

Overall, LangChain simplifies the process of moving LLMs from basic API usage to production-ready NLP systems. Its workflows enhance text generation quality and allow customization for real-world applications.

Now that we've covered the need for tools such as LangChain, let's explore its core components. These building blocks power the development of customized AI workflows.

LangChain's building blocks

LangChain provides a robust set of modular components for constructing complex NLP systems and workflows. These building blocks make it easy for developers to integrate LLMs into real-world production applications.

Now, let's take an in-depth look at these building blocks:

- **Schemas**

  Schemas in LangChain allow you to define the structure of data payload inputs and outputs for each step in your workflow. You can create schemas for text, images, audio, video, and database formats by specifying field names, data types, and relationships.

  Schemas serve as a blueprint for how data should be handled as it flows through your LangChain pipeline. They ensure each component knows what to expect and return.

- **Models**

  The Models component offers abstractions for integrating different LLMs into your workflow, including GPT-3, Claude, PaLM, Codex, and OPT, among others. You can connect custom-trained models and specify parameters such as engine version, temperature, top-p sampling, and more.

Switching between alternative models is simplified by this consistent interface. Models can be chained together, allowing you to leverage different strengths.

- **Prompts**

  LangChain provides libraries of prompt templates tailored for various NLP tasks, such as classification, summarization, and question-answering. These templates can be reused and customized as needed.

  Tools are provided for iteratively developing prompts, analyzing how models interpret them, and debugging issues. Prompts can be generated programmatically or defined manually.

- **Indexes**

  To power performant search across large datasets, LangChain offers tools such as Langchain crawler for creating customized keyword indexes. You can also leverage pre-built indexes for common public corpora.

  Indexes allow you to supply context to models by quickly locating relevant documents or passages using keywords or semantic similarity.

- **Memory**

  LangChain includes memory components for caching interim results, state, and temporary variables to share across workflow steps. Memory can be scoped globally across the workflow or locally within modules.

  Intelligent caching strategies optimize cost and latency by avoiding redundant computations. Persistence options allow state to be retained across executions.

- **Chains**

  Building chains of prompts and models is a core LangChain concept for developing reasoning and conversational workflows. You can construct linear chains, branch based on conditions, iterate in loops, and break long chains into reusable modular blocks.

- **Agents**

  LangChain allows you to encapsulate reusable logic into modular agents for capabilities such as search, question-answering, translation, and optimization. You must invoke these agents from within your workflows to incorporate their capabilities.

  Agents can be fully customized by developing them in Python or JavaScript. Pre-built agents are offered for common needs to accelerate development.

There are also open source no-code platforms such as Langflow and Flowise that enable non-technical users to leverage the advanced NLP capabilities of LangChain for building natural language workflows and applications. For those of you who are not developers, both Flowise and Langflow are good options to get started. In the next section, we will look at these no-code platforms.

LangChain's no-code tools – Langflow and Flowise

Langflow and Flowise both provide visual workflow builders where users can drag and drop pre-built blocks for tasks such as text generation, classification, search, and translation and orchestrate them into end-to-end pipelines.

Intuitive drag-and-drop interfaces remove the need for coding expertise. Users can start from pre-made template workflows or customize flows for their specific use cases.

Langflow and Flowise handle deploying and hosting the workflows on managed infrastructure. They provide monitoring, analytics, access controls, and connectors to extend functionality.

The key difference is that Langflow is focused specifically on LangChain integration, while Flowise has connectors to services beyond just LangChain.

Langflow is written in Python while Flowise is written in JavaScript.

Ultimately, both Langflow and Flowise open up the power of LangChain to non-developers – product managers, growth hackers, marketers, and other domain experts can harness LLMs for NLP.

They make it possible to build sophisticated workflows using LangChain's repository of techniques without engineering resources.

You can get more information about these tools here:

- **LangChain docs**: `https://docs.langchain.com/docs/`
- **Langflow docs**: `https://docs.langflow.org/`
- **Flowise docs**: `https://docs.flowiseai.com/`

To show some of the possible applications, we will explore some scenarios using Flowise.

Exploring Flowise

To see Flowise in action, let's walk through installing it and building some example chatbots:

1. Install Flowise by running `npm install -g flowise`.
2. Start Flowise by running `npx flowise start`.

3.   Open `http://localhost:3000`. You should see something similar to this:

Figure 9.22: Flowise interface

If this is your first time using Flowise, there should not be any chat flows. Chat flows are the applications that you develop.

Under **Marketplace**, you can see some templates for different applications and pre-made tools that you can use:

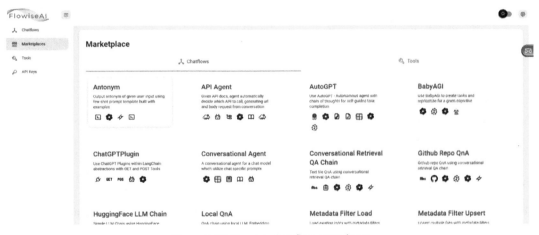

Figure 9.23: Flowise chat flow templates

You can easily create tools using the APIs of the tools you want or need to use. Furthermore, if you create a workflow with Zapier or Make and the entry point to that workflow is a **webhook**, you can use it to set up your own custom tools. A webhook is an automated way for an app or service to provide real-time updates to another app or service when certain events occur. This allows you to build more powerful applications:

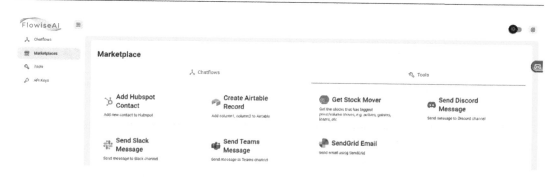

Figure 9.24: Flowise predefined tools

Since Flowise is a visual builder on top of LangChain, it has several block types mirroring the ones of LangChain. For each type, it offers different configuration options, so the user can select the ones that are more appropriate for their specific case. These are the block types:

- **Chat models** such as GPT-3.5 Turbo and GPT-4 are designed specifically for conversational AI applications. They take previous messages as input context and generate a relevant next response.

  These chat-focused models are more powerful and cost-effective for dialogue applications compared to general-purpose "completion" models such as text-davinci-003. Completion models are tuned for single-turn text generation versus multi-turn back-and-forth chat.

  Chat models build on the foundation of models such as GPT-3 and leverage added training data and optimizations tailored for conversation flow and coherence. This allows them to follow dialogue context, incorporate previous responses, and produce more natural, relevant replies.

  For example, chat models can handle tasks such as answering follow-up questions, clarifying intent, and correcting previous statements. Their training also focuses on engagingness, positivity, and consistency.

- **Embeddings** provide a way to convert text into numerical representations that encode semantic meaning. Machine learning models can generate embeddings by analyzing relationships between words and sentences in large datasets.

  These text embeddings capture contextual nuances and similarities that go beyond surface-level word matching. For example, embeddings can map synonyms and analogies close together in the vector space.

  This numerical representation of text makes embeddings very useful for finding semantically related documents. Rather than just matching by keywords, we can compare the vector distances between document embeddings to identify relevant or similar passages.

  Embedding encodings allow us to perform vector similarity searches to retrieve documents containing conceptually associated content. This level of semantic matching is not possible with keyword indexing approaches.

- **Vector stores** are databases that are optimized for managing large collections of numeric vectors or embeddings. They allow efficient storage and retrieval of high-dimensional data points compared to traditional databases.

  Flowise provides integrations with several vector stores, such as Pinecone, Chroma, Supabase, and Qdrant. These can be incorporated into workflows in two main ways:

  - **Upserting document embeddings**: Vectorizer blocks generate embeddings from text or other media. These embeddings can be ingested into the vector store using upsert actions. This populates the index. Upsert is the process of inserting a new record or updating an existing record in a database using a single statement, based on whether the record already exists.

  - **Loading existing indexes**: Pre-built vector indexes can be loaded into the workflow's state. This provides access to search over the indexed embeddings using the vector store's similarity functions.

- **Document loaders** allow you to ingest text content from diverse sources, including PDFs, TXT files, CSVs, Notion documents, Confluence pages, and more.

  Document loaders ingest content from various sources, vectorize it with encoders, and enable retrievers to match relevant documents based on vector similarity. They provide a bridge between unstructured text and performant semantic search.

- **Memory components** allow chatbots to maintain context and recall previous conversations as a human would.

- **Tools** provide reusable functions that agents can leverage to perform actions. They encapsulate logic to interact with external data sources, execute sub-workflows, or access other agents.

  By bundling logic into tool abstractions, developers can incorporate a wide range of capabilities into agents. The agents can focus on coordinating the workflow while reusing existing tools as modular building blocks.

In the following sections, we will explore some simple chatbots that can be created with Flowise.

Assembling a chatbot à la ChatGPT

Probably the simplest implementation of a Flowise flow is to create a chatbot that replicates the functionality of ChatGPT. The advantage of doing this is that you can embed it on any website so that you can provide ChatGPT capabilities for your users.

This workflow has three blocks, as shown in *Figure 9.24*:

1. A conversation chain that requires two inputs: a language model and memory.

2. The language model. Since we want to clone ChatGPT, we selected the **gpt-3.5-turbo-0613** model.

3.   Memory. In this case, **Buffer Memory suffices**:

Figure 9.25: ChatGPT clone workflow

Here, we can see the node (or block) options on the left and the chat in action on the right, where we run a test asking a couple of questions.

A flow can be embedded on a website or be used as an API. This can be accomplished by clicking on the </> icon in the top-right corner. A popup with the following options will appear:

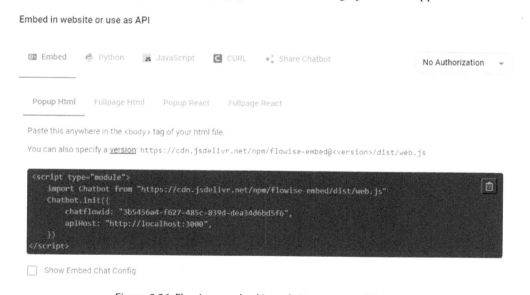

Figure 9.26: Flowise – embed in website or use as API options

In this case, Flowise is running locally on localhost, but it can be deployed to any cloud service, such as Render, Railway, or Replit. It can also be deployed to cloud providers such as AWS, Azure, GCP, and DigitalOcean.

One common application of LLMs is to be able to summarize and ask questions about PDFs and other types of documents. In the next section, we will explore a workflow that allows us to do just that.

Digging for answers in PDFs with LLMs

Many new start-ups and AI agency consulting companies offer services that allow users to chat with their documents and ask questions about their content. With Flowise, you can build such a workflow in just a few minutes.

The workflow looks like the one shown in *Figure 9.26*:

1.   The first thing that we need is a document loader – in this case, a PDF loader. There are other types of document loaders to load text files, CSV, DOCX, web scrapers, and more.

2.   Then, we need a text splitter to break the document into chunks of *N* characters. *N* is a given number of characters defined by the user – 1,000 was chosen in this example. It's good practice to set some overlay to relate a chunk with the adjacent ones.

3.   These chunks have to be stored in a vector database that allows semantic search when needed. I selected Pinecone, which is a popular vector store, but there are several options and they are growing all the time.

4.   To use Pinecone, you need to create an account at https://www.pinecone.io/. Then, you need to create an index and enter the API key, the environment, and the index in the Pinecone node in Flowise. To vectorize the chunks, we need an embedding node. In this case, I'm using the OpenAI one. You need to have an account with OpenAI and generate an API key.

5.   Because we want to ask questions about the PDF, I selected the conversational retrieval QA chain.

6.   Finally, we need an LLM. I chose ChatOpenAI with the **GPT-3.5-0613** model. You need to enter your OpenAI API key in that node as well:

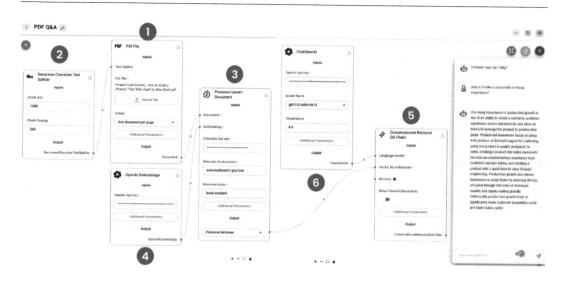

Figure 9.27: Flowise flow to ask questions about a PDF

Once you save your project, you can test using the chat option. In *Figure 9.27*, you can see that it's responding to the question as expected.

You can add more PDF nodes if you want to chat with several documents.

Another simple yet powerful workflow is to allow an LLM to access the internet in real time. There are several nodes offered by tools to do that, such as SERP API, Serper, and Web Browser.

As these two simple examples show, LangChain, Flowise, and Langflow offer powerful capabilities to build sophisticated applications using LLMs. A full workflow could be a custom tool to another workflow. You can even integrate workflows created with Zapier and/or Make in these workflows. Imagine the possibilities.

LangChain recently launched LangSmith, a debugging and monitoring tool for debugging, testing, and monitoring LLM applications, which makes it easier to fix issues with LangChain workflows. We'll explore LangSmith in more detail next.

LangSmith – debug, test, and monitor your LLM workflows

LangSmith provides an end-to-end solution for developing, debugging, testing, and monitoring LLM applications. Its unified platform helps teams move from prototype to production by offering robust capabilities across the LLM application life cycle. Its key features include debugging tools to identify bugs, testing frameworks to validate functionality, monitoring for production apps, visualizations to understand architecture, and exporting data for analysis and sharing. LangSmith aims to enable building enterprise-grade LLM applications from initial prototype through to launch and beyond.

You can get more information about LangSmith here: `https://www.langchain.com/langsmith`.

Innovation in this field is moving very fast. We expect new developments soon. We'll explore some of them in the next section.

The future of LLM integration – plugins, agents, assistants, GPTs, and multimodal models

So far, we have explored integrating LLMs using templates, no-code tools, and developer platforms such as LangChain. However, innovation in this space is rapid. We can expect even more powerful and flexible integration capabilities to emerge. Here are some key developments on the horizon:

- **LLM plugins and extensions**

    Rather than custom coding, expect to see plugins and extensions for directly integrating LLMs into common platforms. We already have plugins for ChapGPT Plus and some of them, such as Code Interpreter, are extremely powerful. Code Interpreter provides a sandboxed Python environment for executing code. While designed for programmers, it can also empower general users to accomplish many tasks.

    For example, you can leverage Code Interpreter to convert PDFs using OCR, edit video files, solve math problems, conduct data analysis and visualization, generate graphs and charts, and more. ChatGPT's Code Interpreter allows you to directly upload local files in various formats.

    Google also launched extensions to Bard. Bard extensions connect Google's conversational AI with its ecosystem of apps, allowing Bard to draw contextual information from services such as Gmail, Maps, and YouTube to provide more useful, integrated responses in one seamless conversation. This connectivity enables enhanced productivity, creativity, and convenience across tasks such as planning, content creation, and learning.

    As LLMs become a standard workplace utility, lightweight plugins will allow you to sprinkle existing workflows into them with little friction. APIs and SDKs will handle the complexity behind simple user interfaces.

- **New LLMs**

    New models will continue to pop up. One example is Google Gemini. Gemini is a multimodal LLM that can process and generate text, images, and code.

- **Specialized LLM agents**

    We will see more modular, specialized LLMs emerge that are pre-trained for particular tasks. These expert agents can provide capabilities such as advanced search, data analysis, optimized recommendations, and automatic report generation out of the box.

Developers can then orchestrate pipelines by combining these best-of-breed expert agents to accomplish complex workflows. Rather than one universal LLM, an agent-based approach plays to different models' strengths.

Along with LangChain, there are other tools tailored for the same purposes that are being developed, such as Superagent (`https://www.superagent.sh/`), LlamaIndex (`https://gpt-index.readthedocs.io/en/stable/index.html`), and many others.

- **Multimodal LLM integration**

    So far, LLMs primarily process and generate text, images, or audio. But models are rapidly improving at uniting text, images, audio, video, and other modalities. We will see tools emerge for tighter integration between LLMs and other media. When OpenAI announced GPT-4 in early 2023, they showed some of the potential of multimodal capabilities. Bard already allows you to load an image and ask it for the context of such an image. We will see more powerful multimodal models in the near future.

Rather than separate utilities, we'll see LLMs become embedded assistants that boost productivity across everyday apps. Tight integration unlocks more contextual recommendations and automation potential.

As LLMs advance, we can expect integration tools to grant broader access to their capabilities while customizing them for specialized domains. Templates and no-code will empower non-developers, while extensibility will prevent vendor lock-in. The next waves of innovation look to make LLMs flexible utilities anyone can apply to their unique needs.

OpenAI's announcements on November 6, 2023, point to some key developments in LLM integration going forward:

- Simplified Assistants API

- Customizable GPTs

- Tighter multimodal connections

OpenAI's new Assistants API provides an easy way to build intelligent agents with capabilities such as code execution, data analysis, and task automation. Developers can quickly create assistants tailored to specific use cases without complex custom coding, by just prompting commands in natural language..

The Assistants API handles ingesting data sources, maintaining conversation context across messages, and leveraging tools such as Code Interpreter and Retrieval under the hood. This lowers the barrier to integrating LLMs into workflows.

With customizable GPTs, users can now craft specialized custom-made GPTs for particular domains and tasks – for example, creating a math tutor GPT or a product copywriting assistant. GPTs make it easy to personalize LLMs without needing data science expertise.

GPTs also let you share helpful AI tools with others through OpenAI's upcoming GPT Store. This marketplace will allow creators to distribute and potentially monetize their custom assistants.

On the multimodal front, access to models such as DALL-E 3 for generating images from text prompts tightly connects text and visuals. The new text-to-speech API similarly bridges text and audio.

As LLMs progress, we'll see models that gracefully unite text, images, audio, video, and data. This interweaving empowers more assistive, personalized, and human-like interactions.

Rather than a one-size-fits-all LLM, purpose-built assistants, GPTs, and integrations tailored to unique use cases appear to be the path forward for delivering value with AI.

Summary

This chapter explored different techniques for integrating LLMs into workflows to automate prompting at scale. We looked at easy template options such as SheetSmart for Google Sheets as well as no-code automation platforms such as Zapier. For more advanced customization, developer tools such as LangChain, Flowise, and Langflow enable building pipelines and applications using multiple LLMs. We walked through sample use cases for competitive intelligence, customer data enrichment, and conversing with documents to see how integrations could work in practice.

Looking ahead, tight connections between conversational AI and everyday productivity apps will enable LLMs to provide more relevant, contextual recommendations and automation. However, while integration unlocks usefulness, it also raises important ethical considerations; we will explore this in the next chapter. As these powerful technologies become further embedded into daily life, principles such as transparency, accountability, and control become crucial.

Part 4:
Ethics, Limitations, and Future Developments

Chapter 10 explores the multifaceted ethical challenges posed by the rise of increasingly capable generative AI systems. As these technologies advance, they introduce risks of perpetuating bias, threatening privacy, disrupting labor markets, exacerbating climate change, and more. However, good governance rooted in human rights can help steer innovations toward beneficial ends. Solutions emphasize ethics by design, algorithmic auditing, thoughtful regulations, and inclusive participation.

Chapter 11 concludes by recapping core concepts from the book, including using conditional prompting for personalization, causality prompting for reasoning, and deanonymization prompting to probe dangers. As access democratizes, responsible oversight and governance will be imperative. Prompt engineering unlocks immense creativity, but we must thoughtfully direct it toward uplifting applications that synthesize the best of human and artificial strengths. The future remains undetermined – our choices today will resonate for generations.

Overall, *Part 4* explores responsible stewardship of these exponentially accelerating technologies. With ethical mindfulness guiding development and governance, prompt engineering promises to unlock AI's potential while upholding human dignity and wisdom.

This part has the following chapters:

- *Chapter 10, Generative AI: Emerging Issues at the Intersection of Ethics and Innovation*
- *Chapter 11, Conclusion*

10
Generative AI – Emerging Issues at the Intersection of Ethics and Innovation

Generative **artificial intelligence** (**AI**) systems represent a new era of AI capabilities. Unlike narrow AI, which is programmed to perform specific, limited tasks without general intelligence or adaptability beyond their narrow focus, generative AI can automatically create a wide range of new content and artifacts such as text, images, audio, and video based on its training data.

Recent advances in deep learning have rapidly accelerated the sophistication of generative models such as GPT-4, DALL-E 3, and Stable Diffusion. While this unlocks new creative potential, it also introduces profound ethical challenges that demand urgent attention as these technologies proliferate across society.

As generative AI capabilities advance, these technologies raise complex questions at the intersection of ethics, technological progress, and social impacts. This chapter explores emerging issues across multiple dimensions – from risks of bias and threats to labor markets to environmental sustainability challenges and deeper philosophical questions about the nature of machine creativity. We will examine key ethical concerns around transparency, accountability, and trust in generative AI systems. The economic impacts will be discussed, highlighting both opportunities and potential displacement risks for workers. Environmental sustainability issues such as energy usage and emissions will also be outlined. Broader societal risks will be explored, along with reflections on what advances in machine creativity reveal about the philosophy of mind. Finally, potential solutions and safeguards are proposed that emphasize collaborative governance and upholding humanistic values as we steer these transformative technologies toward beneficial ends that enrich society. This chapter aims to provide a comprehensive overview of the multifaceted ethical landscape posed by the rise of generative AI.

The following topics will be covered in this chapter:

- Exploring the ethical challenges of generative AI
- Economic impact considerations
- Environmental sustainability issues
- Societal risks and reflections
- The path forward – solutions and safeguards

Exploring the ethical challenges of generative AI

Generative AI introduces two major ethical challenges that require thoughtful solutions.

First, these systems can perpetuate unfair biases if trained on data reflecting societal prejudices. Biased data ingrains prejudices into models, leading them to make discriminatory choices harmful to marginalized groups.

Second, the immense complexity of generative AI makes it very opaque. Even experts struggle to explain how these models make decisions internally. This lack of interpretability prevents properly auditing the systems for issues such as biases. It hinders public trust. In the following sub-section, we will learn more about these challenges.

Trust and accountability challenges of generative AI

One of the most pressing concerns regarding generative AI is the lack of transparency in its complex inner workings. Akin to a black box whose reasoning and decision-making processes remain obscured from view and human understanding, this opacity surrounding how these systems operate and produce outputs makes it extremely difficult to audit algorithms for issues such as bias or establish trust in the results generated, since the steps taken and logic applied cannot be readily interpreted or verified.

While trust and accountability issues pose near-term concerns, generative AI's impacts on the economy raise additional challenges we must proactively address.

Bias and discrimination risks

Most generative AI models derive capabilities solely from their training data. If the data reflects societal biases and lacks diversity, the models will inherit and amplify these problematic biases.

For example, studies have uncovered strong gender and racial biases in leading language models. Biased data gets encoded in subtle but pernicious ways. When deployed across areas such as finance and criminal justice, generative AI could significantly exacerbate discrimination against already marginalized groups.

A study from Boston University and Microsoft Research, published in April 2019 at the AAAI/ACM Conference on AI, Ethics, and Society, found substantial gender bias in GPT-2. The researchers found the model would associate stereotypically gendered words with occupations – for instance, referring to programmers as *he* and homemakers as *she*.

This bias stemmed from the texts the model was trained on, which reflected gender imbalances and stereotypes in society. As a result, GPT-2 would default to biased outputs. So, for instance, if used for resume screening or job candidate recommendations, the model could discriminate against women in technical fields based on these embedded biases.

Mitigating unfair bias requires diversity and inclusion of best practices throughout the AI development life cycle, from curating training data to evaluating for unwanted biases. Achieving fairer outcomes relies on sustained ethical vigilance.

In addition to the risks of perpetuating bias, the opaque and inscrutable inner workings of many cutting-edge generative AI systems severely limit transparency and explainability. This lack of interpretability poses additional obstacles to ethical governance as we cannot properly audit or establish trust in systems whose decision-making processes remain obscured.

Challenges of transparency and explainability

The inner workings of most cutting-edge generative models are not easily interpretable, even by AI experts. While techniques such as explainable AI provide some insights, current methods cannot fully explain the nonlinear dynamics of large systems such as GPT-3. **Explainable AI (XAI)** is a field of research that aims to make AI and machine learning models more transparent and understandable to humans. XAI techniques provide insights into the internal logic, reasoning, and decision-making processes of AI systems, with the goals of building trust, detecting bias, and allowing humans to properly interpret, audit, and oversee these systems.

Without interpretability, users cannot properly audit or establish trust in generative AI. When utilized in sensitive social domains such as healthcare, being able to inspect and query decisions becomes even more critical. More R&D focused on XAI that illuminates black boxes is urgently needed.

While trust and accountability issues pose near-term concerns, generative AI's impacts on the economy raise additional challenges we must proactively address.

Economic impact considerations

Automating a wide range of creative and analytical tasks with increasingly capable generative AI could cause major disruptions in labor markets and incomes over the next decade. However, projections on net employment impacts remain complex and uncertain.

On one hand, studies suggest generative AI could add trillions to global GDP through gains in productivity, personalized services, and stimulating new industries. But other estimates warn that automated substitution of human roles could impact 50% of jobs and displace up to 12 million US workers alone in the next 10-15 years. Fields such as professional services, media, software, and transportation appear especially at risk.

This necessitates wise governance and visionary leadership for just economic transitions. Targeted programs for worker retraining, educational reform, job creation efforts, income/social supports, and public-private partnerships can help impacted individuals adapt and capitalize on new opportunities.

As scholar Mariana Mazzucato has argued, we must "prepare society for AI" rather than just "AI for society" by focusing on human resilience, empowerment, and dignity alongside technological progress. Maintaining inclusive growth requires centering labor rights and economic justice in governance.

In addition to economic considerations, the environmental impacts of developing and deploying generative AI systems demand urgent attention.

Environmental sustainability issues

The massive computational power required by large generative AI models results in substantial energy use, carbon emissions, and resource consumption. Unconstrained, generative AI risks significantly accelerating climate change and pollution.

For example, training a single natural language model can emit over 600,000 pounds of carbon dioxide, which equals the lifetime emissions of dozens of cars. Analysis suggests that by 2025, computational needs for leading models could rival mid-sized nations in emissions.

Prudent governance is urgently required to curb these impacts through renewable energy requirements, efficiency innovations such as model distillation, comprehensive life cycle assessments, carbon accounting, and strong environmental policies and incentives.

Aligning exponential AI progress and climate action will require collective commitment from researchers, companies, policymakers, and the public. We must steward these technologies toward sustainability to safeguard the future of both human and natural intelligence.

While ethical concerns such as bias and transparency pose clear challenges, the rise of increasingly capable generative systems also necessitates reflecting on more subtle but profound societal risks that could emerge. As these technologies proliferate, we must broaden the discourse to preemptively engage with how generative AI could impact society's collective well-being, values, and direction over time.

Societal risks and reflections

Looking beyond immediate ethical concerns, this section contemplates broader risks generative AI may pose to the social fabric and collective values as these transformative technologies advance. We will reflect on ====the impacts on culture, governance, human cognition, and our self-understanding.

Broader societal impacts

Beyond direct harm, the proliferation of increasingly capable generative systems poses risks of more subtle but still concerning societal impacts. For instance, widespread synthetic media could erode public trust or allow state and corporate interests to manipulate popular narratives.

Overuse of generative AI in creative fields may also diminish cultural richness and authenticity over time. Even as communication barriers are lowered, human understanding across diverse viewpoints could paradoxically suffer if public discourse is increasingly mediated by machines optimizing for engagement over wisdom.

The complex interplay between generative AI and human values such as truth, creativity, and belonging remains highly uncertain. We must broaden the discourse on technology ethics beyond technical flaws alone to its ripple effects on democracy, mental health, childhood development, and more.

While generative AI poses risks to society's functioning, advances in machine creativity also compel deeper philosophical reflection on the nature of intelligence.

What machine creativity reveals about cognition

On a philosophical level, the growing creative capabilities of generative systems compel profound questions about the nature of creativity, consciousness, and intelligence. If machines can generate art, music, humor, and literature, how do we characterize the essence of creative cognition?

Some perspectives hold that generative models merely reconstitute patterns from data rather than exhibiting "true" creativity or intentionality. In this view, algorithmic outputs simulate but do not replicate the subjective qualities of the mind, which are essential for original thinking and understanding. Skeptics contend that human creativity intrinsically reflects unique intentional states, values, and life experiences that algorithms inherently lack.

However, other perspectives argue that the capabilities of generative systems reveal cognition as computation alone. If generative models can mimic diverse creative behaviors indistinguishable from humans, perhaps subjective experience is epiphenomenal rather than integral to cognition. In this materialist view, the mind is the machine – there is no ethereal spark of consciousness beyond physical algorithms.

Reconciling these divergent views remains challenging. We have yet to discern whether AI creativity reflects real but alien forms of machine consciousness, is an illusion of intelligence masking mechanistic processes, or exists somewhere in a gray zone in between. How we ultimately judge machine creativity and cognition will profoundly influence societal self-conceptions and ethics in this age of increasingly capable AI systems.

Rather than definitively resolving these debates, we must thoughtfully consider how integrating human and machine creativity can enhance society. With mindfulness, wisdom, and humanistic ethics guiding development and governance, we can positively shape the trajectory of these accelerating technologies.

As we contemplate the essence of creativity and cognition, the governance of generative AI in sensitive domains such as healthcare and defense demands special prudence given the potential for misuse and harm.

Concerns in defense and healthcare

Generative AI also introduces novel challenges in sensitive domains such as defense and healthcare. Potential misuse for military applications, such as autonomous weapons, warrants careful governance, while healthcare applications demand rigorous validation to avoid biased or flawed treatment recommendations that could endanger patients.

Though we face profound risks ranging from labor disruptions to threats to democracy as generative AI advances, we also have opportunities to purposefully shape these technologies for good through ethical collaboration. If anchored in humanistic values such as justice, human dignity, and wisdom, and guided by diverse stakeholders across civil society, government, and the private sector working together, we can steer these powerful innovations toward ends that benefit humanity as a whole rather than further imperil it.

The path forward – solutions and safeguards

Tackling generative AI's multi-faceted ethical challenges demands collaboration between stakeholders across technology, government, academia, media, and civil society. This is how you can move forward:

- Tech firms must commit to ethics by design by implementing internal oversight boards, algorithmic impact assessments for new products, and bias bounty programs to encourage external auditing.

- Policymakers need to enact thoughtful regulations such as requiring transparency reports, prohibiting harmful uses through export control laws, and mandating rights-preserving data practices.

- Researchers should continue advancing techniques such as adversarial testing for bias detection, AI safety research institutes, and proposed standards around transparent documentation and evaluation protocols.

- Workers must influence the governance of AI systems affecting their livelihoods. Labor power has advanced society before and is needed again amid this transition.

- Educational institutions should equip students through required ethics courses, multidisciplinary programs combining tech and humanities, and community outreach on AI literacy.

- Philosophers, ethicists, humanists, and other deep thinkers must guide societal integration of rapidly advancing systems to retain our values amid this process of change.

- Broader civil society participation can be enabled through independent auditing panels, participatory algorithmic impact assessment frameworks, and mechanisms for marginalized groups to provide input and feedback.

The path forward will not be linear as generative capabilities explode in complexity. But by upholding humanistic values, focusing on ethics and dignity, and working together, we can steer these transformative technologies toward beneficial ends that uplift society. The future remains unwritten – through solidarity and wisdom, we shall write the next great chapters purposefully.

Summary

This chapter provided an overview of the multifaceted ethical landscape posed by the rise of generative AI systems. As these technologies proliferate, we face both profound opportunities and risks that demand thoughtful governance rooted in human rights and democratic values.

We explored numerous challenges that must be addressed, from risks of perpetuating bias and threatening privacy to questions of economic equality, environmental sustainability, philosophical identity, and more. But for each challenge, collaborative solutions are possible if we center ethics, empowerment, and human dignity.

By ensuring transparency and accountability around how generative models operate, we can build public trust. With inclusive governance and just transitions for workers, we can share economic gains equitably. Through renewable energy investments and efficiency innovations, we can align AI progress with climate action and sustainability. By upholding our highest values amid disruption, we can steer these transformative technologies toward uplifting ends that enrich our shared future.

As generative technologies continue proliferating, we must remain vigilant about risks in sensitive domains such as defense and healthcare where misuse could endanger human lives and rights. With ethical mindfulness guiding governance, we can realize the benefits while reducing the potential harms.

But we have not a moment to lose. The choices we make today on the ethics and governance of generative AI will reverberate for generations. Will the story be one of cautionary tales or hope fulfilled? The time for wisdom is now – our shared humanity is on the line. Through solidarity, creativity, and moral courage, we can write the next great chapters together purposefully.

The lesson here is that the path forward requires diligent, proactive efforts from all stakeholders. Tech firms must commit to ethics by design and ongoing algorithmic auditing. Policymakers need to enact thoughtful regulations that balance innovation and responsible governance. Researchers should continue advancing techniques that promote transparency, accountability, and safety. Workers must be able to influence how these systems affect their livelihoods. And civil society participation is key for marginalized voices to be heard.

In the concluding chapter, we will synthesize the concepts we've explored so far to provide a comprehensive guide to the emerging art and science of prompt engineering for generative AI.

11
Conclusion

As we near the close of our journey exploring the frontier of prompt engineering, let's summarize the key lessons and look ahead at the future applications and capabilities this technology may enable.

Prompt engineering represents a breakthrough that unlocks AI's potential when thoughtfully directed, as we've seen through diverse examples. Like crafting a recipe, prompt writers carefully hone the ingredients to guide **large language models (LLMs)**.

While models still require rigorous human validation today, prompt engineering promises to greatly augment human capabilities and creativity. Applications could help accelerate discoveries, improve decision-making, and enhance productivity.

However, we must remain cognizant of the risks and limitations. Developing beneficial syntheses of human and artificial strengths calls for care, wisdom, and transparency. Policy incentives encouraging responsible innovation will be vital as access democratizes.

This concluding chapter will do the following:

- Provide an executive summary of the book's core concepts
- Highlight innovative applications of prompt engineering across industries
- Discuss how to craft prompts to achieve the intended outcomes
- Examine responsible oversight needed as capabilities advance

As we conclude this in-depth exploration of prompt engineering, it is evident that this emerging technology represents an extraordinarily promising AI frontier. Although we have only skimmed the possibilities, prompt engineering demonstrates immense potential to fundamentally transform nearly every industry and domain.

Recap of the book's content

In the preceding chapters, we saw glimpses of how thoughtful prompt engineering enables generative systems such as LLMs to deliver immense value. From accelerating content creation to automating coding and unlocking insights in data, prompt engineering makes new applications that were not previously feasible possible. It represents a breakthrough that unlocks AI's potential when thoughtfully directed.

Across diverse areas, tailored prompting adapts AI as a versatile assistant, augmenting human endeavors by automating data processing, generating drafts, and enabling personalized recommendations. For now, indispensable human expertise remains essential during this nascent stage of AI maturity.

Looking ahead, techniques such as conditional prompting for personalization, causality prompting, deanonymization prompting, and AI debate hold promise for safer, more reliable applications. Let's explore these prompting types briefly:

- Conditional prompting involves structuring prompts to condition model outputs on provided user attributes and preferences, allowing generated content to be tailored for individual users.

- Causality prompting aims to imbue generative AI with causal reasoning by crafting prompts that require inferring chains of cause and effect. This could enable systems to answer causal what-if questions and improve decision-making.

- Approaches such as deanonymization prompting aim to surface potential re-identification risks by carefully prompting models to reconstruct redacted information. As capabilities grow, responsible prompting will be needed to probe dangers.

- Techniques such as AI debate train models to argue opposing perspectives from a text, exposing contradictory evidence and biases. This could mitigate the risks of misinformation.

As research continues, we may see human-AI collaboration progressively evolve from simple one-way assistance toward deeper two-way partnership. Already tools such as Excel empower analysts – future creative AI systems could similarly revolutionize fields such as education, research, and medicine by catalyzing discovery.

Expanding possibilities – innovative prompt engineering applications

Across healthcare and other vital fields, prompt engineering, when strategically directed, can automate repetitive tasks and powerfully augment professionals' capabilities and productivity. Our journey revealed flashes of a future where prompt engineering frameworks may allow non-experts to safely harness these technologies, much like tools such as Excel turned non-programmers into software power users.

Healthcare offers one of the most compelling application areas for prompt engineering. Some of those applications are as follows:

- **Clinical decision support**: Well-crafted prompts can help LLMs provide doctors with evidence-based recommendations for the diagnosis and treatment of patients based on symptoms and medical history. This acts as a form of clinical decision support. However, a physician should still validate any guidance.

- **Patient education**: Prompts can instruct LLMs to explain complex health conditions, tests, procedures, treatment options, and so on in simple language to patients at an appropriate literacy level. This improves understanding and adherence.

- **Document understanding**: Using prompts, LLMs can extract key information from medical records, notes, prescriptions, and so on and summarize or highlight relevant details, aiding physicians.

- **Drug discovery**: Prompts can guide LLMs to analyze molecular interactions and 3D protein structures to identify novel drug candidates or repurposed uses for existing drugs.

- **Image analysis**: When prompted properly, LLMs show promise for medical image analysis such as screening radiology scans for abnormalities and suggesting diagnoses for physician review.

- **Epidemiology**: LLMs can rapidly analyze vast amounts of epidemiological data, news, and scientific papers to detect early disease outbreak signals when engineered with the right prompts.

- **Virtual assistants**: Medical chatbots built with LLM APIs can provide conversational guidance to patients on health topics, book appointments, complete intake forms, and so on when appropriately prompted.

- **Clinical trials**: LLMs can help screen patient records to identify protocol candidates, monitor enrollment criteria, and ensure proper informed consent is obtained when directed by prompts.

Other industries, such as engineering, government, journalism, and education, also exhibit great potential to augment human capabilities through prompt engineering. By automating rote tasks, surfaced insights could accelerate discovery and decision-making when strategically directed. Here are some examples:

- **Finance**: LLMs can analyze earnings reports, prospectuses, news, and so on to generate investment recommendations or draft reports when properly prompted. This is useful for investing, trading, and analysis.

- **Engineering**: Prompts can instruct LLMs to recommend materials, designs, or methods for engineering problems by leveraging their vast technical knowledge. This helps with ideating and prototyping.

- **Journalism**: Prompts can guide LLMs to generate rough drafts of articles or summaries of key details from research when provided with appropriate context. This helps with writing.

- **Government**: LLMs can rapidly analyze policies, legislation, regulations, and so on to provide policymakers with summarized insights or draft documents when engineered effectively. This assists in analysis and policy making.

- **Scientific research**: Prompts can steer LLMs to develop hypotheses, design experimental frameworks, analyze results, or draft manuscripts when given research goals and data. This complements R&D.

- **Customer service**: LLMs can answer customer queries, recommend solutions, or escalate issues when unable to help if prompted properly with product knowledge and guidelines. This streamlines support.

- **Manufacturing**: Prompts directing LLMs to propose optimized production flows, inventory levels, or predictive maintenance schedules based on parameters such as demand forecasts help boost efficiency.

- **Human resources**: LLMs can help screen resumes, schedule interviews, suggest interview questions, and draft job descriptions when prompted appropriately. This streamlines hiring and HR workflows.

- **Transportation**: LLMs can analyze traffic patterns, weather data, fleet telemetry, and so on and recommend optimized routes and schedules for delivery vehicles when properly directed. This increases efficiency.

- **Insurance**: Prompts can guide LLMs to extract key details from claims, assess risks, and suggest fair settlement amounts based on policy terms and previous cases. This expedites claim processing.

- **Agriculture**: LLMs can take real-time data on soil conditions, weather, crop growth, and so on and propose interventions such as irrigation, fertilizer, and harvest times when engineered effectively. This supports precision agriculture.

- **Retail**: Prompts can instruct LLMs to generate product descriptions, analyze customer data to tailor recommendations, or optimize pricing and inventory based on demand forecasts. This boosts sales and conversion.

- **Real estate**: LLMs can value properties, flag risks in contracts, suggest listing prices aligned to market data, or draft property descriptions when prompted appropriately. This assists brokers and agents.

- **Cybersecurity**: LLMs can rapidly scan code, analyze threats, identify vulnerabilities, and suggest fixes when directed by prompts written by security engineers. This bolsters software security.

- **Education**: We discussed applications for creating curriculum materials, but LLMs also show promise for personalized and adaptive education when properly prompted.

While these advanced applications demonstrate prompting at the cutting edge, it is also important to take a step back and consider the full range of goals prompts can achieve with LLMs, as we'll explore next.

Achieving intended outcomes – prompt engineering goals

Prompt engineering is most effective when approached as a goal-directed endeavor. Clearly defining the objectives and intended outcomes you want to achieve is an essential first step that informs every subsequent prompt design decision.

Before crafting your prompts, always start by asking yourself – what is the purpose of generating this content or executing this task? What would constitute success? Articulating concrete goals gives your prompt engineering efforts direction and enhances your ability to guide the LLM toward your desired results. Whether your aims are to generate text summaries, synthesize insights from data, suggest personalized recommendations, or anything else, anchoring your prompts in specific goals is key.

Prompt engineering applications serve different types of goals, as depicted in *Figure 11.1.*

Figure 11.1: Prompt goals

While thoughtful prompt engineering enables achieving a vast range of goals by harnessing the potential of LLMs, it remains critical to maintain realistic expectations and responsible oversight, as we'll explore next.

Understanding limitations and maintaining oversight

Of course, we must also remain cognizant of limitations. For now, outputs still require rigorous human validation as today's models fundamentally lack true comprehension of language. Developing beneficial syntheses of complementary human and artificial strengths will be an ongoing pursuit requiring great care, wisdom, and transparency.

The democratization of these technologies through intuitive tools promises significantly expanded access but also poses major risks without thoughtful governance. Policy incentives encouraging participatory community audits of potential societal impacts could promote responsible innovation, as could supporting independent testing and standards bodies to assess factors such as bias and misuse prevention. Requirements for open algorithmic impact assessments prior to deployment may be prudent.

Integrating these models with services via platforms such as Zapier can greatly augment their functions. Chatbots become capable of natural dialogue when powered by LLMs. Automations connect LLMs to diverse data sources and outputs. Tools such as LangChain give LLMs access to customize data sources for enhanced responses. With LangChain, you can create personalized AI agents by training models on your unique data such as calendars, emails, and notes. This enables building tailored solutions that understand your context and preferences at a deep level. The possibilities for customization are immense.

Thoughtful prompt engineering provides immense agency to guide these models toward beneficial outcomes while retaining human oversight. Used judiciously, generative AI promises to augment human capabilities and creativity on a massive scale. Prompts are the key that unlocks this potential.

Summary

This book provided an introductory overview of text generation techniques, but prompt engineering encompasses much more. Emerging techniques also enable generating images, audio, 3D, video, and more. As LLMs grow more multimodal, prompt engineering will unlock even richer creative possibilities.

With LLMs' rapid evolution, we can expect models that are capable of processing over 1 million tokens of text in their context window. This will provide far greater memory capacity and understanding of linguistic context. They will integrate massive multimodal knowledge and become exponentially more powerful and nuanced.

For now, you have the core knowledge to start engineering prompts for different use cases, limited only by your imagination. This book aimed to ignite exciting possibilities for how AI could transform nearly every facet of life and work. Although generative AI is still young, the future looks bright.

Your next step is to start experimenting with the core principles and techniques provided in this book. I look forward to seeing the incredible things you will create by thoughtfully applying prompt engineering. Thank you for learning about this fascinating field – your skills will help shape its future. The story has only just begun.

Index

Packtpub.com

Subscribe to our online digital library for full access to over 7,000 books and videos, as well as industry leading tools to help you plan your personal development and advance your career. For more information, please visit our website.

Why subscribe?

- Spend less time learning and more time coding with practical eBooks and Videos from over 4,000 industry professionals

- Improve your learning with Skill Plans built especially for you

- Get a free eBook or video every month

- Fully searchable for easy access to vital information

- Copy and paste, print, and bookmark content

Did you know that Packt offers eBook versions of every book published, with PDF and ePub files available? You can upgrade to the eBook version at packtpub.com and as a print book customer, you are entitled to a discount on the eBook copy. Get in touch with us at customercare@packtpub.com for more details.

At www.packtpub.com, you can also read a collection of free technical articles, sign up for a range of free newsletters, and receive exclusive discounts and offers on Packt books and eBooks.

Other Books You May Enjoy

If you enjoyed this book, you may be interested in these other books by Packt:

Building AI Applications with ChatGPT APIs

Martin Yanev

ISBN: 978-1-80512-756-7

- Develop a solid foundation in using the ChatGPT API for natural language processing tasks.

- Build, deploy, and capitalize on a variety of desktop and SaaS AI applications.

- Seamlessly integrate ChatGPT with established frameworks such as Flask, Django, and Microsoft Office APIs.

- Channel your creativity by integrating DALL-E APIs to produce stunning AI-generated art within your desktop applications.

- Experience the power of Whisper API's speech recognition and text-to-speech features.

- Discover techniques to optimize ChatGPT models through the process of fine-tuning.

Modern Generative AI with ChatGPT and OpenAI Models

Valentina Alto

ISBN: 978-1-80512-333-0

- Understand generative AI concepts from basic to intermediate level.
- Focus on the GPT architecture for generative AI models.
- Maximize ChatGPT's value with an effective prompt design.
- Explore applications and use cases of ChatGPT.
- Use OpenAI models and features via API calls.
- Build and deploy generative AI systems with Python.

Packt is searching for authors like you

If you're interested in becoming an author for Packt, please visit `authors.packtpub.com` and apply today. We have worked with thousands of developers and tech professionals, just like you, to help them share their insight with the global tech community. You can make a general application, apply for a specific hot topic that we are recruiting an author for, or submit your own idea.

Hi!

I am Gilbert Mizrahi, author of *Unlocking the Secrets of Prompt Engineering*. I really hope you enjoyed reading this book and found it useful for increasing your productivity and efficiency.

It would really help me (and other potential readers!) if you could leave a review on Amazon sharing your thoughts on this book.

Go to the link below or scan the QR code to leave your review:

`https://packt.link/r/1835083838`

Your review will help us to understand what's worked well in this book, and what could be improved upon for future editions, so it really is appreciated.

Best wishes,

Gilbert Mizrahi

Download a free PDF copy of this book

Thanks for purchasing this book!

Do you like to read on the go but are unable to carry your print books everywhere?

Is your eBook purchase not compatible with the device of your choice?

Don't worry, now with every Packt book you get a DRM-free PDF version of that book at no cost.

Read anywhere, any place, on any device. Search, copy, and paste code from your favorite technical books directly into your application.

The perks don't stop there, you can get exclusive access to discounts, newsletters, and great free content in your inbox daily

Follow these simple steps to get the benefits:

1. Scan the QR code or visit the link below

https://packt.link/free-ebook/9781835083833

2. Submit your proof of purchase
3. That's it! We'll send your free PDF and other benefits to your email directly

Made in the USA
Las Vegas, NV
04 February 2025

17531938R10175